My History, Not Yours

D1484257

Wisconsin Studies in American Autobiography

WILLIAM L. ANDREWS
General Editor

Genaro M. Padilla

My History, Not Yours

The Formation of Mexican American
Autobiography

The University of Wisconsin Press

The University of Wisconsin Press
114 North Murray Street
Madison, Wisconsin 53715

3 Henrietta Street
London WC2E 8LU, England

Library of Congress Cataloging-in-Publication Data
Padilla, Genaro M., 1949–
My history, not yours: the formation of Mexican American
autobiography / Genaro M. Padilla.
296 p.   cm.—(Wisconsin studies in American autobiography)
Includes bibliographical references and index.
ISBN 0-299-13970-0   ISBN 0-299-13974-3 (pbk.)
1. Mexican Americans—Biography—History and criticism.
I. Title.   II. Series.
E184.M5P28   1993
920.00926872—dc20   93-3457

This book is for María, friend and compañera,
and each of my beautiful children,
Manuel, Genaro, Jessica, Xochi, Camila

Contents

Illustrations

Preface

When I started writing this book in 1985, I began with the idea of writing a study on recent Chicano autobiography. I thought that some brief mention of earlier autobiographical narrative would suffice to suggest that the rather rich contemporary scene of Chicano autobiography had been anticipated in a few personal narratives from the period after 1848. However, once I found myself reading nineteenth- and early twentieth-century manuscripts, my fascination with the period after 1848 (the year Mexico lost its northern provinces to the United States in a war of conquest) arose such that I gave up study of the present. My attention to the voices of my *antepasados* speaking to me from another time made me listen to the various ways in which my people struggled to represent themselves narratively against social, political, and discursive forces that would just as soon have erased their memory and history in the American social economy that was built over the map of northern Mexico. I found myself absorbed in, or perhaps it was that I was absorbed by, a world characterized by displacement and by the manifold destablizations that we continue to experience today as inhabitants of the same landscape.

Although I wanted to move rather more quickly among a field of narratives, providing a general overview and a scattering of commentaries on many narratives, I found myself again and again resting in one story, listening intently to one life, trying to reconstruct both the social conditions shaping personal experience and the constraints that shaped autobiographical narrative, constraints against which personal narrative was constantly struggling for autonomy. Indeed, during the thinking through of this book, I found myself absorbed in trying to unravel and understand the day-to-day, and year-to-year, complications of personal experience occurring within the social, political, and cultural transformations of the second half of the nineteenth century. But, even though this is a study of auto-biographical narrative, I was not—am not—interested only in the personal particularities of an individual's encounters with the world. I discovered that the personal was always quickly bound up in larger social configurations, in the general transformations, the ruptures, the accommodations, the negotiations of everyday life that people were not only experiencing but trying to control. This book represents my understanding of the ways in which Mexican American autobiography came into formation as a personal and communitarian response to the threat of erasure.

Understanding did not come easily. As I read into and around the social and historical events represented in many of the narratives, I found that I was both fascinated and troubled by some of the people I study here because they were members of the landed classes, *ricos* for whom my own *antepasados* might have labored, people who would have excluded my *bisabuelos* from their world. I more than once decided to abandon the project for political reasons. I would not spend my intellectual life arguing on behalf of people I probably wouldn't have liked in person. But the more I read their narratives, and the more social and political history, newspapers, and letters I read, the more I came to realize that by the end of the nineteenth century just about the only estate left to any of our *antepasados* was one situated in the geography of the past. Theirs are autobiographical narratives of dispossession. Along with those few narratives produced by members of the lower classes, nostalgia for an earlier cultural configuration is the central feature of Mexican American autobiographical narrative. It seems to me, however, that their nostalgia for an earlier world produced not a non-critical reaction to loss, but an oppositional response to displacement, albeit a response often deeply mediated by a language of accommodation. As I intend to show, accommodating language has multiple registers of intent and discrete audiences to which different messages are projected.

One can't—we can't—turn away from the difficulties, the contradictions, and accommodations experienced by many of our *antepasados* without engaging in a form of arrogant dismissiveness much like that responsible for the wholesale suppression of our literary production. Moreover, to do so would doom us to an idea of the past emptied of social complexity wherein we would be willfully deaf to the articulations of discomfort, disillusionment, and anger that structure a rhetorics of accommodation through which our Mexican (American) ancestors were able to negotiate their (and our) place in an alien socio-cultural economy. What I was forced to learn, a concession that has turned into a reading method I wish to convey to others, is that the more deeply I read into the circumstances that produce ideologically contradictory narratives, the more clearly was I able to discern alternate (and alternating) enunciations of opposition by our *antepasados* to the matrix of social constraints within which they lived.

As scholars working in a relatively new field of literary and cultural study, we are in the enviable position of mapping terrain for our own intellectual and cultural posterity. To be part of such a project is a wonderful but also difficult position in which to find ourselves, because, while we are engaged in a first-phase recovery of a rich literary discourse for succeeding generations, we must not excuse ourselves from providing detailed analysis of the cultural material we are recovering—however provisional that interpretive activity may seem given the incompleteness of the archaeological project. My work here argues for the centrality of thick socio-historicized readings of formative Mexican American (autobiographical) narratives and the historical particularities of their production rather than what in much recent criticism impresses me as a leisured superficiality of focusing upon contemporary narrative practices without adequate grounding in the history of our literary traditions.

Finally, although I think of myself as a Chicano and my work as Chicano scholarship, I use "Mexican American" in the title simply because I think it is more historically representative of the people I am writing about than "Chicano," which is a recent self-designation that would have been unfamiliar to the women and men discussed in this book. Even "Mexican American" is only the general rubric for a regionally varied and historically complex group of people who have referred to themselves variously since 1848: "Mejicano (pronounced, dear reader, meh-hee-cah-no, not meX-ee-cay-no), "Hispano," "Nuevomexicano/a," "Californio" and "Californiana," and "Tejano/a," as well as the more accommodating English terms "Spanish American" in New Mexico and California and "Latin American" in Texas. Throughout this book, therefore, I use many of these terms interchangeably, with emphasis on regional self-designations.

Acknowledgments. Not finally but first, I offer special thanks and love to my own wonderful family: María, my compañera, who has unselfishly provided the space and intellectual atmosphere that writing requires, and all of my children, Manuel, Genaro, Jessica,

Xochi, and Camila, who each in his and her own way has gifted my life—all have given me what is most important. Because the writing of this book was carried out through the months and years of everyday life, my family will be relieved (for a short while at least) that I won't be muttering to myself, won't read scraps of ideas tucked into my pockets during dinner, won't say, so automatically, "I can't . . . I have to work," won't be stuck in another century. The family of my days and nights—they have provided all of the joys and aggravations that make life real and substantial. Without their affection and cariño, there would have been no compelling reason to write this book.

There are numerous other debts. Without the assistance of several grants and fellowships, I could not have finished this project. I started the research and thinking for this book at the Stanford Humanities Center in 1984–1985 and I finished drafting it during a Rockefeller Fellowship year at the Southwest Hispanic Research Center at the University of New Mexico in 1990–1991. The year at Stanford was for me both an amazing and a difficult year, difficult personally in ways I won't disclose here and amazing intellectually because it was a profound moment of intellectual dilation, a turning point in my career and in my intellectual life. My year at the University of New Mexico was in all ways wonderful: I was able to return to the cultural homeland and to familia, and I had the benefit of intellectual exchange with people whose ideas, conversation, and scholarship are part of this book—Erlinda Gonzales-Berry, who befriended and encouraged me when I was still just trying to get conference papers accepted and who I now count among the best of colleagues; Tey Diana Rebolledo, who has always graciously shared her ideas and whose arguments with me have always encouraged my work; Rudolfo Anaya, who long ago told me, "Poco a poco se hace"; José Rivera, who, as director of Southwest Hispanic Research Institute, made me and my family's stay in New Mexico easy while I was a Rockefeller resident there; Tobías Duran and Felipe Gonzalez, whose work on the concept of the homeland influenced my thinking greatly; Héctor Torres, whose conversations provided a rich field of thinking; Teresa Marquez, whose archival knowledge and good sense have long been helpful; Enrique Lamarid, whose scholarship on traditional cultural practices has often guided my thinking; and Antonio Marquez, whose *burla* of critical jargon has ballasted my language more than he knows. I would like to thank the staff of both research centers for the substantial help and encouragement that have made the completion of this book possible.

Between those years, I had a President's Fellowship in 1986 at the University of Utah, where I taught before coming to Berkeley. Former colleagues at Utah, Phil Sullivan, Henry Staten, Ann Parsons, and Meg Brady, helpfully read early portions of this work, and Henry Webb, Hal Moore, David Mikkelson, Steve Tatum, and John Nelson first took me to the Utah deserts where I put academia into proper perspective. William Gonzalez, Ed Mayer, Mauricio Mixco, and Ronald Coleman offered me personal and professional friendship and guidance.

I also wish to offer special thanks to the commentary and encouragement offered at the beginning by a group of friends and colleagues who opened my eyes to the possibilities of this study on the formations of Mexican American autobiography: el maestro, Luís Leal, who taught all of us, Francisco Lomelí, María Herrera-Sobek, Ramón Gutiérrez, Juan Bruce-Novoa, Raymund Paredes, Gabriel Meléndez, and Luís Torres. William Andrews, the general editor of Wisconsin Studies in American Autobiography, encouraged this project in its early stages and has waited patiently for its completion. Earlier versions of some of these chapters have appeared in *American Quarterly*, *The Americas Review*, *Revealing Lives: Autobiography, Biography and Gender*, *Criticism in the Borderlands*, and *Recovering the U.S.-Hispanic Literary Heritage*. I wish to thank the publishers and editors for permission to reprint them here.

Those at the University of California, Berkeley, whom I wish to thank are Mitch Breitwieser, whose detailed readings of portions of this study and great sense of humor have proven him a best friend to this work and to my life in Berkeley; my former colleague, Eric Sundquist, who believed in the importance of my work in its early stages; and, likewise, Richard Hutson, Abdul JanMohamed, Elizabeth Abel, Carolyn Dinshaw, Alfred Arteaga, Steven Goldsmith, Sue Schweik, Don McQuade, David Lloyd, Janet Adelman, Hertha Wong and Alex Zwerdling, who all offered the kind of personal and intellectual friendship that provided sustained encouragement. I am especially indebted to Anne Goldman, who not only read but re-read every line of this study over the last few years and offered sustained critical commentary that has constantly challenged and enriched my thinking. Indeed, I am deeply grateful to the Department of English at Berkeley for recognizing the importance of my project at an early stage and for providing the intellectually invigorating atmosphere that enabled the writing of this book. Along with great colleagues, the students at Berkeley, too numerous to mention here, have shaped my thinking during seminars and lectures in a profound manner.

My brother Amado not only read portions of this study and offered sensible editorial advice but, more importantly, has long been the role model I wish other Chicanos could have as they think about the possibilities and difficulties of an academic career; my mother, Esperanza, read most of my work, here and elsewhere, and from the beginning taught us (my four brothers and me) the politically and culturally enabling meaning of education; my father, Manuel, made that education possible by working long years as a blacksmith for the Santa Fe Railroad—having tricked Doña Sebastiana more than once he will see (if not read) this book—*al fin.*

Part 1
The Formation of Autobiography in Mexican American Culture

1
Recovering Mexican American Autobiography

I remember that there was such terror instilled by the Americans that when a dog barked the people killed it, the burros were muzzled so they could not bray, and if the roosters crowed at daylight they killed them. . . . The people fled in terror and the soldiers burned the public markets, the granaries, and everything the people were not able to carry away.

—Rafael Chacón, "Memorias" (1912)

So, that's the way it turns out, that after working so many years, after having acquired an estate, which I certainly didn't dispose of by selling or by any other means, here I find myself in the greatest poverty, living only by the grace of God and through the charity of those who give me a mouthful to eat.

—Apolinaria Lorenzana, "Memorias de la Beata" (1878)

I am willing to relate all I can remember, but I wish it clearly understood that it must be in my own way, and at my own time. I will not be hurried or dictated to. It is my history and not yours I propose to tell.

—Mariano Guadalupe Vallejo on "Recuerdos históricos y personales tocante a la alta California" (1875)

Under the apparent deadness of our New Mexico villages there runs a romantic current invisible to the stranger and understood only by their inhabitants. This quiet romance I will try to describe in the following pages of my autobiography, although I feel an appalling shortage of words, not being a writer, and writing in a language almost foreign to me.

—Cleofas Jaramillo, *Romance of a Little Village Girl* (1955)

I

Although the study of autobiography is flourishing, little has been written about the formation of autobiography in Chicano culture.[1] It is as though individual Mexican Americans had never set their lives to paper, had lived and then disappeared from history without a trace. This is partly true—but certainly not because of illiteracy or disinclination. Chicanos have been silenced not only by the grave but by political transformation, social dispossession, cultural rupture, and linguistic alienation. Yet traces of Mexican American lives

3

do indeed reside in autobiographical narratives that transform life history into textual permanence: memoirs so long out of print they are nearly forgotten; social and cultural histories in which the "I" encloses itself in a language of topographic identity, cultural practice, and political intrigue; diaries, family histories, personal poetry, and collections of self-disclosing correspondence. Lives are scattered on broken pages, faded, partially lost at the margins, suspended in language unread until there is a listener who opens the file and begins. It is my intention, therefore, to initiate a recovery of that autobiographical formation which emerged after 1848, the year a vast part of northern Mexico was annexed by the United States in a war of conquest.

My study hinges on the proposition that when Mexicans were colonized by the United States, when, as David Weber writes, they were "quickly conquered, subjected to an alien political system in an alien culture,"[2] they immediately gave utterance to the threat of social erasure. The rupture of everyday life experienced by some 75,000 people who inhabited the far northern provinces of Mexico in 1846 opened a terrain of discursive necessity in which fear and resentment found language in speeches and official documents that warned fellow citizens to accommodate themselves to the new regime or at least to remain quiet lest they be hurt or killed outright;[3] in personal correspondence in which anger and confusion were voiced to intimates;[4] in poetry, *corridos* (ballads), and *chistes* (jokes) that made *los americanos* the subject of ironic humor, linguistic derogation, and social villainy;[5] and in Spanish-language newspaper editorials and essays that argued for justice and equality for Mexican Americans in the new regime.[6] Autobiographical desire also arose as part of this discursive necessity: memory—shocked into reconstructing the past of another socionational life set squarely against experience in "an alien political system in an alien culture"—gave rise to an autobiographical formation in which the desire for historical presence was marked in everything from the episodic *Personal Memoirs of John N. Seguín* (1858) to the historiographic multivolume "Recuerdos históricos y personales tocante a la alta California" (1875) of Mariano G. Vallejo in northern California; from the autobiographies of two cousins in Texas, José Policarpio Rodríguez and Santiago Tafolla, both of whom fought for the Confederacy, to the "Memorias" of Rafael Chacón, whose narrative describes both the American military invasion and his later service in the Union Army; from the brief personal narratives of the California women Eulalia Pérez ("Una vieja y sus recuerdos," 1877) and Apolinaria Lorenzana ("Memorias de la Beata," 1878) to the fully sustained autobiography of Cleofas Jaramillo (*Romance of a Little Village Girl*, 1955). Unfortunately, these autobiographical narratives remain generally unpublished and unread. Vallejo's "Recuerdos históricos y personales," like Lorenzana's "Memorias de la Beata" and scores of other California narratives, remain in manuscript within the vast holdings of the Bancroft Library at the University of California at Berkeley, and, even though published, both Rodríguez's *"The Old Guide": His Life in His Own Words* (ca. 1897) and Jaramillo's *Romance of a Little Village Girl* have been out of print for decades and are nearly impossible to find. Scores of autobiographical narratives from throughout the West and Southwest therefore remain silent.

The archaeological project to recover the nineteenth-century formations of Chicano autobiography thus begins here. The work of digging through archives—layer by textual layer—gleaning those personal narratives with which we may construct an autobiographical tradition in Mexican American culture is the first requirement of the archaeological project. Discovering, identifying, reading, and categorizing autobiographical narrative is a major undertaking, especially when such work has little and often no precedent. Recent scholarship in Mexican American literary history, carried out almost exclusively by Chicano scholars, is recovering what will amount to a huge inventory of literary material that must, and shall, overturn the ethnocentric assumption that Mexican American culture has a meager literary tradition. Without such a collective and critical undertaking, one would think that there had been no autobiographical voice within a culture that has had a vital literary tradition for hundreds of years. Luís Leal, one of our most prolific and beloved scholars, has been almost single-handedly responsible for encouraging an entire generation of scholars to undertake the kind of archival exhumation that will restore our rich literary tradition.[7] Erlinda Gonzales-Berry, Francisco Lomelí, María Herrera Sobek, Juan Bruce-Novoa, Nicholas Kanellos, Tey Diana Rebolledo, Luís Torres, Charles Tatum, Clara Lomas, Raymund Paredes, Gabriel Meléndez, and Enrique Lamadrid are just a few of the scholars whose work has discovered and described the nineteenth-century origins of our literary production. My reading of nineteenth- and early twentieth-century autobiographical narrative owes its encouragement and much of its critical thinking to this scholarly formation.

Yet only recently has even contemporary Chicano autobiography begun to receive serious attention as a distinct genre.[8] In 1988,

The Americas Review published a special issue, "U.S. Hispanic Autobiography," in which essays on Oscar Zeta Acosta, Ernesto Galarza, Richard Rodriguez, Gary Soto, and Anthony Quinn appear with essays posing theoretical questions about autobiographical ideology, cultural subjectivity in autobiographical narrative, and the autobiographics of recent verse chronicles.[9] Ramón Saldívar has written saliently on "the rhetoric of autobiographical discourse . . . [and] the ideologies that surround" Rodriguez's *Hunger of Memory: The Education of Richard Rodriguez* (1982) and Galarza's *Barrio Boy: The Story of a Boy's Acculturation* (1971) in *Chicano Narrative: The Dialectics of Difference* (1990:155). In fact, the socioideological problematics of autobiographical self-fashioning in contemporary Chicano writing, imbricated with questions about Chicano literary production as a major articulation of resistance to American social and cultural hegemony, appear in nearly all of the current thinking on Chicano autobiography as a genre in which individual experience and collective historical identity are inextricably bound. However, almost all of the scholarship has focused on ideological, identitarian, and rhetorical issues operating in contemporary Chicano autobiography, as though autobiographical consciousness and narrative production, with all of the attendant problems of identitarian inconsistency, ideological contradiction, and rhetorical maneuvering, had developed only in the last two or three decades. This fixation on the contemporary has had the effect, in my estimation, of reaffirming the perception that Chicano literature is a recent phenomenon and, more problematically for our own work, has largely ignored prior personal narrative formations in which ideological complications (historical repression as well as contestatory articulation) comprise the originary worry of autobiographical expression in Mexican American culture.

My aim is not only to encourage the recovery of dormant autobiographical statement but to refigure the complex system of cultural coding, aesthetic desire, and oppositional purpose that since 1848 has produced autobiographical discourse within a dangerous social space. Encouraged by the archival recovery and the critical reexamination of early African American and Native American literary production, I wish to help win back a Mexican American literary tradition that has been ignored and suppressed. Like the work undertaken by Henry Louis Gates, Jr., Joanne Braxton, Houston Baker, Jr., William Andrews, and their predecessors, John Blassingame, Gilbert Osofsky, Arna Bontemps, and Robert Stepto[10] to reconstruct the African American literary heritage, my own work on autobiography is situated within the project, "Recovering the U.S. Hispanic Literary Heritage." This project has as its objective the location, recovery, and publication of literary, folkloristic, periodical, and historical material produced during the Spanish colonial, Mexican, and Mexican American periods which has been out of print for decades (some for a century or more) or which remains in manuscript. Alongside the archival recovery, editing, translation, and publication of this body of foundational literary discourse, we are embarking on a critical and interpretive activity that shall establish the discursive genealogy (its continuities as well as discontinuities) of our literary traditions. The intention of this book, therefore, is to show that the formation of autobiographical consciousness—with all of the ideological and rhetorical stresses it now evinces—originated in prior narrative marking of individual and collective experience.

In its theoretical dimensions, my thinking has been influenced by the rigorous and provocative critical attention Native American autobiography is receiving from innovative scholars like Arnold Krupat, who reads the complex power relations at work in "bicultural composite composition" of Native American autobiography as a contestatory "textual equivalent of the frontier,"[11] and Hertha Wong, who reads Native American "pictography as autobiography." Rather than regarding Native American autobiography as the textual equivalent of the museum in which the noble but vanished Indian is represented as a cultural relic, Krupat (1985:34) argues that it is in the textual "presentation of an Indian voice not as vanished and silent, but as still living and able to be heard that the oppositional potential of Indian autobiography resides." Krupat's assiduous reconstruction of the social, historical, and ideological conditions under which Native American autobiography was (and is) produced provides an exemplary model of analysis, one that has forced us to rethink the naive expectations for cultural representation that have too often been brought to the reading of Native American autobiography. And although she agrees that most Native American autobiography is the product of ethnographic collaborations with white anthropologists and historians, Wong has audaciously challenged the common assumption that Native Americans did not engage in "autobiographical activity" before contact with Europeans. Wong's revisionist work argues that "long before ethnographers came along, Native Americans were telling, performing, and painting their personal histories. One potential preliterate model of autobiography, at least among Plains Indian males, is the pictographic personal narrative. The symbolic language of pictographs allowed preliterate Plains Indians to 'read' about each other from painted robes, tipis, and shields."[12] Reading scores of self-representing pictographic narratives, Wong details the rich tradition of storytelling in which self and communal identity share the same comfortable space of tribal life. She questions the reified assumption that, given the collective nature of tribal life, there was no such category as the individual in precontact Native American society. Moreover, her reassessment of autobiographical consciousness and performance outside the sacred ground of autobiography as a genre of writing that emerges only in Western culture disputes "the ethnocentric definition of self assumed by many theorists of autobiography . . . and [defies] the primacy of the written word" (Wong 1992:24). Wong's project reminds us that the forms of "autobiographical activity" are various, that the very category of the "self" is in many cultures bound up with the idea of community, and, most important, that autobiographical consciousness itself is culturally divergent, socially complex, and multiple in its articulations, owned neither by Western culture nor by writing.

While there are vast differences between the formation of Native American, African American, and Mexican American autobiographical narrative, there are similarities and problems in the extracultural representational function inscribed in each for registering collective opposition to racialist and ethnocentric assumptions. Perhaps the most compelling socioliterary association among the three traditions is what Gates, in describing the collective function of slave narrative practice, refers to as "a communal utterance, a collective tale, rather than merely an individual's autobiography." Given the physical and spiritual demoralizations to which African Americans as a group had been subjected by slavery, individual autobiographers understood that the "character, integrity, intelligence, manners and morals" of the entire community were staked on "published evidence provided by one of their number."[13] For Native Americans, as Krupat points out, while the nineteenth-century collaborative production of Native American autobiographies generally served as "an acknowledgment of Indian defeat," the Indian prisoner whose life story was recorded opened space for narrating the expansionist brutality visited not only on the speaker but on all of his people. The Native American speaker, often a tribal leader, recognized the collective function of the autobiographical occasion, and rather than focusing only on himself, articulated identity within the context of a culture that was being systematically destroyed. Black

Hawk's autobiography, for example, has as "part of the motive force behind" its construction "the performance of an act of textual 'justice,'" citing as it does the "many instances of the 'injuries' done to Black Hawk and his people" (Krupat 1985 : 50). Likewise, after 1848, Mexican Americans were conscious of the historical consequences of such "communal utterance." As Vallejo wrote to his son, his "Recuerdos históricos y personales" would oppose negative representations of Mexican Californians pervasive both before and after 1848. "I shall not stop moistening my pen in the blood of our unfounded detractors. . . . You know I am not vindictive but I am and was born hispano. To contradict those who slander is not vengeance, it is to regain a loss."[14] As we shall see, Vallejo's "Recuerdos históricos y personales" tends toward a strategy of historiographic refutation of "our unfounded detractors," instead of focusing on his own remarkable personal and public accomplishments.

The heavy burden of collective representation, however, created a problem for Mexican American autobiography as it had for African American slave narrative. As Andrews points out, nineteenth-century whites produced and read slave narrative "more to get a firsthand look at the institution of slavery than to become acquainted with an individual slave."[15] Indeed, as Blassingame, Stepto, and Baker have all shown, the struggle for narrative autonomy by African Americans was waged against scores of white abolitionist editors, amanuenses, and publishers who not only sponsored slave narratives but, through the complex authenticating apparatus that framed the narrative, "addressed white readers over the invisible bodies of black narrators," as G. Thomas Couser argues.[16] I would likewise argue that after 1848, Anglo Americans were generally not interested in encouraging the production of, much less in reading, personal narrative that would acquaint them with the perceptions and feelings of Mexicans who had presumably just been granted all the rights of American citizenship. Whereas slave narratives were published and often widely distributed to promote the abolitionist cause, Mexican American personal narratives—for example, the scores of personal narratives collected from Mexican Californians in the 1870s—were meant to function only as supplemental material for American historians and were, therefore, as we shall see, quite intentionally not published. Hence, scores, perhaps hundreds, of Mexican American personal narratives remain in small state and regional historical society libraries and university special collections as well as in major archival repositories like the Huntington and Bancroft libraries. Only when we undertake the difficult work of recovering our autobiographical literature from such archival incarceration will the "collective utterance" of our autobiographical tradition disclose its origins, evolution, and cultural significance. Only by activating Baker's "anthropology of art"[17] for Mexican American autobiography can we, as Andrews advises, began to reconstruct the "full context in which a genre originated, evolved, and took on cultural significance."[18] Like Baker, I believe that "an imaginative reconstruction of a cultural context is mandatory" (1980:xvii) if we are to understand the complex, interrelated codes that constitute the "cultural sign." For Mexican American autobiographical narrative, we must examine the various ways in which autobiographical expression emerged from social rupture and was formed within a matrix of dislocation, fear, and uncertainty that shaped contradictory but exigent responses.

II

The contradictory positions that Mexican Americans have occupied in American society since the U.S.–Mexican War of 1846–1848 have been an obsession in much autobiographical narrative, no matter which region of the West one chooses to examine. The earliest post-1848 narratives record, in their different forms, the effects of the military takeover on the Mexican community in general and on the experiences of individuals. Although there were class stratifications, regional differences, and gender distinctions that nuanced literary discourse in important ways and that must be more finely examined in subsequent scholarship, I will argue that in the period after the American conquest, the life histories of Mexican American women and men articulate an interregional and even interclass sense of individual and communal disjuncture. Whether acquiescent, embittered, confounded, oppositional, self-denying, or assertively defiant, the personal narratives display a range of responses that seek to mediate the nascent national and existential realities imposed on Mexican(American)s in their daily lives by a regime that mouthed a rhetoric of democratic ideals but practiced unrelenting hostility in its relations with them. This historical situation has for over a century sustained a rhetorical site upon which Chicano literary production has had as one of its generative principles the reconciling of vexing contradictions. In autobiographical literature, we see again and again a narrative ground (often a battleground) upon which an individual is contending with social, cultural, and ideological forces that simultaneously so disrupt identity as to unfix it yet, paradoxically, in disrupting identity establish identity as a destabilized condition.

Since autobiographical narrative produced after 1848 was marked by a need to meditate upon the upheaval that traumatized the entire spectrum of Mexican American life, the narrative retrieval of the past may be seen as the direct product of sociocultural stress, often of outright dread of impending personal harm, of a sense that the world was coming to an end—which in many respects it was. The post–1848 personal narratives that I have read and present for study in this book, as a group, exhibit an almost obsessive nostalgic tendency to re-create "los días pasados" as a means of divesting the second half of the nineteenth century of its absurdity. However idealized the pre-American cultural community may appear in these narratives, the autobiographical reconstitution of life before the occupation was less a self-deluding compensation, or naive wish-fulfillment fantasy, than what I consider a strategic narrative activity—conscious of its general social implications—for restoring order, sanity, social purpose in the face of political, social, and economic dispossession. Dispossession was often articulated in an autobiographical sigh of deep sadness and longing for another sociocultural life, but there is always a barely suppressed rage running within the narrative. Throughout the Southwest, nostalgia mixed with anger functioned to mediate the manifold social forces that infringed upon the spirit of those people who resided in the vast territory that became the western United States in 1848 but that geospiritually became a kind of floating island upon which Mexican(American)s were left to work out their historic destinies.

But, of course, our history begins well before 1848. So does our literary culture. So does autobiographical impulse. I begin at 1848 for reasons I shall make clear, but prior discursive formations may productively widen the work I initiate here. Therefore, before drawing the line at 1848, I wish to take a moment to outline indigenous Mexican and Spanish colonial autobiographical articulations that succeeding scholarship may further examine when recharting the terrain of literary culture. After all, reconstructing the history of autobiographical discourse largely entails constructing a tradition. Constructing a tradition likewise demands making decisions that are likely to have socioliterary, cultural, and ideological consequences.

On the indigenous side of the Mexican cultural heritage, many scholars indeed have argued that the pre-Columbian literature of Mexico comprises a cherished part of the Chicano's literary estate.[19] Of course, this rich indigenous literary tradition has been recovered, in the main, only in the modern Mexican period, especially after the Mexican Revolution of 1910 institutionalized the valorization of Mexico's indigenous culture. The Chicano appropriation of pre-Columbian literary material and mythic property has likewise taken place largely within the last twenty-five years, during which time it has exercised wide influence on contemporary Chicano writers, artists, and dramatists who have incorporated the pre-Columbian cultural text into their own cultural refigurations. Suggestive of the kind of "anthropology of art" open to further development, therefore, I will simply brief the kind of "autobiographical activity" measurable in indigenous Mexican culture.

As Miguel León-Portilla has pointed out, while most pre-Columbian literature was collectively produced, there are several hundred lyric poems preserved in pre-Hispanic Náhuatl manuscripts in which an "I"-speaking subject meditates on "divinity and the beyond, the pleasure of conversing with friends, the mystery of death, recollections of princes and elders, adventures in war, love for women and children."[20] Although most of these poems were anonymously scribed, many were signed by famous poets of the time— Nezahualcóyotl and his son, Nezahualpilli, the Lord Tegayehuatzin, Prince Ayocaun, the Aztec warrior Temilotzin, who fought against the Spaniards, Aquiauhtzin, and Cuauhtencoztli. The last, for example, questions outright whether his name will survive, and in autobiographically naming himself, it does survive:

> I, Cuauhtencoztli, here am suffering.
> What is, perchance true?
> Will my song still be real tomorrow?
> Are men perhaps real?
> What is it that will survive?[21]

Such poems speak self-consciousness, historical presence, and ontological desire to such a degree that the lyrics reverberate with a need to know what the "I" is, how it stands within its own experience, and whether friends and succeeding family will remember the space it has filled. This is nothing less than the autobiographical impulse to inscribe one's name and experience upon history. I invite succeeding scholars to engage in a rigorous anthropology of art that will document the autobiographical activity of pre-Columbian Mexico as a project in and of itself and then calculate the refractive influence of an indigenous autobiographical poetics on the contemporary Chicano literary production.

On the European side of the *mestizo* cultural heritage, we can indeed trace a continuous Spanish colonial discourse of conquest, exploration, and settlement between 1492 and the beginning of the nineteenth century which charts the formation of a new subjectivity in the Americas. Certainly, as soon as Europeans set foot on the new continent, the imprint of their boots on the soil marked an appalling presence that would never again be swept smooth. Yet the Spanish presence began to register a shift in its own ontological grid: the eyes scribed startling images of land formations, vegetation, birds, reptiles, and mammals. Another people—dark skinned and with hair "coarse almost like the hairs of a horse's tail," "very well built, with very handsome bodies and very good faces," "very gentle" but "marvelously timid"—peered out from their villages, many running into hiding from the strangers, but some, Columbus wrote in his *Journal of the First Voyage to America*, swam to the Spanish launches in an extravagant display of curiosity.[22] Whether curious or "marvelously timid," however, the encounter with Europeans would prove deadly given the rapacious settlement of the Americas. What the Spanish saw, they made theirs; yet they were also gradually remade by what they saw. This gradual redefining of subjectivity may be read in the scores of exploration and settlement narratives through which the new land and people make an indelible autobiographical mark. Alvar Núñez Cabeza de Vaca's *La relación* (1542), one may say, represents the first autobiographical account of nonindigenous life in the New World. This together with Pedro de Casteñeda's narrative (*Relación de la jornada a Cíbola*, 1582) of Francisco Vásquez de Coronado's massive exploration of what is now New Mexico, Texas, and Kansas between 1540 and 1542, Juan de Oñate's *Proclamación* (1598), Fray Alonso de Benavides's *Memorial* (1630), Fray Eusebio Kino's *Favores celestiales* (ca. 1711), and scores of other military and missionary *relaciones, memorias, diários,* and *viajes* (travel accounts) constitute an enormous field of narrative that may be considered autobiographical in part. After all, American literary historians have identified British travel narratives, journals, diaries, and histories as the first literary productions of the nation; likewise, autobiography scholars have been quick to identify William Bradford's *Of Plymouth Plantation*, John Winthrop's *Journal*, Mary Rowlandson's *Captivity Narrative*, Samuel Sewall's *Diary*, and numerous other histories and personal narratives as part of the nation's autobiographical tradition. Both the Spanish and the British narratives, as well as the full range of the indigenous literary production of the Americas, constitute the beginnings of American literature, since they produce a textual domain shaped by the experience of the Americas.

The project to recover fully the pre-Columbian, indigenous, and Spanish colonial literary traditions must commence, but it is here deferred because the autobiographical formation that I am interested in recovering is of a distinct sociodiscursive order. I would like to suggest, along with literary historians Luís Leal and Raymund Paredes, that such prior traditions be considered not as separate but separately from that literary production that followed the U.S.-Mexican War of 1846–48.[23] Like Leal and Paredes, I wish to argue that a Mexican American literary formation begins with the American violence that ripped the Mexican map in Tejas in 1836 (remember the Alamo?) and then completely blanched the geography of northern Mexico in 1846–1848. For it is the literature written after the invasion by the United States that begins to name us as a people living upon a distinct, startling, and confounding plane of history. Bruce-Novoa's space between the social signifiers—Mexican American—opens at this historical juncture: "We are the space (not the hyphen) between the two, . . . 'the intercultural possibilities of that space.' We continually expand the space, pushing the two influences out and apart as we claim more area for our reality."[24] A Mexican American literary formation that would "expand the space" and "claim more area for our reality" arose from that traumatic historical moment when the United States violently appropriated northern Mexico in the mid-nineteenth century.[25] The year 1848, then, was the beginning and the end, the opening toward a new subjectivity.

As Paredes points out,

> The great divide in Chicano history is the year 1848 when the Treaty of Guadalupe Hidalgo ended twenty-one months of warfare between Mexico and the United States. . . . Although a distinctive Mexican American literary sensibility was not to emerge for several generations, the signing of the [treaty], more than any other event, required southwestern Mexicans to reassess their relationships to the old country and the United States.[26]

After 1848, a crushed social economy led to radical transformation in the cultural epistemology: the disorientation of defeat and the profound rupture of everyday life produced a situation in which subordination would shape a new grid of subjectivity. The violent displacement of a well-established society forced a systemic shift in the modes of cultural self-recognition. In other words, even though most people retained the daily self-identificatory practices of language, social customs, and communal relations, the rupture produced a situation in which Mexican people were forced to adapt to an alien social economy while increasingly struggling to remember themselves with a culture and a history of their own. Among the many modes of reassessment, an autobiographical narrative formation opened at this break, a narrative formation that emerged from rupture itself, from the necessity of sustaining the practices of the past in everyday life while reconstructing life anew within the rupture, transforming rupture into the expanding—and expansive—space of intercultural possibility.

But first there was the problem of immediate survival. As Paredes mentions elsewhere, virtually "all Mexicans [who] elected to remain in their homeland . . . [became] in a single political stroke, Mexican Americans."[27] The sweep of the pen, as Paredes would agree, did not, in fact, enfranchise our forebears as Americans. Rather, most Mexican(American)s experienced profound social dislocation, loss of their traditional homelands, and daily derogation of religious, familial, and cultural practices. The war itself and the rapid Americanization of the West set off social, political, economic, linguistic, and cultural shock waves that generated a rhetorical situation in which Mexicans—now Americans—struggled to reconcile themselves to loss while also marking their resistance to that loss. Pablo de la Guerra, a Californio who became a member of the state senate after the Americanization, summed up the situation in an angry speech before his colleagues in 1856.

> It is the conquered who are humbled before the conqueror, asking for his protection, while enjoying what little their misfortune has left them. . . . They do not understand the prevalent language of their native soil. They are foreigners in their own land. I have seen seventy and sixty year olds cry like children because they have been uprooted from the lands of their fathers. They have been humiliated and insulted. They have been refused the privilege of taking water from their own wells.[28]

Even those *Mexicanos* who sustained filiation with native cultural practices, whose cultural faith, as it might be called, stood firm against the aggravations of *los extranjeros*, had to reconcile themselves to an appalling reality. An autobiographical impulse in Mexican American society, matrixed in native cultural practices, in language and literary traditions (both oral and textual), in topographic identity and familial intimacy, came into existence at the moment when extinction, in the form of social death, loomed on the horizon for the inhabitants of Mexico's northern provinces. But not just social, or symbolic, death. Fear was real and pervasive in 1846 and after. Recall Chacón's words cited in the epigraphs to this chapter.

Before life in the new regime could be rebuilt, the terror of the American conquest had to be reconciled. Such global social rupture led to a destabilization of individual and collective life that, in the discursive realm, required a form of verbal restoration of the community within which the individual had identified his or her very locus of meaning. Memory locked into counterpoint against the terrifying present. The remembered (pre-American) past was sustained in vulnerable suspension against the roiling displacements of post-1848 society. Remembering hurt, but it was necessary for catharsis. Old men and women cried like children but told their stories nonetheless. Yet because anguish burdened memory, memory often faltered when it came to the dispossessions of the post-1848 present, elided the transformative events of the early 1850s, resettled an imaginary geography of the past. In that past, a pre-American social economy all at once became, perhaps only in the defeated imagination, a kind of prelapsarian space, a cultural utopia that would be figured again and again as idyllic against the reality of dislocation. Autobiographical nostalgia for an idealized and unobtainable past arose,[29] to be certain, but nostalgia functioned as opposition to assimilation, while idealizations of a prior cultural habitat operated as articulations of resistance to cultural evisceration. Autobiographical narrative, twined to social and cultural history, therefore, served the reintegrative psychic and social need for sustaining an idea of the past and for fixing a version of history within a cultural text that would mark historical presence in the face of erasure.

III

Beginning at mid-nineteenth century, the autobiographical narratives composed out of a need to reconcile the cultural "self" to a radically discontinuous history assume numerous forms of expression. Although many of the extant materials on which I base my study were composed by members of the upper, landowning classes, there are narratives that disclose the lives of common people— soldiers, working women, small ranchers, adventurers, journalists. Archival recovery, therefore, discovers autobiographical voicings from all classes of the Mexican American society just coming into formation after the American occupation.

Among the earliest autobiographical narratives in the Southwest are José Antonio Menchaca's "Reminiscences" (ca. 1850) and
Juan Seguín's *Personal Memoirs* (1858), both of which are ambivalent and often bitter defenses of complicity in the Anglo-Texas rebellion of 1836. Seguín's brief personal narrative, for example, is an
anguished attempt to come to terms with a string of events that
within the space of a few years saw him transformed from a member
of the landed Tejano elite who fought for Texas independence from
Mexico (because, as he says, he believed in American democratic
ideals) to an outcast who suffered political and economic dispossession. Ironically, Seguín was forced to retreat to Mexico when his life
was threatened by Americans, and then, absurd as it may sound, he
fought on the side of the Mexican army when it recaptured San Antonio, where he had just served as American mayor. As I argue in
chapter 2, Seguín's *Personal Memoirs* is in many of its details the
prefigurative narrative of the forms of personal and cultural schizophrenia witnessed in succeeding Mexican American autobiographical narratives.

In Texas alone there are other narratives that exhibit the transformation of the cultural subject discovered in the Seguín memoirs. Santiago Tafolla's unpublished "Nearing the End of the Trail"
(ca. 1890) is the life history of a man who ran away from home when
he was twelve, spent his youth traveling in the eastern United States
with an Anglo benefactor, settled in Texas, and then fought on the
side of the South during the Civil War—only to be forced to desert
when he and fellow Mexicano Confederate troopers learned they
were about to be lynched by white soldiers because they were
"greasers." José Policarpio Rodríguez's narrative *"The Old Guide"*
(ca. 1897) describes his life as a "Surveyor, Scout, Indian Fighter,
[and] Ranchman" and ends as a conversion narrative much in the
Augustinian tradition. As it turns out, Tafolla and Rodríguez were
cousins who both became Protestant ministers late in life and who
remember each other in their respective narratives. Another duo
who met on and off the pages of their memoirs were Jesse Pérez,
Texas lawman, and Catarino E. Garza, journalist, union organizer,
and revolutionary. Garza's "La lógica de mis hechos" (The Reason-
ing of My Activities) is a 280-page handwritten manuscript that describes the social conditions of Mexican Americans in South Texas
and St. Louis, Missouri, between 1877 and 1889 and his own efforts
to help establish the *sociedades mutualistas* (mutual aid societies)
before he returned to Mexico to participate in the Revolution of
1910. And Pérez, strangely enough, was a member of the Texas
Rangers in the 1890s when that group was terrorizing the Mexican

American communities of South Texas. In the early 1920s, Pérez struggled with a typewriter to compose his "Memoirs," part of which recount those occasions when he chased Garza along the border as Garza and other revolutionaries ran guns from Texas into Mexico. However, unlike other Rangers, Pérez never saw his "Memoirs" published—perhaps because the very notion of a Mexican Texas Ranger was a contradiction in terms.[30]

In New Mexico, Padre Antonio José Martínez wrote and published his autobiographical brief, "Relación de méritos," on his own (and the first) printing press in New Mexico in 1838.[31] Martínez's "Relación" describes his birth in Taos, New Mexico, in 1793, his boyhood in a landowning family, his marriage to María de la Luz Martín, who bore him a daughter but soon thereafter died, leaving him a widower who decided to become a priest at twenty-four. Not only did Martínez become a priest but he became the politically influential and widely revered prelate who was excommunicated from the church in 1861 by Archbishop Jean-Baptiste Lamy because he resisted the liturgical Americanization in New Mexico that denigrated the Mexican clergy and robbed the people of locally established religious practices. Citing the library of doctrinal texts that constituted his intellectual personality, the "Relación" describes Martínez's sociointellectual formation and the theological knowledge that would eventually put him at doctrinal odds with a bishop who had been sent to New Mexico with the express purpose of Americanizing the Mexican Catholic populace. Although Padre Martínez was a member of the constitutional convention and the territorial legislature, when he defended the religious cultural practices of his people, he was vilified by Lamy and his assistant, Reverend Joseph Machebeuf, and driven ignominiously from his pulpit in Taos. In 1927, Willa Cather's *Death Comes for the Archbishop* perpetuated and perhaps forever hardened the image of Padre Martínez as a brutal, self-aggrandizing, and ugly man who dictated the lives of his Mexican parishioners and stood in the way of American progress. Although recent biographical scholarship is restoring Padre Martínez's historical and cultural significance,[32] his own extant writings, scores of letters and essays as well as his "Relación," have yet to be collected and published.

In addition to Padre Martínez's, there are other journals and narratives by New Mexican political and military figures that require further examination. In 1833, five years before Martínez published the "Relación de méritos," Rafael Chacón (the subject of chapter 5) was born outside of Santa Fe to a family who had deep roots in *Nuevo México* and who, like most other *Nuevomexicanos*, lost their homeland after the American conquest. Chacón was a thirteen-year-old cadet in the Mexican militia when the Americans invaded New Mexico; after 1848, he mustered in as a soldier in the American army, fighting in the only Civil War engagement in New Mexico territory and campaigning against the Navajo and Apache; after his retirement from the military in the 1860s, he struggled to build a home for his family under difficult economic and social conditions. Chacón, who wrote his "Memorias" between 1906 and 1912, remembers the terror instilled by the invading Americans as well as his service in the American army, where he and his fellow Nuevomexicanos were treated disrespectfully. However, what I found most appealing about Chacón's "Memorias" are not the military exploits Jacqueline Meketa, his translator and editor, finds remarkable but rather the sense of cultural and familial devotion that motivates the composition of a personal document he hopes will textually sustain the family name in a time of social uncertainty.

After the turn of the century, there is a group of New Mexicans whose lives spanned the last quarter of the nineteenth century and whose autobiographies chart the transformation of the social and political life of the territory. Miguel Antonio Otero, Jr. (1859–1944), the son of a prominent Santa Fe *político,* went to school in St. Louis and went on to become territorial governor of New Mexico from 1897 to 1903. Although not produced until the 1930s, Otero's autobiographical trilogy charts his experience from 1859, when he was born in St. Louis, Missouri, to his years as territorial governor of New Mexico at the turn of the century. *My Life on the Frontier, 1864–1882* (1935), provides a fascinating account of Otero's boyhood on the Missouri and New Mexico frontier where he met such legends as Wild Bill Hickock, Buffalo Bill Cody, and Billy the Kid. *My Life on the Frontier, 1882–1897* (1939), relates his experiences as a young man rising to affluence and political power in New Mexico, ending with notice of his appointment as territorial governor by President William McKinley. And *My Nine Years as Governor of the Territory of New Mexico, 1897–1905* (1940) records in detail his years in office as the first Hispano governor of the state since the American conquest, his futile attempts to gain statehood for New Mexico, his help in organizing Theodore Roosevelt's Rough Riders (among them, many Nuevomexicanos whose loyalty to the U.S. was still in question), and his rise to national prominence during the late territorial period in New Mexico.[33]

From the 1920s through about 1950, a group of women in New Mexico wrote books in which cultural traditions, family and community customs, and social history are combined with personal narrative. Their versions of personal life history and culture are mostly a form of narrative pageantry in which the Spanish colonial past is imagined as a vital element of New Mexican Hispano identity with, like many of the men's, little reference to Indian and Mexican heritage. Nina Otero Warren's *Old Spain in Our Southwest* (1936), Cleofas Jaramillo's *The Genuine New Mexico Tasty Recipes: Old and Quaint Formulas for the Preparation of Seventy-five Delicious Spanish Dishes* (1939), *Sombras del Pasado/Shadows of the Past* (1941), and *Romance of a Little Village Girl* (1955), Aurora Lucero White-Lea's *Literary Folklore of the Hispanic Southwest* (1953), and Fabiola Cabeza de Baca's *The Good Life: New Mexico Traditions and Food* (1949) and *We Fed Them Cactus* (1954) are all books that may be characterized as a hybrid of personal narrative, folkloristic transcription, recipe book, and family, community, and general sociocultural history. Cultural traditions and daily customs are not only transcribed but given personal, familial, and historical context in *Old Spain in Our Southwest, Sombras del Pasado/Shadows of the Past,* and *The Good Life.* Recipes for traditional foods are contextualized by personal and familial *recuerdos* (memoirs) to such a degree that culinary and cultural knowledge are inextricably bound. As Tey Diana Rebolledo points out, such knowledge tends to be topographically distinct and gendered. "Recipes are integrated with accounts of folk life, as if the female sense of rootedness and place is passed down through the distinctive foods nature offers."[34] Personal narratives like *We Fed Them Cactus* and *Romance of a Little Village Girl* are likewise tied to such traditional narrative practices as relating *cuentos* (folktales), *romances* (narrative ballads), religious drama like the *pastorelas* (pastoral plays), and *recuerdos* in which the personal life is matrixed within a family genealogy of *tíos* and *tías* (uncles and aunts), *abuelas y abuelitos* (grandparents), *primas hermanas* (first cousins), *padrinos* (godparents), and *compadres* (family friends). In fact, community, family, and personal histories are usually so integrated that while cookbooks like Jaramillo's *Genuine New Mexico Tasty Recipes* and Cabeza de Baca's *The Good Life* are ethnographic texts, they are also what Anne Goldman calls "culinary autobiographies." Goldman describes such narrative as a complex form of cultural and self-representation. "Reproducing a recipe, like retelling a story, may be at once cultural practice *and* autobiographical assertion. If it provides an apt metaphor for the reproduction of culture from generation to generation, the act of passing down recipes from mother to daughter works as well to figure a familial space within which self-articulation can begin to take place."[35] Intergenerational exchange of cultural knowledge thus constitutes a form of cultural subjectivity rooted in an enduring sense of place, in a sense not only of rootedness but of ownership of cultural terrain.

These narratives, nevertheless, do tend to read the past nostalgically, evoking a harmonious cultural domain while occluding the social fragmentations of the present. There were moments while reading many of these narratives when I wanted to dismiss this body of writing for what Paredes rightly refers to as its "hacienda mentality." Yet Rebolledo reframes our thinking about such narrative production by reminding us that during this period (1930s–1950s) most "women had no education and even those who did had little leisure to write. Nor were they encouraged to write; they were confined to fairly rigid gender roles, carefully watched and cared for. It is a wonder they wrote at all" (1987:99). More recently, Rebolledo has gone a step further to argue that this group of women were neither "naive" nor "innocent" in their writing, that in fact they established a set of "narrative strategies of resistance" that are "constantly subverting the 'official' text" of Anglo-American writing about Nuevomexicanos that offered little more than romanticized representations of a people whose "quaint" customs and culture were ostensibly disappearing in the modern Anglo world. Rebolledo agrees with my contention elsewhere that this group of women writers construct a sentimental and nostalgic view of the past that is a form of embryonic resistance; yet she convincingly argues that women's strategies of resistance were not merely "'sparks' of dissent" but rather complex and powerful narrative articulations of self and culture that opposed the Anglo-American hegemony.[36] Given my interest in exploring the oppositional function of nostalgia, the sociodiscursive politics of idealizing the past is an issue I will consider in chapter 6.

As I argue in chapter 6, while it is clear that in many respects Jaramillo and other New Mexican writers of this period mimicked an Anglo-American discourse that romanticized the Spanish Southwest, their writing nevertheless also operated as a vital form of resistance to Anglo-American ethnocentrism. What I wish to propose, therefore, is a contextually reaccentuated reading of Jaramillo's autobiography, a reading that restores the discursive grid in which a subordinate text appears and in so doing discovers the sociodiscursive forces that conspire for control of the text, encouraging its cultural romanticizing and historical concealment, muting it where it raises troublesome questions, and eliding unpleasant socioideological issues. The proliferation of nonnative, Anglo-American cultural discourse in New Mexico between 1900 and 1940 led to what Michel Foucault identifies as "systems of exclusion for the control and delimitation of discourse," which, in effect, exercise a "power of constraint upon other forms of discourse."[37] This "system of exclusion," I contend, was so powerful that the literary activity of an entire generation of Nuevomexicanos was at once selected, organized, and controlled by a powerful nonnative discursive network that dulled their ability to see straight to the heart of their own historical and material condition, or, to the extent that they did, muted their capacity to speak without fear of nullification or erasure.

Of course, the hegemonic effects of such a system of exclusion had already been installed well before 1900. In the 1870s, Hubert Howe Bancroft, book dealer, document collector, and professional historian, solicited scores of personal narratives taken from the *Californios,* as many of the California Mexicans called themselves. These narratives undergird his massive *History of California,* published in seven volumes between 1884 and 1889, as well as *Pastoral California* (1888),[38] an often ethnocentric and romanticized history of pre-American California society. As Bancroft himself wrote of the project in *Literary Industries* (1890), he and his field assistants collected some "two hundred volumes of original narrative from memory by as many early Californians, native and pioneers, written by themselves or taken down from their lips, . . . the vivid narratives of their experiences."[39] Most are personal narratives collected as oral dictations by Bancroft's field researchers, Enrique Cerruti and Thomas Savage, who during a period of some six years traveled a wide circuit from San Francisco to San Diego transcribing the lives of the Californios.[40] There are, by my count, nearly one hundred Californio personal narratives of lengths varying from ten pages to some that are hundreds of pages. I must confess not only my sense of wonder but my sense of resurrective power at discovering scores of disembodied voices, textualized lives stored away during the 1870s in Bancroft's manuscript library: María Inocente Pico de Avila, "Cosas de California"; Juan Bernal, "Memoria de un Californio"; Josefa Carillo de Fitch, "Narración de una Californiana"; Rafael González, "Experiencias de un soldado"; Apolinaria Lorenzana, "Memorias de la Beata"; José del Cármen Lugo, "Vida de un ranchero"; Felipa Osuña, "Recuerdos del pasado"; "Eulalia Pérez, "Una vieja y sus recuerdos"; Pío Pico, "Narración histórico"; Vincente Sánchez, "Cartas de un Angelino"; Pablo Vejar, "Recuerdos de un viejo."[41] These and scores of other personal narratives still await the kind of exhaustive recovery, editing, translation, and publication that will rescue them from archival obscurity.

This Californio manuscript collection constitutes a major narrative formation, solicited by Bancroft but composed in collaboration or alone by individuals who wished to relate the history of their community in their own language and from their own cultural perspective in a manner that often contested popular and historiographic representations of Mexican Californians, which by the 1870s were highly derogatory at worst or condescending at best. Mariano G. Vallejo, Juan Bautista Alvarado, Juan Bandini, Pío Pico, and Antonio María Osío were some of the men of power and influence in pre-American California who composed sustained collaborative narratives in which the "self" figures prominently in the social transformation that was displacing them even as they wrote. Vallejo's "Recuerdos históricos y personales" occupies some five volumes of nearly one thousand pages of historical and personal impressions of California society before and after the American occupation.

Chapter 3 focuses at length on the production of the Vallejo narrative during the 1870s when Bancroft identified him as the single most important figure in pre-American California. What especially interested me was tracing Vallejo's development of a set of strategies for controlling historical and self-representation, strategies he had begun to develop in his earliest contacts with Americans during the 1830s when he saw that American immigration into California would transform the country. Vallejo's "Recuerdos históricos y personales," like those personal narratives of many other Californios, reveals contradictory responses to the Americanization of northern Mexico. Impressed with American democratic rhetoric and proclaiming his own republican ideals, Vallejo had encouraged the American annexation in the 1840s. As I argue in chapter 2, when he was taken prisoner during the Bear Flag Revolt in 1846, his treaty articles and letters to his family demonstrate a strategic manipulation of multiply coded statements that, on the one hand, assured his American captors that his intentions coincided with their own and, on the other, exposed their violations of trust and their violent abrogations of the democratic rhetoric they mouthed while they were forcefully taking the country.

Still hurting from such betrayals in the 1870s, Vallejo initially refused to cooperate with Bancroft and was reluctant to write his historical memoirs, but recognizing the stakes involved in historical and self-representation, he ended up spending two years traveling with Cerruti to gather official documents for Bancroft, whose comprehensive history of California could not be written, Vallejo knew, without his rich archive of official documents and his own memoirs. The result is a personal narrative in which different ideologies and different emotions meet on the page, the residue of republican political ideals and self-interest intersecting with the reality of socioeconomic displacement and cultural decimation. Yet however ideologically ambivalent, Vallejo's "Recuerdos históricos y personales" is historiographically confrontational and insistently revisionist in its affirmative view of Californio society and culture before the American conquest. Indeed, together with his tireless efforts to gather official documents and encourage other men and women to gather their memories for posterity, Vallejo's composition of the "Recuerdos históricos y personales" constitutes a deliberate act of historiographic preemption against an aggregation of negative representations of Mexican Californians that rationalized the American conquest and the deforcement of his people after 1848. Rather than strictly self-serving, therefore, his writing and document gathering constituted a forceful act of opposition to contemporary as well as future historiographic erasure. As he wrote to his son, Platon, when he was nearly finished with the huge five-volume undertaking, "The history will come out and it will be as you've heard me say many times, the truth impartially written so it can serve posterity as a guide."

Vallejo's narrative confirms Georges Gusdorf's proposition that "memoirs are always . . . a revenge on history."[42] For Vallejo, the "Recuerdos históricos y personales" was a form of discursive revenge on negative representations of Mexicans that were being constructed during his own lifetime as well as a form of prior "revenge" on the negative history he had good reason to believe would be written about his people after him. I have no doubt that Vallejo collaborated on his narrative to gratify his own ego; after all, he claimed that Bancroft's projected *History of California* could not be written without the name *Vallejo* at its center. Vallejo was indeed among that class identified by Gusdorf as "the minister of state, the politician, the military man [who] write in order to celebrate their deeds (always more or less misunderstood), providing a sort of posthumous propaganda for posterity that otherwise is in danger of forgetting them or of failing to esteem them properly" (1956:36). Yet Vallejo also recognized the stakes involved for all of his people when he wrote "Recuerdos históricos y personales" and encouraged other

Californios to relate their narratives. Vallejo's work indeed functioned as "a sort of posthumous propaganda for posterity," but it was
also a keen response to the historiography of his own moment. In
this respect, "Recuerdos históricos y personales" may be read as a
preemptive narrative strategy intended not so much to forestall as
to masterscript Bancroft's history. His unyielding supervision of
"Recuerdos históricos y personales" was nothing less than a battle
for control of historiographic (and self-) representation that would,
at the least, guarantee textual historical presence after he and his
people had vanished, as it was supposed they would. In a letter to
a friend, he wrote that unless they wrote their own histories, they
would "disappear, ignored of the whole world."

The Bancroft collection also contains about fifteen narratives by
women that describe events before and during the Americanization
of the territory from a gendered perspective that both criticizes patriarchal constraint in Mexican society and yet refutes common assumptions that Mexican women were not bothered by the conquest.
Indeed, one of the reasons there are not more narratives is because
many women were so angry with the Americans that they simply
refused to collaborate in giving their life stories. As Leonard Pitt
writes in his classic study, *The Decline of the Californios*, "The
widows of the Carrillo brothers stiffly refused any recollections, and
Señora José Castro bristled at the merest suggestion that she should
contribute information to clear her husband's clouded reputation."[43]
Rosalía Vallejo de Leese did speak, but, she was so incensed, it is
through clenched teeth that she tells of the American conquest.
"Those hated men inspired me with such a large dose of hate against
their race," she recalls, "that though twenty-eight years have
elapsed since that time, I have not forgotten the insults heaped upon
me, and not being desirous of coming in contact with them I have
abstained from learning their language."[44] Notwithstanding their
ambivalence, other women like María Inocente Pico de Avila, Catarina Avila de Ríos, Apolinaria Lorenzana, María de las Angustias de
la Guerra, and my favorite, Eulalia Pérez, said to be 139 years old
when her life story was recorded, are among some dozen women
who offer revealing views on gender relations in Californio society
and disclose their own strategies of self-empowerment.

In chapter 4, I trace the manner in which women subverted a
testimonial procedure intended to elicit information from them for
what Bancroft referred to as the "women's sphere"—a sphere of do-
mesticity, self-effacement, silence. As Sidonie Smith argues, "Since
the ideology of gender makes of woman's life script a nonstory, a

silent space, a gap in patriarchal culture, the ideal woman is self-effacing rather than self-promoting, and her 'natural' story shapes itself not around the public, heroic life but around the fluid, circumstantial, contingent responses to others that according to patriarchal ideology, characterizes the life of woman. . . . From that point of view, woman has no 'autobiographical self' in the same sense that man does. From that point of view, she has no 'public' story to tell."[45] However, as Smith continues, women have long resisted such voicelessness and have reconstructed themselves as figures possessed of a will to power in the world. Rather than subordinate themselves to domestic memory, that is, to voices within the "women's sphere" that would make their "life script a nonstory, a silent space, a gap in patriarchal culture," Mexican American women—speaking their lives to Bancroft—invariably voiced resistance to the patriarchal domination that characterized social relations in Mexican California and assertively figured themselves as agents in the social world they inhabited along with, not at the side of, men. So, at the directive of Bancroft's assistants, Pérez's and Lorenzana's personal narratives may begin with descriptions about their domestic work in early California missions, but voice quickly opens toward recollection of their tough-minded independence and will toward self-sufficiency in a male-dominated society. From de la Guerra, Bancroft's interlocutor, Thomas Savage, wished to solicit information on "government matters" and political events because of her affiliations with powerful public men—her father, her brothers, and her first husband. What one witnesses in the women's narratives is that women like de la Guerra remember themselves as agents in political events rather than as domestically passive witnesses to men's activities in the public realm. In fact, de la Guerra figures herself and other women as sociopolitically perspicacious and courageous, whereas the political patriarchs of the country were, she charges, more often than not blind to the threat of American encroachment, enfeebled by political corruption and embarrassingly cowardly when "it came time to defend the country."

As with nearly all nineteenth- and early twentieth-century autobiographical narratives by Mexican Americans, the archaeological recovery of the Californio life histories requires lifting them from their lowercase status, chipping away the Bancroft text that encases them, brushing the dust off their covers, and, by publishing and reading them, restoring the presence of their voices. Felipe Fierro, Vallejo's contemporary and the editor of the San Francisco newspaper *La Voz del Nuevo Mundo*, recognized the gravity of recording life histories when he pleaded with his readers to participate in the Bancroft project, not for Bancroft's benefit but in anticipation of the day their stories would be given a public life of their own. Fierro's editorial comments to the Californios in *La Voz* on March 7, 1876, echoed in other parts of the West: "De ese modo llegará el día en que los sucesos, lo mismo que los servicios de los buenos ciudadanos, sean dados a la luz de una manera digna de ellos" (In such manner the day will arrive when the events, as well as the contributions of these good citizens, will be given public light in a manner deserving of them).[46]

Fierro's editorial articulates an understanding on the part of an entire generation that they must inscribe themselves upon history, or disappear. The "public light" Fierro envisioned, therefore, would function as more than an obligatory contribution to the historiography of California. Fear of being systematically erased by an ethnocentric society generated an autobiographical impulse in post–1848 Mexican American society through which people seized the opportunity to textually mark their individual names as well as their culture upon American history. Such was the case because by the 1870s, when their life histories were recorded, most of the Californios had been despoiled. An established way of life was disintegrating, being rubbed out, erased even at the moment the life was being narrated, transcribed, textualized. It is the disjuncture between a valorized pre-American life and the profound sense of loss after the invasion that provided the autobiographical moment when past and present could be reconsidered, conjoined, reconciled to some degree by scores of people trying to make sense of their experience. I read these personal narratives as legitimate autobiographical enunciations by individuals whose voices have not been merely forgotten but, like the people themselves, suppressed. Rather than affixing any degree of historical truth value to their testimony, or arguing the merits of their representativeness of Mexican Californian culture, my primary concern is to recover the voices of these ghosts. They make their own claim to autobiographical recovery simply because, within the confines of oral testimony meant to subordinate their stories to Bancroft history, these women and men marked their narratives with individual presence. The narratives bequeathed by these individuals may have been used by Bancroft as social history, but it is the ever-present "I" within that transforms them from oral history into the genre of life writing we call autobiography.

Nevertheless, among the issues that come into question when thinking about the Californio personal narratives is their *autobio-*

graphical integrity. The degree to which these dictated narratives direct, distort, or otherwise decentralize the autobiographical subject is, I believe, an important issue. In brief, I argue that whereas for Bancroft the collection of these personal narratives was foundational research for his *History of California* project, for the narrators themselves it was the critical and perhaps only occasion for re-creating the life of the self, together with the world inhabited by that self. Yet precisely because some of the narratives to which I refer were neither self-composed nor meant to function strictly as autobiography, claiming autobiographical status for certain texts once again raises the proprietary issue of genre that must be clarified. To echo one of the questions Krupat (1985:31–32) asks about Native American autobiography, "To what extent is it responsible to treat works presented as contributions to history and ethnography as works of literature?" Such an issue is of immediate concern for anyone intent on explaining the sociocultural, ideological, and discursive conditions that underlie the formation of autobiographical consciousness in Mexican American society. The dilemma confronted by Krupat, H. David Brumble, and other scholars of Native American autobiography who have had to consider the autobiographical fashioning of native people by Anglo-American amanuenses, whether historians, anthropologists, poets (John J. Neihardt), or journalists, serves as both warning and instruction for my work. As Krupat saliently points out, "Indian autobiographies are collaborative efforts, jointly produced by some white who translates, transcribes, compiles, edits, interprets, polishes, and ultimately determines the form of the text in writing, and by an Indian who is its subject and whose life becomes the content of the 'autobiography' whose title may bear his name" (1985:30). One can no longer naively read collaboratively produced narrative without thinking about editorial construction with all of its customary manipulations, performative stagings, transcriptional excisions, translations (not to mention mistranslations), additions, and refashionings. Certainly, the problematics of Hubert Bancroft's collection of scores of California personal narratives from oral dictations—with all of the editorial mechanics of formulaic questioning (masked in most narratives but noticeable when comparing statement clusters on certain crucial historical events), the selecting out of many informants whose memories were considered faulty, the hurried pace of collection mentioned in the prefatory statements of the field collectors and evinced by numerous transcriptional truncations— requires recognition and analysis of the power differential inscribed within the very formation of autobiographical articulation.

Yet although we must assess the interpolations of editorial construction, we must also recognize that, as Krupat suggests,[47] bicultural collaboration is a site of contention for authority over narrative self-representation (at the ground level of speech), as well as the site of socially symbolic contestations over the Mexican American's political, cultural, and social status in the United States. The disclosure of individual experience and the overlay of individual personality on the description of external sociopolitical events mark the Californio narratives with distinct autobiographical authority, just as the signature of the "I" identifies authorial status in various autobiographical enunciations, markings, and representations throughout the narratives. Autobiographical authority, I would therefore argue, need not be thought of as issuing only from the hand that scribes personal experience but rather from what I believe is a deep human desire to shape and control narrative, to modulate its articulation by that small stubbornness of voice that insists on its own story and that reconstructs the past in a register that claims ownership of the past, especially when ownership of the present is endangered.

Central to the reclaiming of the Mexican past was the narrative habit of remembering oneself within a community of the past. It is no surprise, therefore, to see that many of the nineteenth- and early twentieth-century narratives that comprise the beginnings of Chicano autobiography construct a culturally matrixed subjectivity in which the "I" is subsumed within a narrative of regional or cultural history. This displacement of a self-absorbed "I"-centered narrative by narrative in which the cultural subject is refigured within a collective matrix may be regarded as a filial act. The collective "I" indeed sustains itself by narratively restoring the cultural ecology in which it lives: the history of the cultural community constitutes the history of the "I," or, to put it another way, the "I" is but an empty cipher, a floating signifier without content until it is grounded by a collective identitarian utterance, by an act of cultural recuperation of the kind Jaramillo (in one of the opening epigraphs) refers to as describing a "current invisible to the stranger and understood only by their inhabitants," or, as in the case of Vallejo, reading oneself into the Spanish colonial and Mexican social and political history of California. Indeed, such narratives reside outside the formal boundaries scholars have traditionally reserved for autobiography as a singularly, self-disclosing text, "a retrospective prose narrative produced by a real person concerning his own existence, focusing on his individual life, in particular on the development of his personality."[48] As more and more autobiography scholars, especially feminist and

Third World practitioners, are arguing, traditional genre constraints have been exclusionary and must be renegotiated, wedged open to alternate forms of self-representation—historiography, cultural ethnography, folkloristic narratives—that do not focus exclusively on the development of individual personality so much as on the formation, and transformation, of the individual within a community.[49] Hence, narratives that some scholars would consider more properly within the domain of social history or cultural ethnography but that I believe a culturally historicized and contextually reaccentuated reading will discover to be a kind of communitarian autobiography must not be categorically dismissed as nonautobiographical. This is not to argue that Mexican American autobiographical expression is devoid of ego (Vallejo telling Bancroft's scribe, "I will not be hurried or dictated to. It is my history and not yours I propose to tell.") but rather that in the years after 1848, the Mexican community underwent such a global assault that even powerfully self-assertive individuals like Vallejo were put in a position of reading their own lives against the ruins of their social world. Therefore, we must read for autobiographical content within a complex narrative matrix in which individuals who composed or related their communal histories were simultaneously composing the history of the self and its shaping, twisting, reconfigurating response to social transformation in a voice (voices, really) that appropriated the exogenous historiographic and ethnographic discourses through which they were licensed to speak.

IV

Autobiographical demarcation for Mexican Americans after 1848 must be read as desire to reconstitute the self of an earlier presence, as desire to reconstruct the habitation of an earlier life, of a past made habitable again in the memory's imagination even as, or especially when, memory was confronting the excoriations of the past in its waking moments. There is, as I have suggested, a danger in remembering the past as idealized social space. Nostalgia for an earlier world emerged from grief for a world lost. As Janet Varner Gunn argues of *Black Elk Speaks*, everything Black Elk "relates to Neihardt is being spoken . . . from the retrospective standpoint of that lonely hill of his old age after he and his people have been displaced from [what Gusdorf calls] 'the mythic framework of traditional teachings' to 'the perilous domain of history.' . . . [And thus] this erstwhile traditional man occupies a place between his loss and his

finding, a space he fills with his speaking."[50] For Gunn, such autobiography occupies a "liminal space where what has been lost can
only be recalled and what might be possible, only anticipated. Especially alluring for such autobiography in such an in-between place
is a temptation toward nostalgia" (137). In part, I agree with Gunn
when she says that part of the illusion of such nostalgia is that
"were it able to eject itself from temporality, the self would find
some unspoiled Eden (the 'enchanted realm' of childhood) awaiting
its arrival," and corollary "to the nostalgic pull towards a perfect
past is the allure of utopian imagination, which must ignore both
the past and the *nunc stans* of the present in its catapult into some
illusory future devoid of all tenses" (137–138). However, the world
of the past reconstructed in Native American and Mexican American autobiographical narrative constitutes remembrance of a prior
social economy, a cultural geography that however non-Edenic was
no illusion.

The autobiographical formation in Mexican American culture
often figures the past as utopian, but this is because post-1848 life
was a nightmare; so if the social economy of pre-American life was
fashioned as coherent and sane, it was because the present of the
American regime was culturally incoherent and socially insane.
Juan Seguín, Mariano Vallejo, and Cleofas Jaramillo, over the duration of a century, each knew that claiming ownership of the past
(however that past was fashioned) must fill a space emptied of presence by American social domination and, its adjunct, a historiography of the American conquest that discursively decimated Mexican
people. Fully cognizant that Mexican Americans must write their
own history or, as he wrote to Anastacio Carrillo, "disappear, ignored of the whole world" (Pitt 1971:278), Vallejo wrote nine hundred pages of personal memoirs in the 1860s only to have the manuscript burn in a fire that destroyed his home in 1867. Then, while he
was traveling throughout California in the 1870s, writing his own
memoirs once again and encouraging men and women of this generation to dictate their personal narratives as well as place them in
archives, Vallejo beseeched people to remember and restore the past
against misrepresentation and betrayal. As Pitt writes, because they
"perceived themselves not merely as the victims of annexation or
assimilation, but of deliberate betrayal and bone-crushing repression," Mexican Californians like Vallejo emphasized "injustice, violence and broken promises in their memoirs" (1971:278, 283). Indeed, nostalgia appeared in their memoirs as a revisitation of a
coherent and harmonious past, but even memoirs that masked the

anger that produces nostalgia in the first place were politicized by loss and anger. Rather than uncritical celebration of an idyllic and unobtainable past, therefore, nostalgia may be seen to function as ideological opposition to having their world destroyed.

What I want to argue, therefore, is that negative—and negating—readings of what may be termed narratives of nostalgia for life in an idealized past would press the burden of ideological acquiescence on the Mexican American subject without carefully considering the political, economic, social, and discursive grids of domination that dictated the everyday lives of Mexican Americans, pressing them into subordination in the discursive realm just as in the material realm. What I wish to think about in parts of this study is the formation of socially subordinate and discursively imprisoned personal narrative. What happens when the autobiographical impulse finds its self-constitutive operations undermined by the very discursive practices that make autobiographical presentation possible? What happens when a conquered people find themselves in a situation where memory is encouraged to speak itself into textual permanence but only in an idiom that marks the boundaries of permissible utterance? Given the discursive domination to which the subordinate cultural subject must make supplication if she or he wishes to survive in any form, the autobiographical "I" is likely to find itself represented by a voice that masks painful feelings about social displacement. The "I" is made alien to itself, existing as it does implicated in a discursive world outside of its own making or control. We discover an "I" that reveals its incarceration within a network of discursive practices invented by cultural imperialists whose goal has been and continues to be to lock it into a cell of alien linguistic culture, social economy, and ideology, into a consciousness that participates in its own submission, and, where necessary to material and social survival, to the self-figurations in a utopian past.

As I have already suggested, the post–1848 military domination of northern Mexico was only the initial blow that gave way to various forms of coercion through which the conquest sought to complete itself. As in all wars of conquest, the dominating culture—from the moment it forces another group supine—must subvert the structure of the group's ideological consciousness as much as possible. It must make the subjugated culture forget the details of its domination as a way of making it believe that it has not surrendered so much as availed itself of a more progressive sociocultural national experience. In short, it seeks to bring the subject group to consent. Where there is dissent from sectors of the subjugated group, perhaps from those who occupy the lower social strata and whose resentments are not compromised by having to protect their class status, the dominating culture must bring the precolonial elites into closer proximity with its structures of power, must make these dispossessed elites deceive themselves into thinking they occupy positions of authority, must turn that carefully monitored authority against those sectors that openly resist. The dispossessed elites, in addition to the modicum of political power they are granted, are also fitted with a socioideological discourse that not only accedes to their dispossession but becomes the official cultural discourse through which the suppressed group makes sufferable its subordination. Domination and suppression, the reality of the group's material and social condition, is often narratively occluded, or transformed into a narrative of life in an imaginary pre-American past through which aristocratic pretense, genealogical invention, and political self-deceit articulate resistance in language often ideologically deaf to itself.

What residue of culturally resolute subjectivity can we look for in narrative that has been denatured, robbed of much of its historical memory, made prisoner of an illusory and idyllic past? Since cultural hegemony is seldom complete—that is to say, since every subject, or prisoner, wishes to be free—there are moments where dissent discloses itself in even the most acquiescent discourse. We must look for disruptions in the narrative, revealed perhaps only in whispers of resistance, quelled immediately but signaling like a flash through the dense texture of language and reified memory. In such disruptions, we discover those gaps in the narrative where the native cultural "I" voices resistance against the dominant Other through the bars of the ideological prison in which it is confined.

Understood as a response to displacement and erasure, narratives in which nostalgia emerges as discursive countervalent to loss may be read as expressions of opposition rather than as unmediated and noncritical reflexes to displacement. To remember is not only the act of not forgetting but the act of not being forgotten, just as remembering the past as utopian cultural terrain reveals the very conditions of cultural dislocation that made a necessity of retrospective communitarian idealization. The narrative reconstitution of an earlier world may be troubled by "utopian imagination," but the original trauma of displacement (the American conquest of 1846–1848) and an unrelenting assault on the cultural habitat establish a form of autobiographical consciousness in which Mexican American writers understood that their posterity's future was staked in establishing a version of the past, a historical text, that must stand against erasure at worst or negative historical representation at best. Nostalgia for the past ends in the future when it reveals a recognition that there are stakes involved in the reconstruction(s) of the cultural past, idealized or not. Post–1848 Mexican American autobiographical narrative projects a future condition, therefore, in which a Chicano reader in the late twentieth century reads personal narrative "de una manera digna de ellos."

Unless we wish to think of Mexicans as either blind or stupid, I believe we must recontextualize our reading of their narratives to understand their social and discursive situations. We must recognize that colonized Mexicans were often speaking out of both sides of their mouths with visionary social purpose. As I argue in chapter 2, what may at first appear as ideologically subordinate speech actually constitutes multiaddressed utterance in which pragmatic appeasement reads at one surface of language and contestation reads at other surfaces. Such strategic utterance, I maintain, constitutes a form of rhetorical duplicity that first appropriates a public "voice" for an individual from an otherwise "silenced" group and then turns that voice to oppositional purpose. Discursive duplicity functions to communicate different stories to different audiences, with an implicit understanding that one's own people will, to follow Fierro's comments, someday read them "de una manera digna de ellos"; that is, in a manner that restores the difficult conditions under which they were produced and through which they must speak to us—the future audience to which Fierro referred and for which Vallejo hoped.

V

Given what I have suggested here about the multivoiced narrative strategies deployed by Mexican American autobiographers to sustain a dignified cultural self, it is also necessary for scholars to assess the autobiographical disclosure of cultural denial that characterizes some autobiographical narrative. Since a good deal of the autobiography composed by Mexican Americans has been a sorting out of cultural identity, or identities, as well as a consideration of the position that individuals occupy, or are allowed to occupy, in American society, it should be no surprise to discover autobiographical texts inhabited by *Mexicanos* posing as loyal Americans. Such *Mexicanos* have, from the moment a part of their nation collapsed in 1848, presented the spectacle of the cultural "other" trying various means of transformation into "Americans." Richard Rodriguez, author of the widely discussed *Hunger of Memory*,[51] is by no means the first Chicano autobiographer who has publicly disaffiliated himself from his culture so as to assume the mask of the "middle-class" American. Rodriguez's autobiography has provoked a spate of commentary over the issue of cultural loyalty and the individual's public, in this case, textual, responsibility to the group.[52] Such textual self-denial represents the desire to create a new self through language, as though to write oneself into a different life, to shed one skin for another through an incantation of self-describing words. The only obstacle to complete assimilation for such "Americans" has been their rejection by those "real Americans" who, for instance, 150 years ago reminded Juan Nepumuceno Seguín that he could pen himself as "John" and drop his strange middle name to "N" but that he was still just a "Mexican." Notwithstanding the incessant reminders of marginal social acceptance, however, a succession of *Mexicanos* from Seguín to Rodriguez have invented "American" personas with which they make their way in North American society.

Whether Rodriguez and his antecedents—a Tejano Confederate soldier, a Mexican Texas Ranger, or a culturally self-denying "Spanish-American" territorial governor—should be disavowed is an issue readers must decide for themselves. However, precisely because their lives refuse to conform to some of the images we have created for ourselves, especially in recent years when we have radicalized that self-image, their autobiographies do force us to recognize variations of the Chicano self. Reading Mexican American autobiography during its first one hundred years forced me to expand the image of the *Mexicano* I had constructed, an image that was obviously too easily divided between self-serving elites and humble, working-class *Mexicanos.* I expected culturally ambivalent "Spanish-American" politicians: Seguín and Vallejo had prepared me for that. So Miguel Antonio Otero, appointed territorial governor of New Mexico by McKinley in 1897, came as no surprise. But a *Mexicano* Confederate soldier? Never. That a *Mexicano* would ever be part of the Confederacy had simply never crossed my mind; as it turns out, there were many Confederate sympathizers in the *Mexicano* community, especially in Texas, and as I have discovered, at least two men—Santiago Tafolla and José Policarpio Rodríguez— who wrote about their experiences in the Gray. Even more surprising, no, dumbfounding, was the discovery of a *Mexicano* Texas Ranger. Whereas I had simply assumed that the only relation between *rinches* (Texas Rangers) and *Mexicanos* was that of the lynch mob to its victims, Jesse Pérez's "Memoirs" provided a shock: Pérez was a member of one of the most anti-Mexicano groups in the Southwest, mostly for the money, of course, but also because he liked thinking of himself as a Ranger. It allowed him to share in a power network from which Mexicanos had been excluded, and unfortunately, it constructed an ideological consciousness in him that largely alienated him from his own community.

Rodríguez's "*The Old Guide*" intends to be more than an account of his long experience as a soldier, scout, Indian fighter, ranchman, and guide; it is, in the end, a traditional Protestant narrative of a sinner's life before his conversion. The central event of his life, as he records it, is his conversion, experienced in true Pauline fashion while he is riding his horse, and his subsequent decision to give up everything to preach the word of Christ. In addition to the sociopolitical dimensions present throughout the text, Rodríguez's narrative must be examined for the configuration of spiritual life it seeks to identify. But conversion does not take place without familial and cultural repercussions. Rodríguez's transformation put him at odds with his immediate family as well as with the larger, predominantly Mexican Catholic community who regarded him with suspicion because he had given up a vital part of his Mexican heritage as seated in religious practice. As Rodríguez writes, his wife "burst into tears and told the children that their father had gone crazy," and, outside of the family, his "conversion made a great sensation among my neighbors and friends; and . . . the report that I had gone crazy was believed by many. It was so different from anything they had ever heard of, and from any idea about religion that they could not explain it in any way except by saying that I had lost my reason."[53]

In Pérez's case, his association and ideological identification with the Rangers seem to indicate that perhaps he was *agringado* (assimilated) enough to have crossed the line. Yet the language of his memoirs is, it seems to me, one of the most striking representations of thickly accented Mexicano English I have ever read. No matter that he was a Ranger, he surely betrayed himself as a Mexicano every time he opened his mouth.[54] Would it be too speculative to think that Pérez was the unknowing dupe, the Mexican go-between who was used by the Rangers to effect their policies against other *Mexicanos* on either side of the border? I think not. Here, then, Pérez's autobiographical language complicates, actually subverts, his own autobiographical intent. Whereas many other Rangers had their memoirs published,[55] Pérez was silenced, one suspects, because he sounded too much like a "Mexican." Such an image—a Mexican Texas Ranger—would simply not do, since it did not accord with the mythic figure of the Ranger as a tall, broad-shouldered, fair-skinned son of Texas.

As much as each of these Mexican Americans represent themselves as "fellow," or "assimilated middle-class" Americans (as in the case of Richard Rodriguez), there are repeated narrative intrusions where they worry through the obstacles that function to identify them as "other" and effectively exclude them from the mainstream. On one hand, their narratives may be read as culturally self-denying texts; on the other, a different text superposes itself which discloses evidence of cultural confusion and divided loyalties—the condition of a destabilized identity to which I earlier referred. We must train ourselves upon such contradictions to arrive at a literary and cultural analysis that will make clearer the formation of our inherited literary discourse. These early narratives are worthy of close analysis because they show how statement is structured, first, by the actual conditions of physical threat and, then, by what must have felt like the overwhelming, nearly dispiriting, crush of an "alien culture." Necessity established the contradictory conditions by which later autobiographical expressivity would structure representation through multivocality and through what is contained in such multivocalities: ideological contradiction, nostalgia as the expression of dislocation, proclamations of loyalty to an "alien political system in an alien culture," rhetorical gestures of accommodation sublated by the autobiographical encodations of rage, heterogeneous narratives of cultural, historical, and self-representation that function as a prospectus for a future mediated and often mangled by ethnocentrism, exclusion, and physical violence.

As I argue in chapter 2, therefore, Vallejo in California, Juan Bautista Vigil y Alaríd in New Mexico, and Juan Seguín in Texas each wrote carefully crafted articles of capitulation to the American invaders in which, subjacent to appeasement and accommodation, personal and general resentment, fear, and anger in the Mexican populace are voiced as palimpsest. As early as 1858, we find an autobiographical document in Juan Nepumuceno Seguín's *Personal Memoirs* which appears to direct different messages to different cultural audiences. On the one hand, Seguín's narrative reads like a schizoid cultural document, a textual vortex of confusion, contradictions, dissimulation, and self-deceit. On the other, its very contradictions, like those in Vallejo's "Recuerdos históricos y personales," appear purposive if one considers that Seguín is simultaneously addressing an American and a Mexican audience and a Mexican American audience not yet born—his "Posterity." Although the narrative seems motivated by Seguín's desire to win the sympathy of "the American people" so as to reestablish his social standing in San Antonio after the U.S.-Mexican War, it also functions as a cipher to the Mexican community, signifying that its dealings with the Americans will be troubled, its proclamations of loyalty to the American state rejected, its land despoiled and stolen, its families reduced to begging as was his. Seguín's *Personal Memoirs* may be read, then, as both an acquiescent and a subversive text, a narrative meant to appease one cultural audience while warning the other. Such a rhetorical stratagem proceeds from the necessity of engaging in a form of cultural double-speak when there are high personal stakes and contending communities involved. Françoise Lionnet provides an apt metaphor for the sociodiscursive efficacy of such multiply coded statement with her concept of rhetorical *métis:* "an art of transformation and transmutation, an aesthetics of the ruse that allows the weak to survive by escaping through duplicitous means the very system of power intent on destroying them. . . . Such practices had to be learned . . . as survival tactics within a hostile environment that kept them subjugated, relegated them to the margins."[56]

The rhetoric of accommodation, however seemingly mired in nostalgia and implicated in an apologetics of complicity with the Americans, must be read as oppositional *métis* alongside other forms of narrative resistance to American hostility and hegemony. The *corrido* (ballad) tradition along the border in Texas, for example, stages an ideal of personal, especially masculine, heroics that expresses collective desire for sustaining presence against physical threat and sociocultural erasure. As Américo Paredes long ago argued, the significance of *corridos* such as the ballad of Gregorio Cortez is that they sustain collective psychological belief on the part of powerless people confronted on a daily basis by social, political, and legal injustice.[57] However, to selectively privilege only narrative practice that *imagines* open resistance to the *rinches* by a "warrior hero" seems to me to opt for only one form of symbolic action when in everyday life opposition takes many forms. The warrior hero may indeed have provided some of our *antepasados,* as well as us, their posterity, with a form of symbolic action against oppression, but what power we have seized from such a ballad tradition of armed warrior heroes is heavily more imaginary than real, more deeply symbolic than acted in the world of segregated schools and restaurants with signs reading "No Mexicans Allowed," or against an exploitative labor economy in which men and women contained their anger and frustration because they needed even poorly paying jobs to keep their families whole. To derogate or dismiss Seguín, Vallejo, Jaramillo, Pérez, or José Policarpio Rodríguez because they do not provide us with heroic narrative resistance seems to me not only a mistake but a form of arrogance that blinds us to the difficulty most of our *antepasados* encountered in the everyday social world.

Recognizing the social and discursive pressures that forced my *antepasados* to comply with the dominant group—*los americanos*—forced me to reconsider my own initial disaffection with such figures as Seguín, Vallejo, and Jaramillo to arrive at an understanding of part of my own history. This is to say that like other Chicano critics of my generation, I have been troubled and in no small way alienated by Seguín's apologetics, Vallejo's and even Angustias de la Guerra's class privilege, and Jaramillo's aristocratic *Spanish* pretenses. After all, my own family's experience in New Mexico can hardly be considered an aristocratic romance: my mother's family was part of a displaced Nuevomexicano migrant group of the 1920s and 1930s who cut sugar beets and harvested potatoes in southern Colorado ("Your grandpa wasn't afraid to do any kind of work—era muy macho. And I worked alongside him from the time I was a girl," my mother, Esperanza Lopez, wrote to me not long ago), and my father (Manuel Padilla) only went to the sixth grade before he joined his brothers laboring in the Santa Fe railroad shops in Albuquerque. Perhaps I should have no truck with Vallejo, a man for whom my father would have worked as a blacksmith at best, or with Jaramillo, who might have looked at my mother's dark face and dismissively seen more Indian than Spaniard. But that would be too easy. Whether I like it or not, reading Vallejo's and Jaramillo's and Seguín's autobiographical narratives provides filiative traces of my own historical and cultural "I," the self that discovers its genealogical flesh in the lives of my parents as well as in those narratives that are my textual *parientes* (relatives). It may be that in retrospect I see more clearly than they the sociodiscursive effects of subordination, but it is they whose lived and textual experience, however mediated by the exigencies of daily reality, wedged the opening for wider resistance in another time and place. Given the dangerous situation in which they found themselves, it is a "wonder they wrote at all," to echo Rebolledo.

To raise troubling antecedent texts—whether those of Pérez, Jaramillo, or Seguín—to incorporation within the Chicano literary tradition, therefore, requires more than summarily, or begrudgingly, recognizing their presence with the chronology of our literary production. The narrative exhibition of what Antonio Gramsci refers

to as subordinate, or "subaltern," consciousness is an embarrass-
ment only when we do not fully unravel the extraordinary nexus
of domination and control that our *antepasados* experienced. The
corrido tradition with its figure of the male warrior hero is one form
of socially symbolic resistance, but there are other figures of resistance as well—Angustias de la Guerra describing how she and
other women responded to the American invasion, Chacón and other
Nuevomexicanos enduring privation and American hostility in the
service of the U.S. military, Jaramillo trying to return the spectacle
of the Santa Fe fiesta to native custom. The autobiographical formation I am interested in examining here, therefore, discloses contradiction, uncertainty, fear, a desire to read the past as utopian ideal
over and against a gringo version of the past as barren terrain for the
taking, autobiographical narrative that fashions an image of prior
social and cultural coherence as a mode of resistance within the everyday social and discursive world. The marks of contradictory consciousness are all too common in the autobiographical narratives of
the period I examine. Historical memory evokes articulations of resistance to the dominant culture and within the same breath gestures of retraction (but already their Chicano posterity has heard and
remembers the other voice). We must account for the complex narrative voicings of socially subordinate writers without losing ourselves to a form of progressive intellectual snobbery that ignores or
dismisses those flashes of opposition in early autobiographical discourse that are a textual signal of embryonic consciousness, articulations of antecedent resistance that we must carefully listen to so
as to hear—"de una manera digna de ellos"—how our *antepasados*
negotiated a terrain of uncertainty.

Although the politics of much of our recent analysis may indeed
read itself as openly and courageously opposed to the bigotry our
people have had to confront historically, as Chicanos we must remind ourselves that the language our own writing takes tends also
to accommodate itself to the often viciously hegemonic require-
ments of the academy, which demands that we mimic a particular
way of speaking, thus thinking, if we are to be heard at all by our
colleagues. Operating during a period in which we speak within a
space that licenses contestatory articulation, we must nevertheless
remember that our license is relative to the authority exercised
within the profession by what I call the "tweeds," those who have
as little regard for Chicano scholars (and our scholarship) as factory
and farm owners have for *their* Mexicans (although the product of
their labor is probably more appreciated than is our scholarship).

The lesson, therefore, should be that however accommodating our *antepasados* seem to us now, Rebolledo's unequivocal "wonder that they wrote at all" should guide our thinking about the sociodiscursive dilemma in which they found themselves and through which they assiduously sought to preserve in writing those elements of cultural practice, however romanticized, that affirmed an identity distinct from that of the dominant culture.

Whether they are the personal narratives collected by Bancroft or those numerous other autobiographical documents located in Texas, Colorado, and New Mexico and throughout the West, the textual recovery of nineteenth- and early twentieth-century personal narratives can no longer be delayed. And although the archaeological project itself is just beginning, it must be accompanied by an interpretive activity that will describe the inter- and intracultural forces that have shaped the Chicano cultural subject and the narrative it constructs for itself.

The work of memory and the struggles of self-representation that address us through a rhetoric of accommodation—Lionnet's *métis* of the "aesthetic of the ruse"—begins in Texas in 1836 and in California and New Mexico in 1846 when the American military illegally crossed the border into northern Mexico.

2
Autobiographical Prefigurations
The Encodations of Accommodation

Autobiographical consciousness in Mexican American culture opens when the world inhabited by our *antepasados* was forced to surrender itself to the United States, but under coercion learned a language of subversion, developed complex narrative strategies for dealing with defeat without being defeated, and crafted multiple modes of self-representational articulation that would speak to us from the grave. Because autobiographical impulse comes into formation as a response to sociohistorical rupture, we must begin by looking at the immediate responses to that nightmare of history for nineteenth-century Mexicans of the far northern *provincias,* the outward posts of nearly forgotten Spanish colonial frontiers, the emerging but unstable territory where the Mexican map grated against that of ever-invasive North Americans who wanted not to share the map but to redraw it entirely. We must begin with those painful and confusing events that tore Mexico in half, because it was that tear which, as I have already suggested, ruptured everyday life, altering social and cultural practices as it pulled the map out from under the feet of some 100,000 Mexican citizens.

As Saldívar argues in his study of Chicano narrative, "History is the subtext that we must recover because history itself is the subject of its discourse" (1989:5). History's discontinuity, the split and abrupt dehiscence of a people's social practices and cultural habitat in 1846, "turns out to be the decisive determinant of the form and content" (ibid.) that autobiographical narrative assumes in its obsessive attempt to reconcile the personal life with historical disjuncture. The immediate rhetorical responses to the American conquest disclose the formation of multiply coded statements that measured the accommodations of the moment against a vision of an altered and frightening future. The work of memory and self-representation, addressing us through a rhetoric of Lionnet's aesthetic of the ruse, begins in Texas in 1836 and in California and New Mexico in 1846 when the American takeover of northern Mexico began.

During the 1830s, the American settlement of Texas, the opening of the Santa Fe Trail into New Mexico, and the development of coastal commercial exchange in California brought North Americans and Mexicans into contact. In Tejas, American immigrants outnumbered Mexicans in 1830 by 20,000 to 5,000, and by 1834, these immigrants moved to secede from Mexico; after initial Mexican victories at the Alamo and Goliad, the Americans defeated President Antonio López de Santa Anna's troops at San Jacinto, forced his surrender, and by 1836 the Texas Republic was formed. During this period, Texas Mexicans like José Antonio Navarro, Erasmo Seguín, his son Juan, and other landed Mexican families incorporated themselves into the secessionist movement, believing they would share power in a republican form of government, only to find that they were, and always would be, "Mexicans"—neither trusted nor tolerated by their fellow American citizens. Juan Seguín, for instance, who had fought at the side of the Texans and had then been elected mayor of San Antonio in 1841, had to flee to Mexico in 1842, his life threatened by citizens who would not stand for a "Mexican" telling them what to do. In California, on the morning of June 14, 1846, a ragged group of Americans rode into the village of Sonoma, roused the *comandante-general*, Mariano G. Vallejo, and his fellow citizens, arrested Vallejo and other officials, proclaimed the formation of a new republic—the Bear Flag Republic—and promised the people of Sonoma that "as enemies we will kill and destroy you, but as friends we will share with you all the blessings of liberty." In Nuevo Mexico, people who had been settled in villages for some two centuries, were, on August 19, 1846, summarily told by an American general at the head of 1,500 troops that they were no longer Mexicans but American citizens; by fiat of proclamation they were "absolved" of Mexico, but unlike Texas and California, which were admitted to the Union at midcentury, they were left suspended in territorial status for sixty-six years because they were *too* Mexican to become members of the United States.

Let us begin in New Mexico on August 19, 1846, move back through Vallejo's startled encounter with the Bear Flaggers on June 14, and back again to Juan Seguín's account of events in Texas between 1836 and 1846 in the *Personal Memoirs*, an autobiographical narrative that prefigures the form and content of Mexican

American autobiography that follows. The discursive response to the American conquest, with all that it prefigured for Mexican people settled in the northern provinces, flashed immediately in a theater of rhetorical exchanges between conqueror and conquered, an exchange of statements in which Americans asserted their peaceful intentions with force of arms and in which Mexicans encoded resentment and resistance through the documents of submission they were forced to sign. The surrender statements made by Vigil y Alaríd in Santa Fe, Nuevo Mexico, and Vallejo in Sonoma, California, in June 1846 disclose in microtext the rhetorical strategies that mark later development of a particular discursive habit in Mexican American autobiographical narrative, which toward the end of this chapter, I argue, may be best characterized in the *Personal Memoirs* of Juan Seguín.

For Vigil y Alaríd, Vallejo, and Seguín, as for succeeding Mexican Americans, the conditions of public discourse are subject to fear, ambivalence, confusion, and uncertainty. Their personal statements disclose disillusionment with an American democratic rhetoric that is given the lie by the reality of hostile social relations. Their words betray a muttering recognition that they have been made fools, duped into believing in a sociopolitical and cultural alliance with American immigrants only to be summarily displaced from power, shoved off their property, their language and cultural practices derided. Vigil y Alaríd's and Vallejo's statements of surrender, followed by Seguín's apologetic *Personal Memoirs*, are documents that emerged from social situations that made a necessity of multiregistered address. Moreover, it seems to me that because there were contending communities and high personal stakes involved in intercultural address, such narrative palimpsesting created sociodiscursive bifocality, in which the reader's social situation and cultural-linguistic position obscured one surface and illuminated another. The *Personal Memoirs*, I will argue, may be read as narrative simultaneously intended to appease Anglo and Mexicano audiences by addressing different concerns for each, allowing one audience to read accommodation and appeasement, the other a warning. As I will show, Seguín's narrative operates as perhaps the first autobiographical articulation of divided subjectivity, of personal identity skewed by the continuity of the cultural border grating against the remapping of national borders, of daily life wedged by accommodation and yet by resistance to material and social change.

The articulatory schizophrenia apparent throughout Vigil y Alaríd's, Vallejo's, and Seguín's public statements of surrender is sociodiscursively predictable: they must speak contradiction because they are at the historical locus of contradiction; they must articulate ambivalence and divided loyalty because they occupy the historical site where divided subjectivity is formed, upon which intercultural tensions are fastened as fragmentation and confusion, where self-deceit and deception are joined, where accommodation and anger fill the same phrase, and where, in the social world, an unrelenting movement between borders, countries, cultures, and languages establishes subjectivity as difference. The textual vortex of necessary contradiction establishes the script for succeeding Mexican American personal narrative in which autobiographical statement marks the confounding situation of people undergoing deforcement, political and social displacement, and cultural destabilization. Such narrative necessity discloses the socially schizophrenic situation in which Mexicans found themselves after 1848.

II

> General:—The address which you have just delivered, in which you announce that you have just taken possession of this great country in the name of the United States of America, gives us some idea of the wonderful future that awaits us. It is not for us to determine the boundaries of nations. The cabinets of Mexico and Washington will arrange these differences. It is for us to obey and respect the established authorities, no matter what our private opinions.
>
> The inhabitants of this department (New Mexico) humbly and honorably present their loyalty to the government of North America. No one in this world can successfully resist the power of him who is stronger.
>
> Do not find it strange if there has been no manifestation of joy and enthusiasm in seeing this city occupied by your military forces. To us the power of the Mexican Republic is dead. No matter what her condition, she was our mother. What child will not shed abundant tears at the tomb of his parents? I might indicate some of the causes of her misfortunes, but domestic troubles should not be made public. It is sufficient to say that civil war is the cursed source of the deadly poison which has spread over one of the grandest and greatest countries that has ever been created. To-day we belong to a great and powerful nation. Its flag, with its stars and stripes, covers the horizon of New Mexico.
>
> —Juan Bautista Vigil y Alaríd, August 19, 1846

Juan Bautista Vigil y Alaríd, acting governor of New Mexico when General Stephen W. Kearny marched into Santa Fe on August 18, 1846, responded to the American conquest in words that measure accommodation against confusion and muted resentment produced of fear coursing through the New Mexican populace. When notice reached Santa Fe that the commanding general and governor, Manuel Armijo, had failed to defend the country the day previous some fifteen miles from the city, the acting governor had no choice but to advise his people to stay in their houses while he went out to meet the enemy. The Army of the West, 1,500 soldiers strong, marched into Santa Fe to take possession of the territory, and they were prepared to destroy every town and village in the department should there be any hint of resistance. Rather than present themselves as a conquering army, however, Gen. Kearny, in the classic imperial mode, proclaimed himself and his army protectors: "We come as friends, to better your condition and make you a part of the Republic of the United States. We mean not to murder you or rob you of your property. Your families shall be free of molestation; your women secure from violence. . . . I advise you to attend to your domestic pursuits, cultivate industry, be peaceable and obedient to the laws. . . . I hearby proclaim that, being in possession of Santa Fe, I am therefore in possession of all New Mexico. . . . You are no longer Mexican subjects." With boundless promise of incorporation set against the outright threat of physical disincorporation by a surrounding army, who among the citizenry of Santa Fe would not make a smile and, like Vigil y Alaríd, swear allegiance to these new friends? Vigil y Alaríd, representing the desires of his people to stay alive, answered Kearny's proclamation point by point by accommodating point.

This theater of conquest had opened a few days earlier when Kearny, standing on a rooftop before the startled citizens of Las Vegas, a town about sixty miles northeast of Santa Fe, proclaimed his intention to take possession of the entire territory: "Mr. Alcalde and people of New Mexico: I have come amongst you by the orders of my government, to take possession of your country and extend over it the laws of the United States. We consider it, and have done so for some time, a part of the territory of the United States. We come amongst you as friends, not as enemies; as protectors, not as conquerors." Yet in the next breath, Kearny ordered his "friends" to remain unquestioning and acquiescent, quietly "attending to their crops and their herds"; should they fail to do this, the consequences were clear: "But listen! he who promises to be quiet and is found in arms against me, I will hang. . . . There goes my army; you see but a small portion of it; there are many more behind; resistance is useless." Kearny's "I came, I saw, I conquered" proclamation ended with him asking the alcalde and his captains to submit an "oath of allegiance" in a public display before the township, which R. E. Twitchell writes they were loath to do: "Beyond all question the alcalde and the two captains did not fully appreciate the situation in which they found themselves. The captains did not protest, but looked with down-cast eyes upon the earthen roof upon which they were standing. Noticing his attitude, General Kearny said to one of them, in the hearing of all the people: 'Captain, look me in the face, while you repeat the oath of office.' The oath was administered, and General Kearny, attended by his staff, descended, mounted and galloped away to the head of the column."[1] The people of Las Vegas had been made to play their part in the peaceful conquest of New Mexico. Now Kearny and his army would march into Santa Fe to reenact the drama.

Vigil y Alaríd, enacting the role of conquered subject, produced on the very site of conflict a statement of surrender measured to appease the conquering army while reminding the Americans that they must maintain the ideals of their forefathers, not because he and his fellow Nuevomexicanos wished to share those ideals but rather to secure survival in the face of destruction. "Today we belong to a great and wonderful nation, its flag, with its stars and stripes, covers the horizon of New Mexico," Vigil y Alaríd proclaimed. But in the next breath, he signaled anxiety about the American military presence: "We are cognizant of your kindness, of your courtesy and that of your accommodating officers and of the strict discipline of your troops." Looking at the surrounding troops and "cognizant" of his people's fear of a rain of destruction, Vigil y Alaríd simultaneously complimented Kearny's troops and made them responsible for their actions: "We know that we belong to the Republic that owes its origin to the immortal Washington, who all civilized nations admire and respect." Note the rhetorical switches throughout Vigil y Alaríd's proclamation of allegiance: before he says, "Today we belong to a great and wonderful nation," he recalls the Mexican Republic, the deceased matria, as "one of the grandest and greatest countries that has ever been created." Vigil y Alaríd makes peace at the site of forced historical transformation, because along with the U.S. flag that with "its stars and stripes covers the horizon of New Mexico" the horizon is covered by a conquering army. Indeed, should there be any doubt that the U.S. flag was to cover the horizon henceforth, Kearny made things clear on August 22: "The undersigned has come to New Mexico with a strong military force, and an equally strong one is following him in his rear. He has more troops than is necessary to put down any opposition that can be brought against him, and therefore it would be but folly or madness for any dissatisfied or discontented persons to think of resisting" (Twitchell 1909:79). For Vigil y Alaríd and his fellow

Nuevomexicanos, therefore, the reality of the conquerors' power had been made explicit: "Today we belong to a great and powerful nation," a powerful nation that was in the process of conquering the region through sheer force of power rather than through democratic annexation. Vigil y Alaríd's article of submission—"No one in this world [no one in his right mind, he might as well have said] can successfully resist the power of him who is stronger"—must be read as a response to Kearny's order for New Mexicans to "remain quiet and peaceable" lest they be "considered traitors and treated accordingly" (ibid., 80).

Vigil y Alaríd had already personally learned that the American will to power, subtly masked by a rhetoric of friendship, was in reality an exercise in domination. Although President James K. Polk had ordered the officers of conquest to leave the existing government officials in their positions as a gesture of goodwill, Kearny immediately reorganized the government of New Mexico, replacing Vigil y Alaríd with Charles Bent, the American consul in Santa Fe. A few years earlier, Bent and another American had walked into Vigil y Alaríd's home and beaten him with a horsewhip, after disputing charges made by Mexican officials that Bent had summarily overlooked illegal trafficking along the Santa Fe Trail and had then encouraged the Texas invasion of New Mexico in 1841. Bent himself casually described the beating in a letter: "I asked him how he dare make such false accusations against uss [sic] he denied them being false. The word was hardly out of his mouth when Workman struck him with his whip, after whiping him a while with this he droped it and beate him with his fist until I thought he had given him enough, whereupon I pulled him off. he [Vigil] run for life."[2] As the historian Benjamín Read (1910:226–227) points out, "Bent y su compañero no solo no respetaban las canas de un anciano indefenso sino que abusaban de las leyes de una nación amiga" (Not only did Bent and his companion not respect the gray hair of a defenseless old man but they abused the laws of a friendly nation). Rodolfo Acuña is more precise about Bent's abuses of power and outright attempts to subvert Mexican rule: "A large enclave of United States citizens near Taos, led by Charles Bent, formed what was called the American party. The party, hated by the Mexicans, openly supported the Texas cause. . . . Bent was accused of contraband and theft, collusion with the Texans, harboring thieves, and selling firearms to the Indians."[3] Of course, the seriousness of these charges and the well-known enmity between Bent and key Mexican officials did nothing to sway

Kearny. Bent was summarily appointed New Mexico's first territorial governor, one might argue, as a patent symbol of domination.

Such were intercultural power relations when Kearny marched into Santa Fe. Vigil y Alaríd's accommodating statement of August 19 relative to "the power of him who is stronger" must therefore be recalculated, both with respect to the beating he sustained at the behest of Bent and to his understanding of what would take place if Mexican(American)s did not remain "quiet and peaceable." After all, the American army was composed largely of Missourians and Texans who, like Bent, hated Mexicans. The "anciano" Vigil y Alaríd remained quiet and peaceable, but as Howard Lamar writes, "Underneath [the] outward show of peace and prosperity many proud New Mexicans bridled with resentment at the loud, pushy Americans" (1966:66–67). And within a few months, pockets of resistance were organized throughout New Mexico. Plans for an insurrection in Santa Fe were discovered and smashed on Christmas Eve, 1846, but in January 1847, Governor Bent was assassinated in Taos by nationalists whose audacious action inspired other villagers to take up the fight against the Americans. The uprisings in the villages of Arroyo Hondo, Santa Cruz, Embudo, Las Vegas, and Mora were quickly smashed by American artillery and well-armed cavalry, but as Lamar suggests, widespread discontent and armed resistance "did dramatize to Americans that they had major cultural barriers to overcome before New Mexico could be really theirs" (ibid., 70). For many Nuevomexicanos, intercultural barriers were so entrenched in their memories of the period that even though they participated in the American regime, they never forgot the widespread resentment and fear of the Army of the West, an army that had come as friends to "absolve" them of their allegiance to Mexico and to protect them as long as they remained quiet.[4]

There is one final irony I must comment on. Unlike Seguín and Vallejo, both of whom participated in the formation of the new regime, Seguín as mayor of San Antonio and Vallejo as a constitutional delegate and state senator, Vigil y Alaríd as much as disappeared from public view after his submission speech of 1846. Like those *alcaldes* of other villages along the road to Santa Fe, he had stood before Kearny promising to "obey and respect the established authorities, no matter what . . . [their] private opinions." But his own opinion of Americans was so negative that he immediately retired from public life. Wayne Harper, who writes about Vigil y Alaríd's career after the Americanization, points out that he "did not get along with the Americans or their territorial officers. He could not accept their self-proclaimed superiority or style of governance. That is the major reason why he never returned to politics. The other reason for non-participation was he would not renounce his Mexican citizenship."[5] The form resistance took in Vigil y Alaríd's case shows just how meaningful the "private opinions" of colonized Mexicans would soon prove—as we shall see for Vallejo and Seguín.

Indeed the irony of Vigil y Alaríd's proclamation welcoming American incorporation and the "wonderful future that awaits" announced itself when he and some two thousand other Nuevomexicanos chose both to retain their Mexican citizenship and to remove to Mexico in 1849. Under Article VIII of the Treaty of Guadalupe Hidalgo (1848), those Mexicans "established in territories previously belonging to Mexico" did not have to leave U.S. territory to retain their property but could stay in their homeland, retaining "the title and rights of Mexican citizens." Vigil y Alaríd might have remained in Santa Fe, but his "loyalty to Mexico and dislike of the American overlords influenced his decision to move to Mexico" (Harper 1985:165). So he sold his properties in Santa Fe and made the long trek into Mexico, where he settled in Aldama, a village near Chihuahua, in 1849. He opened a *botica* (apothecary) and took up practice for three years until he moved to Mesilla, a town just south of the border that had been settled by another group of discontented Nuevomexicanos in 1850. "There are reports of his owning a store in Mesilla and being obnoxious to any Anglo," Harper writes (166). But once again, historical irony would undermine him and his fellow Mesilla citizens: in 1854, President Santa Anna again sold his countrymen like sheep when he closed the Gadsden Purchase, which turned over another piece of Mexico, including the Mesilla Valley, to the United States for a railroad line. Rather than move deeper into Mexico again, and because he missed his *parientes* in Santa Fe, he returned to his home where during the late 1850s he struggled, unsuccessfully, to recover his and other people's Mexican land grants (ibid., 167–173).

When he died in 1866 at the age of seventy-four, Juan Bautista Vigil y Alaríd, it appears, had been forgotten. "There was nothing to mark his passing, not even an obituary. . . . There was no notice in the papers or mention in the Territorial Legislature that the man who had surrendered New Mexico and was its first acting governor had died" (ibid., 175). Even today, about the only thing Vigil y Alaríd is remembered for is the proclamation of submission of August 19, 1848. Unlike Seguín and Vallejo, there is no personal narrative by which we may measure his thinking about that day's accommodation, his later refusal to betray his Mexican citizenship, his removal to Mexico, or his final struggle to recover lost land. We have only the speech of August 19 and a few facts about his post-1848 life to show us that he and other Nuevomexicanos neither automatically surrendered their loyalties to the homeland nor remained quiescent about their rights. Vigil y Alaríd's proclamation operated as an early example of multivoiced encodation, a rhetorical appeasement that made the occupation sufferable. With resentment embedded in accommodation, he quietly articulated the Nuevomexicano's fidelity to a homeland that would not be summarily dissolved by conquest, governmental reorganization, or dispossession at the material level.

The Nuevomexicano's continuity of cultural practice, the willful self-enveloping of culture and language throughout the occupied territory, indeed proved that the "major cultural barriers" to which Lamar refers were, in fact, carefully sustained by Mexicans throughout the nineteenth century and deep into the twentieth in various forms of counterhegemonic discourse. In fact, some sixty years after the occupation of Nuevo Mexico, the territory had still not been granted statehood because Nuevomexicanos were *too* Mexican: their loyalties to an ideal of a cultural homeland would not dissolve with Kearny's or his American successors' plans for swift transformation. And although they had indeed become subalterns politically, they adapted speech and social gestures to sustain cultural identity in the face of American hostility to things "Mexican." Long after the crushed uprisings of 1847, after the American abrogations of the Treaty of Guadalupe Hidalgo, after efforts at Mexican repatriation, and during the unceasing disfranchisements, Nuevomexicanos sustained native social and cultural practices that strengthened the community's resistance to American domination. In the century that followed the conquest, New Mexicans would both remember themselves in an accruing body of oral narrative and develop personal and folkloristic narrative expressions of their cultural experience.

In the year that New Mexico was granted statehood (1912), Chacón would finish his "Memorias," an autobiography that covered his birth in 1833, his childhood memories of the conquest, his mustering into the American army in the 1850s and service in the Union Army during the Civil War, and his retirement in southern Colorado—which he (and many of us) still regard as culturally and familially continuous with New Mexico. His "Memorias" is a crucial example of the formation of autobiographical consciousness split by contending sociocultural regimes: he writes from the standpoint of a veteran widely honored in 1912 for his service to the American army; yet he remembers that when the American army marched through New Mexico in 1846–47, "there was such terror instilled by the Americans that when a dog barked the people killed it, the burros were muzzled so they could not bray, and if the roosters crowed at daylight they killed them. Only at night were fires permitted in order that the enemy not discover the smoke from the huts." Kearny's injunctions in Las Vegas and Santa Fe that people remain quiet and peaceable was taken to heart, Chacón remembers sixty years after the occupation, because elsewhere the Americans had "burned the public markets, the granaries, and everything that people were not able to carry away."[6]

One hundred years after the occupation, Cleofas Jaramillo, Nina Otero (de Warren), Aurora Lucero (de White-Lea), Fabiola Cabeza de Baca, and other women would write about the cultural homeland in folkloristic autobiography that sustained cultural practice as autochthonous social knowledge in the face of Anglo-American appropriation and distortion. Yet Kearny's order to remain "quiet and peaceable" remains in force within their work, which like Vigil y Alaríd's originary statement of appeasement, operates as a form of accommodation to Americans who controlled the social and material domain and with it the Nuevomexicana license to speak. A century after the conquest, accommodative narrative functioned as a rhetorical site of guerrilla resistance to domination. As Jaramillo wrote in her prefatory remarks to *Romance of a Little Village Girl*, "Under the apparent deadness of our New Mexico villages there runs a romantic current invisible to the stranger and understood only by their inhabitants." The "quiet romance" of her autobiography both accommodates itself to the historical force of subordination and turns accommodation toward resistance as an instantiation of Lamar's comment on the subterranean response to the American occupation: "Underneath [the] outward show of peace and prosperity many proud New Mexicans bridled with resentment at the loud, pushy Americans" (1970:66–67). During the 1930s and 1940s, Jaramillo and other women would work side by side with many "loud, pushy Americans" who were restoring Spanish colonial churches and territorial buildings, collecting Nuevomexicano folklore, and reconstructing (read, constructing) a history of the region that wrapped old intercultural wounds in a gauze of highly romanticized figurations of a Spanish colonial past that simply erased the year 1846 when Mexican citizens were ordered to remain quiet, or die. Jaramillo's "quiet romance," like Vigil y Alaríd's message, articulates a people's desire not only to survive in the face of domination but to reclaim ownership of a culture "invisible to the stranger and understood only by its inhabitants."

III

"Sonoma was a tiny little cluster of adobe houses and could have been captured by Tom Sawyer and Huck Finn. The conquerors found General Vallejo asleep."

—Bernard DeVoto (1943)

"These Bear Flag men, more or less conscious of their independent responsibilities, lived through a very curious episode of California history—one that seemed to some of them afterwards ineffably glorious, and that in fact was unspeakably ridiculous, as well as a little tragical, and for the country disastrous."

—Josiah Royce (1886)

"Doubtless God had decreed that June 1846 was to be the blackest month of my life."

—Mariano Guadalupe Vallejo (1875)

By nearly all accounts, the Bear Flag Revolt, which opened the U.S. conquest of California, was an unnecessary provocation of comic proportions. At least the American narrative versions are funny. For Californios like Vallejo, of course, the Bear Flag incident was not at all humorous. But let us begin with the comic.

The early morning of June 14, 1846. Dawn. Everyone in Sonoma is sleeping. A group of some thirty Americans rides out of the hills into the pueblo of Sonoma ready to do war with the Mexican troops, whom they have been told are about to deport or destroy American immigrants. They are ragged mountain men, hunters and trappers mostly, Americans who arouse as much fear for their looks as for their arms; men who John C. Frémont described as having "nothing to lose but everything to gain," men Rosalía Vallejo de Leese described in her memoirs as "wearing on their heads caps made with the skins of coyotes or wolves, some wearing slouched hats full of holes, some wearing straw hats black as charcoal. The majority of this marauding band wore buckskin pants, some blue pants that reach only to the knee, several had no shirts, shoes were only to be seen on the feet of fifteen or twenty among the whole lot."[7] These marauders charge into Sonoma expecting armed opposition from Mexican regulars they had been led to believe were about to drive them out of the country. But there are no Mexican troops. There is only Mariano Guadalupe Vallejo, the thirty-eight-year-old *coman-dante-general de la alta California*, a father of eight children, a man wealthy in Sonoma and Napa land, livestock, and material possessions, a widely influential *jefe político* (political chief) who seems to have struck a bargain with the devil: he had been friendly toward the same American immigrants who were now about to seize him as a prisoner of war.

But what war? Although the United States had indeed initiated war against Mexico in Texas a few weeks earlier, California was many thousands of miles away, and Mexican officials had not yet been apprised of formal hostilities. And anyway, why seize Sonoma and Vallejo, a man who had angered many of his own countrymen because he had for years been too friendly toward American immigrants? In what would become the classic travel narrative on California, *Two Years Before the Mast* (1840), Richard Henry Dana remarked that "Don Guadalupe Vallejo, a young man, and the most popular, among the Americans and English, of any man in California . . . spoke English very well, and was suspected of being favorably inclined to foreigners"[8] as early as 1835. Ten years later, in the spring of 1846, Vallejo had spoken before his countrymen in favor of annexation to the United States, and, therefore, while he may have been popular with many Americans, his position vexed Mexican officials as well as his brother, Salvador, who always distrusted American motives. As we shall see, Vallejo was also wary, but he was more pragmatic than many Californios, more politic and accommodating, clearer about what he foresaw as the inevitability of American immigration, which had begun with hundreds in the 1830s and, word had it, would soon turn into thousands of Americans crowding over the Sierra Nevadas into his own Sonoma and Napa valleys by the end of the 1840s. It does not require much guesswork to see that by the time he met the twenty-year-old Dana on San Francisco Bay in 1835, on the "first [day] of entire sunshine in over a month," Vallejo, whose bay it was by command, knew perfectly well that some day soon the entire area would be the site of significant commercial activity. Dana's wonder as he looked around him on that Sunday in 1835 must have echoed Vallejo's own.

> If California ever becomes a prosperous country, this bay will be the center of its prosperity. The abundance of wood and water, the extreme fertility of its shores; the excellence of its climate, which is as near to being perfect as any in the world; and its facilities for navigation, affording the best anchoring grounds

in the whole western coast of America—all fit it for a place of great importance.[9]

This was California. Whether reached by mountain passage over the Sierras or by way of Cape Horn, California offered a prospect that Americans would not relinquish until it was theirs. California would be taken from the Mexicans, just as the Spaniards had taken it from the native tribes scattered across the map. So by June 1846, the map was about to be redrawn once again at the instigation of Frémont, U.S. topological engineer, and, as it turns out, also an American officer with secret orders to provoke a fight with the Mexicans that would destabilize the country, forcing the issue toward a war the United States could not lose.

Out of the hills, then, with no more than roused spirits about vague rumors of expulsion, the group of thirty horsemen rode into Sonoma against a general and his troops. But it was a comic fiasco. Frémont's men were neither soldiers nor settlers; neither very patriotic nor politically conscious. Rather, they were a species of nineteenth-century Hell's Angels, wild-eyed men loose on the map, reminiscent of Crevecoeur's barbarian "back-settlers," those "half cultivators and half hunters" on the fringe of wilderness whose "shocking violations" and "sudden devastations" have "so often stained our frontiers."[10] Something would have to be done to justify the morning's sudden violation by such men. As has often been the case with American foreign policy, a good story would be required to shore up the petty reality of the event. Jingoist narrative practice would have to intervene in military matters, the event narratively reshaped to suit the American version of its necessary history. Such narrative retrospective required time, however, or at least distance from the event itself that would allow ideological exigencies to mediate the event for retelling, because, as Josiah Royce writes, "Even after the motley company had spent a number of days together, few could give any connected account of what had really brought them there. The few that could give any connected account, however, are the ones who endow the whole affair with its true humor."[11] Decades later a memorial would be constructed in Sonoma celebrating the Bear Flag heroes, heroic stories would justify the statues and plaques, and, therefore, heroism would necessarily be evoked by imagining Sonoma as a fortress and Vallejo as an enemy commander-in-chief.

American political rhetoric would take care of American political needs. As Bancroft pointed out, "In narratives of the time, and later, it was customary to magnify the exploit of June 14th, by speak-ing of Sonoma as a Californian stronghold, a fort, a garrisoned town, taken by surprise, or even by a 'gallant charge without shedding of blood, so skillfully was the movement planned.'"[12] The shaping of history began with the earliest official correspondence concerning the events in June 1846. In San Francisco, William A. Leidesdorff's dispatch to the American consul, Thomas O. Larkin (June 19), on the seizure of Sonoma registers a decidedly less informative than unequivocally nationalist imperative: "There is no doubt that the most determined and chivalric spirit actuates the men . . . which forbids them to commit any act of violence, or cast injury upon anyone. . . . Hoping there is not so much excitement with you as we have here."[13] On September 8, 1846, the *Monterey Californian* ran a banner story reading, "Each man having felt the oppression of the then existing govt [*sic*], and the certainty of an increase of those oppressions, with a clear sense of their danger, their rights, and their duty, they rushed to the rescue with one impulse and one object. The watchword was equal rights and equal laws, and they nobly sus-tained their principles."[14] And by early 1847 the Committee of Citi-zens promptly published the *History of the Bear Flag Revolt*, a nar-rative placing blame for the provocation on the Mexicans, who, predictably, were charged with marching "up the Sacramento River, with the design of destroying the crops, burning the houses, and driving off cattle belonging to the foreigners. . . . It was quite appar-ent that further and more decisive action was necessary to secure the lives and property of the immigrants; and it was determined to seize the fort of Sonoma."[15] The fact is that the excitement of im-pending war in the north rumored by Leidesdorff and celebrated by the American newspapers and the Committee of Citizens was the excitement of imperialism without opposition, since, to continue with Bancroft, "there was no garrison at Sonoma. The soldiers for-merly in service there had been discharged some years before. . . . Some of the citizens even were absent from the town, and there was no thought of even posting a sentinel. . . . A more peaceful burg than this stronghold of the Frontera del Norte on that Sunday morning it would be difficult to find" (1884–1889, 5:111).

Back to the scene of conflict. Awakened by the noise of horses and shouting men, Francisca Benicia, Vallejo's wife, sensing that Mariano was in danger, pleaded with him to dress quickly and es-cape through the back door. Honor would allow no such thing. Or perhaps, since it was not clear just what was happening outside and given Vallejo's well-known hospitality to strangers, Vallejo opened the doors to the *osos* (bears), asking to know what business they had with him and with the town so early in the day and demanding to speak to whomever was in command. However, since Frémont had directed the show from afar, none of the invaders could really say who was in command. As Bernard DeVoto writes, Dr. John Semple, a wild-looking man nearly seven feet tall, Ezekiel Merritt, and William Knight, brought along as an interpreter of sorts, entered the general's home and "told Vallejo that he was a prisoner of war. He had some difficulty understanding what war he was a prisoner of and set out brandy for his captors, so that they could talk it over."[16] Vallejo's brother, Salvador, and Victor Prudon, another young Mexican officer, were also arrested and brought into the *sala* (parlor). Then Jacob Leese, Vallejo's American brother-in-law, was detained, first as interpreter and then finally as prisoner.

Contemporary accounts give warrant to Bancroft's, Royce's, and DeVoto's comic deflation of what has been taught to California children as the glorious Bear Flag Revolt of 1846. While discussions were taking place inside, the group of men outside, restless and impatient, had tapped into a barrel of liquor and were ready to get on with the liberation of California. William B. Ide, soon to proclaim himself president of the California Republic, wrote in his memoirs that the men who rode into Sonoma were confused about their aims, less high-minded than high-spirited, and less interested in liberating California for democracy than in liberating brandy for an early morning drunk. Of those first few hours in Sonora, Ide writes,

> The sun was climbing up the heavens an hour or more, and yet no man, nor voice, nor sound of violence came from the house to tell us of events within: patience was ill, and lingered ill. . . . "Oh! go into the house, Ide, and come out agin and let us know what is going on in there!" No sooner said than done. There sat Dr. S. [Semple], just modifying a long string of articles of capitulation. There sat Merritt, his head fallen; there sat Knight, no longer able to interpret; and there sat the new made captain [John Grigsby], as mute as the seat he sat upon. The bottles had wellnigh vanquished the captors.[17]

Ide goes on to describe the morning's events, saying that "disorder and confusion prevailed" among the men outside: "One swore that he would not stay to guard the prisoners—another swore we would all have our throats cut—another called for fresh horses, and all were on the move"(1967:127). Ide rose to the occasion, however, assuming the mantle of leadership (no one else wanted to lead, it seems), and delivered a rousing speech that ended, "I will lay my bones here, before I will take upon myself the ignominy of commencing an honorable work, and then flee like cowards, like thieves, when no enemy is in sight. . . . We are robbers, or we must be conquerors!" (127–128).

By about 11:00 A.M., the events of that Sunday morning take on Royce's reading of the "ridiculous," the "tragical," and the "disastrous," for no sooner had the articles of capitulation been signed than the confused and half-drunk American patriots outside refused to free the prisoners as guaranteed in the articles. Despite a carefully negotiated treaty by the Californios, the moment the doors opened, the articles were revoked by the rest of the *osos* outside who demanded that the Vallejos, Prudon, and Leese be taken under guard to Sacramento. After the prisoners were whisked off to John Sutter's fort, the Americans splotched together a flag "made of plain white clothe and ornamented with the red flannel of a shirt from the back of one of the men, and Christened with the word 'California Republic'" (Ide 1967: 130), the centerpiece of which was a picture of a bear, darkened, the story has it, with blackberry juice and so crudely drawn that the American marauders as well as the Mexican citizenry joked that it looked more like a hog than a bear.

Laughable or not, after raising the new flag and before issuing the proclamation of the California Republic, Ide rounded up "as many of the surrounding citizens as possible" and when he had their attention, by placing them "between four strong walls (they were more than twice our numbers)," went on to share a democratic vision with them, which they were to accept for their own good or face destruction. Speaking in the third person, Ide proclaimed that "although he had, for the moment, deprived them of that liberty which is the right and the privilege of all good and just men, it was only that they might become acquainted with his unalterable purpose. . . . 'We will restore you the liberty of which we have deprived you, after we have convinced you . . . that as enemies we will kill and destroy you! but as friends we will share with you all the blessings of liberty. Go. You are free as the air of heaven'" (ibid., 132–133). As it turns out, Ide was talking into the air more than to the Mexican citizens of Sonoma, since as he admits, "the address was not the twentieth part interpreted." Common to the colonial endeavor, nevertheless, this minor failure of interpretation was resolved by oratorical nuance, the address presumably giving "expression that would have been understood by every nationality and tongue under heaven" (ibid., 134).

This dangerous carnival atmosphere had prevailed since dawn, leaving the people of Sonoma uncertain about what was being said, amused at one moment with the spectacle of the bear flag and fearful the next for being detained en masse, worried about their families and concerned for their property, much of which had been "purchased on credit" by the *osos*, who needed, Ide writes, "ten thousand pounds of floor" and "a supply of beef."[18] The citizens of Sonoma—future citizens of the American republic—were arrested but arrested, presumably, only to be apprised that no one wished to "deprive them of their property, nor disturb their social relations one with another." The next morning, Ide issued a formal "Proclamation of the California Republic," which, in addition to ensuring "the security of life and property," would "encourage industry, virtue and literature" (ibid., 140). This June morning in 1846 was a moment of decisive conflict, less at the level of military conflict than on the ground of social discourse as a site of conflict, rhetorical hegemony practiced as war, language as the machinery of conquest. Years later, when these new Mexican American citizens went before the "Government" to square accounts for all the credit they extended on June 14, their claims—to their surprise but no one else's— were denied, no matter how judicious or eloquent their language. So although obviously it is not just at the level of language that conflict must be analyzed, language as a locus of antagonism, contention, and deceit may be seen to emerge from the verbal and scripted exchanges that took place in Sonoma in June 1846.

If we step back into Vallejo's residence for a moment, the centrality of language as the site of intercultural contention can be seen to operate with social significance in a manner that anticipates a reading of Vallejo's later "Recuerdos históricos y personales" (1875) as counterhegemonic discourse. Remember that immediately on opening the doors of his home, General Vallejo was informed that he was under arrest. Sensing the incongruous danger, Vallejo surrendered but also opened negotiations with his captors and—while passing around brandy—succeeded at winning a guarantee that protected his family and township in exchange for promising to refrain from hostilities. Within the articles of capitulation, Vallejo managed to insert a significant passage, penned in Spanish, in which the Bear Flaggers were implicated in an unprovoked and dangerous seizure of Sonoma. The articles contain three paragraphs, those in English written by Semple but the first written by Vallejo himself; the Spanish paragraph stands as a symbolization of resistance, marking the prisoner's ability to voice opposition to and censure of the American marauders within a confined, and dangerous, rhetorical space.

Dana's statement, published to the world, about Vallejo's ability to speak "English very well" is crucial here: Vallejo might "very well" have had the article transcribed into English by Semple, but he did not. Perhaps this is where opening his cabinet and serving the "richest wines and brandy" (Ide 1967:124) came in handy as a means of pacifying and lulling the Americans into quiescence while he composed a coded oppositional micro-narrative of the event. The subtle inclusion of the Spanish article disclosed the flagrant nature of the armed assault against the peaceful town that would soon be set against American versions of Sonoma as an armed garrison. I include the entire paragraph as it was written in Spanish because it seems to me that Vallejo knew that he must code in Spanish, practicing linguistic duplicity through syntactic nuance and repetition of key phrases that, even if readable by his captors, would placate them while documenting their rapacity.

> No. 1 "Conste por la presente que, habiendo sido sorprendido por una numerosa fuerza armada que me tomó prisionero y á los jefes y oficiales que estaban de guarnición en esta plaza, de la que se apoderó la expresada fuerza, habiendo la encontrado absolutamente indefensa, tanto yo como los señores oficiales que suscriben comprometémos nuestra palabra de honor de que estando bajo las garantías de prisioneros de guerra no tomaremos ni a favor ni contra la repetida fuerza armada de quien hemos recibido la intimación del momento y un escrito firmado que garantiza nuestras vidas, familias é intereses y las de todo el vecindário de esta jurisdicción mientras no hagamos oposición. Sonoma, Junio 14 de 1846.[19]

"Be it known," Vallejo writes, "that we were surprised by a large armed force that took me, as well as those officers charged with protecting the plaza, prisoner" even though, he repeats, this "armed force" (*expresada fuerza*) rode into Sonoma and finding it "absolutely defenseless"—or, in other words, "absolutely peaceful"— took advantage of (*apoderó*) the situation. Given the unprovoked and hostile takeover, Vallejo understandably offers his "word of honor that under the guarantees of prisoners of war we will neither take arms for nor against the aforesaid armed force." Two significant messages are embedded within the accommodating language of the article. First, he writes, "comprometémos nuestra palabra de honor," "comprometémos" here signifying that their "word of honor" was offered under duress of being made prisoners of war. Second, the sentence carries a double complement and a double meaning: "la repetida fuerza armada" is repeated for the third time, the second part of the phrase building on the threat posed by this "armed force"—"la repetida fuerza armada de quien hemos recibido la intimación del momento"—a phrase initially ambiguous until "the intimation of the moment" is contextualized by what is taking place, namely, that the prisoners and their families are being held by dangerous men ready to destroy them and the town at a moment's provocation. To this point, the message signals the coercive and dangerous situation in which Vallejo and his fellow Sonomans found themselves. Vallejo then effects a reversal of power relations when, in addition to receiving his captors' word of honor (*intimación del momento*), he elicits a "signed affirmation guaranteeing the lives of our families and interests [properties, livestock, etc.] as well as that of our people here in this jurisdiction." Not bad manuevering for a "prisoner of war." Vallejo had bartered brandy and verbal acuity for crucial written guarantees from the *osos*, whose word of honor was not to be trusted—as he immediately learned when his successful negotiating did not go past the door.

Vallejo and his officers were taken to Sutter's Fort where they were imprisoned for nearly two months in cramped, flea-infested rooms, "fed with coarse food, . . . allowed no communication with friends or family, . . . the few letters allowed to pass from the prison closely examined by Frémont's men."[20] Vallejo's few letters to his family, however, like the Spanish article of capitulation, disclose nuances of multiple address that split them into multiple versions, these versions opening toward a narrative of resistance mediated by a perilous situation that required countercoding through muted speech, a mode of speaking through clenched teeth in a language perhaps understood at basic semantic levels by his captors but fugitive in its nuanced repetitions and demarcations of anger scribbled into the underside of Spanish phrases.

In one of his first letters to his brother, José de Jesús, Vallejo ironizes his accommodating language, seeming to be neither displeased with his situation nor opposed to the impending upheaval.

I am sending this letter to you with the object of relieving your mind about the fact that we have not been killed, at least up to this time. . . . We believe that fundamentally this is the beginning of a complete turnover in the country; but not without a change founded on justice and on the law that will be a relief from the present miserable state of things. . . . Our own persons, our families and our property has been solemnly guaranteed to

be returned to us in due respect so we ought to rest assured of
it under the safeguard of law as well as under the good faith of
men so I hope it will turn out and your loving brother begs you
to publish this letter.[21]

Since he specifies that José should publish the letter, it is reasonable to assume that the acquiescent intonations within it function to ensure, first of all, its publishability, and through its publication and distribution, an encoded articulation of the imminent
danger they find themselves in. Knowing that his letter would be
read by his captors, Vallejo voiced his opposition in multiple registers calculated to appease these captors while addressing another
distinct message to his own people. The opening sentence functions
as a negation of the accommodating sentiments expressed moments
later; that is, everything he says about "a change founded on justice
and on the law" must be mediated by the fact that he and his fellow
prisoners were in danger of being murdered at any moment. This is
the central message to his family. What follows addresses itself to
Frémont and other Americans as an accommodation to and affirmation of the democratic rhetoric that, as those American versions
of June 14 I have referred to, justified the taking of Sonoma, and soon
California, for the glory of the American republic and the good of
the benighted Mexicans in California. Vallejo's rhetorical play opens
a space for critique through which he lays the burden of national
idealism and moral conscience on the Americans, who rather than
reading a censorious letter discover instead an affirmation of those
democratic ideals that, by their hostile actions, they have abrogated.

   The Spanish article of capitulation and his letters from prison,
therefore, constitute a rhetorical site of embryonic resistance in
1846, anticipating the complex narrative operation of the "Recuerdos históricos y personales tocante a la alta California" composed
some thirty years later when Vallejo, suffering the final humiliations of material and political displacement, expanded the article of
capitulation into some five volumes, or one thousand pages, of
multiply coded resistance, simultaneously expressing accommodation, uncertainty, frustration, and anger toward the American
annexation-conquest. The dangerous situation in which Mexicans
in California found themselves after 1846 established, or rather
forced, a set of situational rhetorical practices for organizing experience under the American regime that allowed Vallejo and his fellow Californios to mark resistance within the space of coerced collaboration. They were forced to develop discursive strategies for

leaving a mark of presence where speech alone would evaporate, a signed mark describing what happened at Sonoma on June 14, 1846, together with the other painful events that were to take place afterward.

Yet although, as he would say thirty years later, the history of California could not be written without the name "Vallejo," when called on by Bancroft to give his version of California, Vallejo, already embittered and distrustful, refused. Only patient and cunning maneuvering by Bancroft would overcome the seventy-year-old man's reluctance to cooperate in the historiographic enterprise; after all, other American writers had devastated the Californios in their books. Why should Bancroft prove any different from the other Americans who had befriended, then betrayed, him? Writing the past would require an act of courage on Vallejo's part because memory turned to nightmare when he remembered the betrayals, disappointments, and reversals he had experienced after June 14, 1846, which as he wrote in "Recuerdos históricos y personales," "God had decreed . . . was to be the blackest month of my life." But it was precisely because it had been the blackest month of his life that he must complete his memoirs and encourage other Californios to complete theirs. Convinced of the social significance of narrative conflict, Vallejo would urge many of his compatriots and *parientes* to narrate their memoirs of pre-American life as a demarcation of presence and will to permanence that, he wrote to his son, would "serve posterity as a guide" (Emparan 1968 : 129). The collective Californio memory must reconstruct a narrative of the past that would contend for authority over and against other accounts that denigrated Mexican culture and social manners, that represented the Californios as an indolent and degraded people. Dana may have complimented Vallejo and a few other Californios, but in general his descriptions of Californio social, cultural, and political practices are derogatory: although California had long been a self-sufficient economy, for instance, he insisted that "the Californians are an idle, thriftless people, and can make nothing for themselves" (1840 : 75); of their "domestic relations," he wrote, "The men are thriftless, proud, extravagant, and very much given to gaming; and the women have but little education, and a good deal of beauty, and their morality, of course, is none of the best" (ibid., 162).[22] When Vallejo did compose his historical memoirs, he had a clear recognition of the stakes at hand: the ownership of the past was being decided during his lifetime. Vallejo knew that within the text of his narrative battle would be waged against those American versions of history that were constructing a set of representations about the past intended to legitimize the American conquest and valorize American pioneers while demoting the Mexican Californios. Fully cognizant of the power relations at stake in historical and personal narrative practice, therefore, Vallejo set out to mark his own life, not so much against the erasure of the grave but rather against social erasure and textual nullification.

IV

I address myself to the American people; to that people impetuous, as the whirlwind, when aroused by the hypocritical clamors of designing men, but just, impartial and composed, whenever men and facts are submitted to their judgement.

I have been the object of the hatred and passionate attacks of some few disorganisers who, for a time, ruled, as masters, over the poor and oppressed population of San Antonio [Texas]. Harpy-like, ready to pounce on every thing that attracted the notice of their rapacious avarice, I was an obstacle to the execution of their vile designs. They, therefore, leagued together to exasperate and ruin me, spread against me malignant calumnies, and made use of odious machinations to sully my honor, and tarnish my well-earned reputation.

A victim to the wickedness of a few men, whose imposture was favored by their origin, and recent domination over the country; a foreigner in my native land; could I be expected stoically to endure their outrages and insults? Crushed by sorrow, convinced that my death alone would satisfy my enemies, I sought for a shelter amongst those against whom I had fought; I separated from my country, parents, family, relatives and friends, and what was more, from the institutions, on behalf of which I had drawn my sword, with an earnest wish to see Texas free and happy.

In that involuntary exile, my only ambition was to devote my time, far from the tumult of war, to the support of my family, who shared in my sad condition.

Fate, however, had not exhausted its cup of bitterness. Thrown into a prison, in a foreign country [Mexico], I had no alternative left, but, to linger in a loathsome confinement, or to accept military service. On one hand, my wife and children, reduced to beggary, and separated from me; on the other hand, to turn my arms against my own country. The alternative was sad, the struggle of feelings violent; at last the father triumphed over the citizen; I seized a sword that galled my hand. (Who amongst my readers will not understand my situation?) I served Mexico; I served her loyally and faithfully; I was compelled to fight my own countrymen, but I was never guilty of the barbarous and unworthy deeds of which I am accused by my enemies.

Ere the tomb closes over me and my contemporaries, I wish to lay open to publicity this stormy period of my life, I do it for friends as well as enemies, I challenge the latter to contest, with fact, the statements I am about to make, and I leave the decision unhesitatingly to the witnesses of the events.[23]

In 1858, Juan Nepumuceno Seguín, aka John N. Seguin, had good reason to compose an apologia clarifying divided motives and contradictory actions. In 1834, he had joined with Stephen Austin, Sam Houston, and other American immigrants, along with prominent Tejano landowners like José Antonio Navarro and Lorenzo de Zavala, to overthrow Mexico's possession of Texas.[24] In 1836, he was in the Alamo on the eve of General Santa Anna's successful storming of the fort, but as he writes in the *Personal Memoirs*, he was ordered away to gather reinforcements which he returned with—too late. After the fall of the Alamo, his first act was to collect the remains of the dead and give them an honorable military burial. A few months later, he was among the heroes of the Battle of San Jacinto in which the Mexican troops were surprised during the afternoon siesta and soundly routed, Santa Anna himself ingloriously captured. In fact, he was instrumental, he claims, in devising the battle strategy: "At noon, General Rusk came to partake of dinner in my tent. When he had done eating, he asked me if the Mexicans were not in the habit of taking a siesta at that hour. I answered in the affirmative" (Seguín 1858:12). By 1838, in recognition of his patriotic service in the formation of the Texas Republic, the town of Walnut Creek honored him by changing its name to Seguín, and in the same year, he was elected "Senator to Congress" for the Texas Republic. Then, at the expiration of his senatorial term, he was elected "Mayor of the City of San Antonio" in January 1841.

All seemed to be developing well for Seguín and for an independent Texas Republic—or so Seguín and other Tejanos were naive enough to believe. The truth is that things were going to hell for Tejanos throughout their native land. For during the five years following the overthrow of Mexican rule, instead of securing full incorporation in a new bicultural republic, Texas Mexicanos saw their situation become worse and worse. Although Seguín and other Tejanos had proven their loyalty to the Texas cause, for many Americans they remained Mexicans who, as one American wrote, "wear the semblance of friendship—with a slight peeping out of the cloven foot now and then."[25] Suspect and distrusted no matter their offers of service and friendship, Tejanos were treated like the enemy by "the American straggling adventurers, who were already beginning to work their dark intrigues soon after 1836 against the native families" (Seguín 1858:18). By the time he was elected mayor of San Antonio, the "first city of Texas" had become, in his words, "the receptacle of the scum of society." Daily life turned to nightmare for the native Tejanos: "At every hour of the day and night, my countrymen ran to me for protection against the assaults or exactions of those adventurers. Some times, by persuasion, I prevailed on them to desist; some times, also, force had to be resorted to. How could I have done otherwise? Were not the victims my own countrymen, friends and associates? Could I leave them defenceless, exposed to the assaults of foreigners, who, on the pretext that they were Mexicans, treated them worse than brutes?" (ibid., 19). Just who were his countrymen and who were his enemies was fast blurring. In the 1820s, he had befriended the immigrant Americans, thinking of them as compatriots in a republican cause and embracing them as "fellow-citizens," but by 1842, they had reverted to "foreigners" who treated his fellow "Mexicans" like animals. In the spring of 1842, Mayor Seguín was himself accused of showing his cloven foot, first for refusing commercial favors to certain Americans and then for alleged conspiring with Mexico to regain Texas. As he writes, the allegations against him were based on ethnocentric hostility: "The rumor that I was a traitor was seized with avidity by my enemies in San Antonio. Some envied my military position as held by a Mexican; others found me an obstacle to the accomplishment of their villainous plans" (ibid., 30). Seguín, who was insulted and then openly threatened on the streets of San Antonio, had become a particularly dangerous Mexican. Forced to flee from home and office, "hiding from rancho to rancho" with "every party of [American] volunteers en route to San Antonio [declaring] 'they wanted to kill Seguín'" (ibid., 25), he became a foreigner in his native land.

Seguín came to represent the strain and tear of intercultural division; he became the prototypical Mexican American cultural subject on which racial hostilities commenced and were to be executed on succeeding generations; he became the figure in the flesh of a people made foreigners in their native land. Although officially still mayor of San Antonio, Seguín could not return home "without peril." His family estate had been despoiled, his father, wife, and children threatened with violence. He had been made a dupe, had discovered that his idea(l) of an independent Texas Republic, jointly ruled by Anglo-American and native Tejanos, was only a delusion, a *pendejada* (a stupidity). "I had to leave Texas," he writes, "abandon all, for which I had fought and spent my fortune, to become a wanderer. . . . I was in this country a being out of the pale of society" (ibid., 25–26). There was, he knew, only one thing to do—flee to Mexico, the country he had turned against in 1834, the enemy in 1836, his only refuge in 1842. Strange irony that he would feel safer in a "foreign country" among the enemy than anywhere in Texas. And ironically predictable that although he should have been immediately executed as a traitor when he crossed the border, he was jailed (hardly "thrown into a prison . . . to linger in a loathsome confinement") and then, choosing conscription rather than confinement, put in Mexican uniform for General Adrian Woll's invasion of San Antonio in September 1842.

As he freely admits in *Personal Memoirs*, he was more than a conscript; almost at once he was put at the head of a regiment and ordered to take San Antonio "at all hazards," which he did. The Anglo-Texans, his compatriots in 1836, had become the enemy; his enemy at the Alamo and at San Jacinto had become his compatriots. Mexico, more than a temporary refuge from which he could justify himself to his fellow Texans, became home again, at least until 1848 when the Treaty of Guadalupe Hidalgo sealed the loss of Mexico's extensive northern provinces to the United States. Seguín returned to San Antonio, redeclaring his American loyalties and audaciously arguing that "during my absence nothing appeared that could stamp me as a traitor," even though it seems obvious, even now, that his loyalties were at best divided. Openly admitting that he loyally fought against and then for Mexico must have first amazed people in San Antonio and then angered them. Notwithstanding what must have seemed obvious to everyone, however, Seguín resolved to stay in San Antonio to restore his good reputation. Although he had a few influential Anglo friends who sided with him, there were continual whispers, and then during "the electoral campaign, of August, 1855," Seguín writes, "I was frequently attacked in the newspapers and was styled in some 'the murderer of the Salado'" (ibid., 31). Rather than "enter a newspaper war," he decided to write a public memoir, "a short and clear narrative of [his] public life in relation to

Texas" which, he believed, would sweep away the "attacks of scribblers and personal enemies" who continued to accuse him of infidelity to Texas and the United States but which, it turned out, would also affirm his filial relations with his Tejano countrymen as well as with Mexico itself, which continued, and would continue, to represent home and family for Seguín and other Mexican Americans.

The *Personal Memoirs*, therefore, was published in 1858 when Seguín was attempting to reestablish his name and reputation in San Antonio. It was a dangerous sociorhetorical move because everyone in the city knew that he had joined the Woll expedition of 1842 to retake San Antonio. Seguín's cultural dilemma is nowhere more apparent than in the Janus-voiced rhetoric of the Preface and final Remarks. It is here that one of the central paradoxes of the Mexican American experience, evident in much post-1848 autobiographical discourse, emerges in one of the earliest personal narratives written by a Mexican(American) trying to prove himself a loyal American citizen and yet a loyal Tejano. The Preface arouses immediate suspicion. Here is a Tejano representing himself as "John Seguin," a misunderstood and wronged citizen of the United States who would prove his innocence and loyalty if only given the chance to clarify, hence revise, the facts about troubling events. Indeed, his narrative would provide incontrovertible evidence that he was not at heart a traitor in 1842, at least not out of choice. But just whom did Seguín imagine his audience to be in 1858 when he asked the citizens of San Antonio to understand, or believe, his "situation"? "(Who amongst my readers will not understand my situation!) I served Mexico; I served her loyally and faithfully; I was compelled to fight my own countrymen but I was never guilty of the barbarous and unworthy deeds of which I am accused by my enemies" (ibid., iv). In the fullest sense, Seguín was attempting to construct an ideal (sympathetic) audience. Of course, the paragraph is shot full of contradictions, but contradiction operates to fashion an idea of the frail and divided nature of human motive that, Seguín reasons, will open the ventricles of compassion in the "just, impartial and composed" readers he wishes to constitute. "Any reasonable reader," Seguín contrives, must understand that "the father triumphed over the citizen," must understand that Seguín, a loyal Texas patriot equally loyal to Mexico, sustained his honor in both situations and should, therefore, be commended for his dual loyalties. Such a reader would reconcile the fact that Seguín refused imprisonment "in a foreign country," imprisonment that would indeed have confirmed his loyalty to the Texas Republic, and would then simply overlook, or forget, that he served as an officer in the Mexican army.

Why, one must wonder, would a man who wished to be reconciled with the "American people" make such a self-incriminating claim. Why not just lie? But, of course, he was lying even while being honest: he must admit what was well known but only by appealing to familial conscience as well as to an ideal of masculine honor that would soften admonishment and prove him the honorable and honest man Texas should be proud to claim. Chronologically tracing his movements during the hostilities conferred documentational strength to his appeal, but his principle rhetorical strategy was to figure himself a loyal Texan forced (as a Tejano) to seek refuge in Mexico, a "foreign country." Notice the rhetorical ploy, however: by arguing the irony that only in Mexico was he secure from assassination by his American "fellow-citizens," he turns the burden of guilt around, making those "fellow-citizens" responsible for his coerced situation. His words increasingly resonate with chagrin and resentment toward the very audience he addresses. Careful not to sound too vindictive, however, he says that he is merely addressing the "passionate attacks of some few disorganizers" (ibid., iii), exposing "the wickedness of a few men," and therefore appealing to that large (silent?) majority of "American people" who, although sometimes "impetuous as the whirlwind," are "just, impartial and composed, whenever men and facts are submitted to their judgment" (ibid.). Reading this qualification against the fact that he had to seek refuge in Mexico rather than anywhere in Texas generalizes his narrative anger toward the very audience he constructs, implicating them in his "situation" by hinting the destructiveness of their impetuosity toward him and other Tejanos, who "on the pretext that they were Mexicans [were] treated . . . worse than brutes." When he writes that he was denied his constitutional rights and was unsafe anywhere in Texas, his anger is unequivocally generalized: "Exiled and deprived of my privileges as a Texan citizen, I was in this country a being out of the pale of society, and when she could not protect the rights of her citizens, they were privileged to seek protection elsewhere. I had been tried by a rabble, condemned without a hearing, and consequently was at liberty to provide for my own safety" (ibid., 26–27).

So, indeed, John (or is it Juan?) Seguín rhetorically contrives his way back across the border after complicitous exile among the enemy, but contrivance emerges from necessity. How else give language to his situation but by speaking contradictory experience both anguished and angry? After all, his chosen countrymen treated him as an enemy in San Antonio, while the enemy—the Mexican Republic—became a refuge from Texas. It is little wonder, then, that

Seguín's *Personal Memoirs* explodes at the very surface with contradiction, with half-lies, self-deceit, competing claims, anger voiced through reasoned appeal, placating his American audience and in the same breath implicating them in his people's losses.

Yet there is another audience Seguín addresses: those people who must have struggled to read the English narrative published at the San Antonio Ledger Book and Job Office, his own Tejano community. For this other audience, the *Personal Memoirs* discloses Seguín's recognition that his ruin (and theirs) was irreversible. Reading Seguín's textual bequest not as self-serving apology but as sociopolitical apologetics intended to implicate the very audience he addresses suggests that Seguín intentionally deployed a form of narrative duplicity that would function to allay the suspicions of his "American" readers while also incriminating them in his, and his people's, dispossession. Moreover, it seems to me that the depositional structure of the text anticipates a readership not yet present: a cultural "posterity" whose own historical situation will require an insider's version of events, a personally experienced version that projects a warning far beyond 1858. Such a narrative operates as a cipher (coded if not encoded) directed to his own people, warning them that their dealings with the Americans will remain troubled, their land despoiled and stolen, their families reduced to wandering beggars. Figuring himself as the prototypical betrayed Tejano, Seguín offers a warning that no matter how much they assert their loyalty to the American state, Mexican(American)s will be dispossessed, made foreigners in their native land, brutalized "on the pretext that they [are] Mexican." Addressing himself to an American audience in a conspicuously accommodating voice, signing himself "John" rather than "Juan," does not make him the exception to that brutalization; rather, it reveals the extent of dispossession, the intensity of his disillusionment notwithstanding his surrender of language and name.

The *bios* is torn against itself, is so contradictory and self-competing that auto/graphy must trace division and disillusionment, must reconstitute subjectivity as it emerges from those destabilizing social conditions that divide and confound the cultural habitat, making contradiction exigent to daily survival. The publication of John N. Seguín's *Personal Memoirs*, written in English, reads against itself as the necessary self-negation that must accompany his address to a posterity who will read (and understand) the contestatory desperation of a Tejano made foreigner to himself. By reading the *Personal Memoirs* as confessional narrative, Seguín may be seen as disclosing his social stupidity and expiating himself be-

fore the Tejano community. Even though to many of his contemporary readers the *Personal Memoirs* must have seemed little more
than self-serving fraud, a reader (this reader: his posterity) who historicizes Seguín's situation comes to understand that sociocultural
necessity produces rhetorical contradiction as a mode of negotiation
in the world.

Although an autobiographical brief, Seguín's *Personal Memoirs*
lays open the terrain of Mexican American autobiographical discourse from the mid-nineteenth century through well into the
twentieth century in autobiographical narrative that traces the personal and collective trauma produced by the American annexation:
the vertiginous shifting of borders, allegiances (re)formed by Tejanos
summarily violated by Seguín's "American straggling adventurers,"
material loss measured against cultural continuity, memory of prior
stability rooted in an idea of home buttressed against dispossession
and alienation. The *Personal Memoirs* structures autobiographical
articulation as a discursive matrix of intercultural conflict, contestatory desire, humiliation, and anger registered within acquiescent
speech, of communitarian guarding of language and cultural practice in the face of derision and legislative nullification. The confusion of his frenetic crossing and recrossing of the border, his appeal
to two cultural audiences—living together but divided by the hostility of the conquest, by language, social manners, cultural practice—shapes narrative as both socially strategic and ideologically
confused. Seguín's contradictory narrative functions as an embryonic autobiographical articulation prefiguring Mexican American
narrative formations in which destabilization on all sociomaterial
levels restructures cultural identity and discursive necessity.

After Seguín's narrative of 1858, one can trace a line through
Mariano Vallejo's "Recuerdos históricos y personales" of 1875, Apolinaria Lorenzana's "Memorias de la Beata" of 1878, Rafael Chacón's
"Memorias" of 1912, and Cleofas Jaramillo's *Romance of a Little
Village Girl* of 1955 to describe the ways in which Mexican Americans have developed a way of speaking personal experience within a
cultural matrix. Even when memory assumes a nostalgic register
that occludes historical material events, nostalgia itself operates to
metaphorize resistance by posing a prior condition both forever lost
and forever desired. Yet even when nostalgia sets in immediately—
while the event and narrative are conterminous—personal narrative
often functions as a document, not only recalling home but trying
to reclaim home as a material reality. Seguín argues that his home
has been destroyed, that he, his family, and his people have been

made foreigners in their native land, and that given such abjurations of his proven loyalty to Texas, he should by all rights be restored to his material and social status once his narrative is impartially reviewed. But there would be no restoration except in the narrative imagination. Vallejo, Lorenzano, and Chacón also disclose a narrative longing for an earlier place, a home broken. Writing the cultural past of the "I" constitutes a willful act of reclamation in which narrative can and must restore a home where, as Jaramillo writes a century later, there are only "melting ruins." Nostalgia, then, opens as an evasion of history only to loop back to history by redrawing the map of an earlier habitat, by narratively remapping the geography of a social space in which Californios, Nuevomexicanos, or Tejanos had developed distinct cultural ecologies. In either case, the idea of home and homeland remains a fierce social symbol, its loss a source of anguish just as it remains a source of belief for autobiographers recalling and, hence, reconstructing the homeland in the narrative imagination in the century after 1848.

Let me close with a few remarks on the social significance of the play of names and the joggling of Seguín's bones. The *Personal Memoirs* as signed by "John N." represents a signatory strategy intended to win approval at first glance by Seguín's intended American readership, but Seguín's *gringo* signature in 1858 masks his given name: Juan Nepumuceno, the name he carried within the family and which even well after 1858 he carried across the border into Mexico where he died in 1890. The name fluctuates between one cultural affiliation and another, measuring the social necessity of adaptation and cultural self-annihilation, the English name subordinating the Mexican name in the contest of languages following the fall of Mexican Texas in 1836 but subordinate only at the surface of social relations (as strategic appeasement) while in the circle of the home his family and friends called out to him "Juan," even in 1858 as he signed himself American "John." The Mexican sound of the name reclaimed in 1862 when, disillusioned once again and angry with Texas, he rode over the border into Mexico to serve in Benito Juárez's army. John (again?) when he returned to Texas in 1873 and successfully petitioned for military pension. Then Juan in 1883 when he returned to Mexico to live with his son, Santiago, who was mayor of Nuevo Laredo. Certainly Juan in 1887 when he audaciously applied for a pension for his services in the Mexican army, this time refused because, after all, he had been a traitor to his country in 1836 and once again after 1848.[26] The signature, thus, the real and socially metaphorical ground upon which the future contest between Mexican and American cultures would continue unceasingly into the present.

But the body itself signified the sociometaphorical apotheosis of destabilization in the flesh: Seguín's corpse remained fluctuant even after his death and burial in Nuevo Laredo, Mexico, in 1890 (a final affirmation of identity he must have thought on his deathbed), nullified by the unearthing of his bones and their return to Seguín, Texas, in 1974 when he was ceremoniously reclaimed as a hero "because of his service to Texas in gaining independence from Mexico."[27] (If bones carry desire and memory in the dry rack of skull, where is home now?) Seguín's final ride into Mexico, where death's decision was undone by the Texas Historical Society's exhumation of his bones, refigures the idea of the Mexican(American)s' confounding encounter with history just as his *Personal Memoirs* prefigures autobiographical discourse even up to the present as an articulation of the sociodiscursive schizophrenia experienced by Mexican Americans whose lives still sway between borders, real and imagined.

Part 2
History, Memory, and
Self-Representation

3

"It is my history, not yours I propose to tell"

History as Autobiography in Mariano G. Vallejo's "Recuerdos históricos y personales tocante a la alta California"

> I was literally speechless with astonishment and joy when Cerruti said to me, "General Vallejo gives you all his papers." Besides the priceless intrinsic value of these documents, which would forever place my library beyond the power of man to equal in original material for California history, the example would double the benefits of the gift.
>
> —Hubert H. Bancroft, *Literary Industries* (1890)

I

Between that dark day in 1846, when his keenly penned article of capitulation was nullified by the *osos* waiting outside his home, and 1874, when he gave all of his papers to H. H. Bancroft, the world Mariano Guadalupe Vallejo had made for himself as a young man had nearly disappeared, his once immense property and wealth had nearly vanished, his political presence had turned from that of real influence into honorary condescension by the Americans who were, piecemeal, assuming title to his property. Yet Vallejo was an important public figure, not for any office or estate of the present in 1874 but for his estate and office of the past. As Bancroft remembers in *Literary Industries* (1890), his own autobiography, Vallejo was chief among those whose knowledge of early California he must have for the definitive and monumental history of California he wished to write. Recognizing also Vallejo's long and vast political sway in Alta California, Bancroft knew that he must possess a great many state documents, official correspondence, and mission and presidio papers indispensable to a history of the period. Therefore, to cajole Vallejo into giving his knowledge and documents was among Bancroft's principal aims during the early 1870s: "To the searcher after California truth Vallejo was California, to the student of California's history Vallejo was California" (Bancroft 1890:384). Vallejo, living on the small acreage of his once vast estate, may have represented California, but California was no longer his; for, as Bancroft writes,

> within the period of his manhood he had seen California emerge from a quiet wilderness and become the haunt of embroiling civilization. He had seen arise from the bleak and shifting sand-dunes of Yerba Buena cove a mighty metropolis, the half of which he might have owned as easily as to write his name, but of which there was not a single foot he could now call his own, and where he wandered well nigh a stranger; he had seen the graceful hills and sweet valleys of his native land pass from the gentle rule of brothers and friends into the hands of foreigners, under whose harsh domination the sound of his native tongue had died away like angels' music. (Ibid., 377)

Before 1846, Vallejo might easily have written his name over the map of what is now the San Francisco Bay area and the Sonoma and Napa valleys, but by 1874, he had been despoiled so extensively that he had been forced to sign away most of his land and remained confined to his beloved Lachryma Montis home in Sonoma, which was also heavily mortgaged. Between 1846 and 1874, Vallejo had worked long and traveled widely in an effort to represent Californio interests in the new state government: he was elected one of six Mexican delegates to the California Constitutional Convention (Monterey, September 1849); in 1851, when he was still worth $1 million,[1] he offered land and $370,000 for the building of the State Capitol; in 1852, he was elected mayor of Sonoma. During the 1850s, he sent two of his sons to private schools in the eastern United States and gave money and a building for a private school in Sonoma where his daughters and other girls could receive an education (Emparan 1968:89). In 1859, he once again visited with Richard Henry Dana in San Francisco and then traveled to New York City, Philadelphia, and Boston in 1865 where he met President Lincoln a few months before his assassination. He led a life of sumptuous affluence and enduring political influence, it seemed, even after the American conquest.

But that was the outside story, the public narrative through which Vallejo represented himself as a prominent and vigorous public figure. The story inside was quite different. Like numerous other Californios up and down the state, Vallejo's material and political losses were quickly outrunning his gains by the 1860s. Although

Mariano Guadalupe Vallejo, ca. 1850s. Photograph courtesy of The Bancroft Library, University of California, Berkeley.

things were getting bad, Vallejo was usually gracious and pleasant—at least in public, where he kept up the cheerful semblance of a man not only reconciled to the Americanization but pleased by the socioeconomic possibilities of the transformation. Inside he fumed. As in 1846, his letters provided an intimate and recondite rhetorical space through which articulations of displeasure and anger were voiced to his family, to whom alone he felt comfortable disclosing a private terrain of confusion, chagrin, and uncertainty about his dealings with what he regarded as a money-obsessed American society. In 1859, Vallejo, in a public display of reconciliation with the Bear Flaggers, rode in his Paris-built carriage with Frémont on the anniversary of California's admission to the Union, but during the same period, letters to his wife, Francisca, and to his son, Platon, disclose (in private) that he was steadily losing ground to squatters and lawyers, that his trips to the East Coast were less for pleasure than increasingly desperate, and usually futile, economic excursions into a world where money, it seemed, drove people socially insane. The "glittering beauty of New York Harbor at night," he wrote in one letter, is undone by the calculated coldness in social manners.

> This city of New York is a town in which every one walks, goes and comes in the streets without recognizing or talking to one another and hub-bub and confusion is such and the noise so great that one talks in shouts to be heard. . . . Everyone is money mad; it seems to me that the people are crazy. Friendship is for the sake of self-interest alone and I have not regarded it so up to now and it makes me unhappy, just to think about it. The madness they have is desperate madness.[2]

Back in California, this money madness had irreparably undone social conventions. There is an alarming sense in his letters that the world he had known, a world of civility and kinship, had, in the new American society, hardened into an obsession with getting and hoarding money. In one letter, after losing a land claim before the U.S. Supreme Court, he disclosed his own participation in the economic madness surrounding him: "So much money invested in Law—for nothing. . . . To remain poor because the most powerful government in the world has squatted on my most valuable pieces of property. . . . I have suffered much physically and mentally, making unheard efforts to sell and to get money to take home but the Devil Money has disappeared from the country. Everyone barks, cries, and whines for it. Some days past I was in Monterey. There are families in such misery that were it not for fishing, they would die of hunger" (Emparan 1968:109). And in 1864, the same year that he proudly saw his son, Platon, receive his medical degree from Columbia University, Vallejo wrote a letter to Francisca in which he bemoaned the foreclosure of his estate and the general economic gloom of their future: "I see that a frightful crisis is coming close and one must prepare to see it in time. . . . Nothing is clear; on the contrary all the future is dark, threatening a monetary storm. . . . There is not one peso here, nor is one to be had. This letter is for you alone" (ibid., 109). Unlike the 1846 letter from prison in which he voiced one message to his intimates and another to his American captors, his letters to family after 1850 are increasingly monotoned in the singular meaning of that word. That is, letters to Platon and Francisca provide a private space in which he could report his grievances, and his grief, without recourse to coding. The sociorhetorical intricacies of multiple meaning operating in his letters and public discourse elsewhere addressed to, or through, American ears are flattened out in his private correspondence, as though his letters to family have become the last refuge of a beleaguered and deeply disappointed husband and father.

Vallejo was too much the public figure, however, to let do with expressing his grievances in private letters alone. During his travels to San Francisco and throughout the state, he saw that what had befallen him had befallen other elite families and that the lower classes were even more desperate. Widely read, he knew that Mexican Californians were pervasively represented negatively in the press and in the gathering California history produced after 1850.[3] By the 1860s, therefore, his interest in history had taken a decidedly serious turn. In addition to time-consuming travel and legal wrangling to save his property, he began writing his memoirs in 1867 which he hoped to publish as an insider's history of California. He had written some nine hundred pages when a fire roared through his home on the Sonoma plaza, destroying the manuscript along with his library of some 12,000 books. Nothing, it must have seemed, could be saved from destruction. After this loss he was silent until Enrique Cerruti, employed to collect research for Bancroft, presented himself on March 24, 1874, with a letter of introduction in which he lavished praise on Vallejo and requested an interview with the "General." Yet, precisely because the rupture between his pre-1846 status and his situation in 1874 was so deeply felt, so painful (not just because of the humiliation he had suffered at the hands of the Bear Flaggers alone but because he had suffered repeated humiliations through the 1850s and the 1860s), by the time Cerruti rode into Sonoma in the winter of 1874, with the single purpose of gaining his favor and winning his papers and memory for Bancroft, Vallejo's trust had been broken so often that he was wary.

Still, he welcomed Cerruti into his home. As it turned out, he genuinely liked Cerruti's worldly air, his gift for conversation on political as well as literary matters from the world beyond California. The two men talked long, lavish hours together, conversing in Spanish over dinner or riding through the Sonoma countryside discussing books, European politics, and early historical events in California. Cerruti, it appeared, was one of the few men interested in Vallejo's knowledge and intelligence rather than in his property: Cerruti dined with the family, told the children tales of his adventures, stayed late into the evening but always returned to his hotel room in Sonoma, and never asked for loans or proposed business deals to be backed by Vallejo—a common enough occurrence for those visiting Lachryma Montis. Cerruti did want something, nonetheless. More and more he brought the topic round to California's Spanish colonial and Mexican period and listened as Vallejo talked for hours about his role in the formation of northern California, relating one incident and anecdote after another, bringing Cerruti into the imaginative sphere of the past, with Cerruti taking brief notes or returning to his hotel where he would write as much as he could remember. When he politely asked to see historical documents, however, Vallejo "retired within himself, and remained oblivious to the most wily arts of the tempter" (Bancroft 1890:388), telling Cerruti that there were no documents, or so few as to be unimportant. Of course, Cerruti was being baited by Vallejo, who had long known that he was in the employ of Bancroft, whom, Vallejo knew, was in the business of collecting historical documents and rare books.

Because Vallejo well understood how much was at stake in shaping historical and personal representation, he developed a form of political-literary strategizing through which he would oversee the construction of California history, in which he and his people were central. He would test Cerruti (and by extension, Bancroft) until he could be sure his collection of inestimable official papers would be handled with respect and care, and then he would once again begin the project of writing California's history—this time with the help of an amanuensis. As part of an elaborate but serious game, Vallejo would leave the room momentarily during their conversations and return with a few documents that he allowed Cerruti to read. Occasionally, he allowed Cerruti to copy a short document in the parlor.

Soon he had Cerruti taking small bundles of papers to his hotel room for copying. Upon returning one set of documents, thicker bundles were loaned, until Cerruti discovered that rather than scattered remains, there were two or three trunks full of papers. He pleaded with Vallejo to allow him to have the papers sent to San Francisco where Bancroft's small legion of copyists might save them for posterity, telling him that he could not possibly copy so much alone. Vallejo agreed and added even more documents. However, when Cerruti suggested that it would be easier to give his entire repository of historical documents into Bancroft's keeping, Vallejo bristled, telling Cerruti, "No Sir. . . . Think you, that I regard these papers so lightly as to be wheedled out of them in a little more than two short months by one almost a stranger" (Emparan 1968:123). There was a major breakthrough commandeered by Vallejo: even though he would not give his papers outright, Vallejo said that he was finally ready to give his recollections. Cerruti at once took up pen and notebook but had to be reminded by Vallejo that his personal history was not casual testimony to be recorded in haste. If he was to write his memoirs, he would do so judiciously, comparing and cross-referencing memory with the documents he had entrusted to Cerruti. Although he had been wheedled out of his land and most of his money, what remained of Vallejo's estate were his memories of a past over which he had exercised vast power, along with a few trunks crowded with documents, letters, and official notes that would bolster the currency of those memories.

In June, while Cerruti and Vallejo were working on the first chapters of what would become the five-volume "Recuerdos históricos y personales tocante a la alta California," they visited Bancroft's library and workshop in San Francisco. Vallejo was ushered into Bancroft's office, where "the history of California, with the Vallejo family as a central figure" (Bancroft 1890:394), was discussed at length. As part of the tour, Bancroft had arranged for the original documents pertaining to the Spanish colonial enterprise in the Americas to be placed before Vallejo: Queen Isabel's orders to Columbus, Columbus's letters of the discovery, Spanish exploration chronicles, and cartographic descriptions of early California coastal expeditions. Vallejo then spent considerable time watching as some eight men seated around a table worked at copying the documents he had sent. "It was very evident," Bancroft writes, "that General Vallejo was impressed and pleased. Here was the promise of a work which of all others lay nearest his heart. . . . It was a work in which he was probably more nearly concerned than the author of it. If I was the writer of history, he was the embodiment of history. This he seemed fully to realize" (ibid.). As the tour came to an end, seeing that Vallejo had finally been won over by the care lavished on new world manuscripts, maps, and historical documents, with his own storehouse of papers treated as a central and significant part of the library's holdings, Cerruti once again suggested that the original documents would be safe and well cared for in Bancroft's library. All at once, Vallejo relented. "He deserves them. Tell him they are his."

This was a profound moment for both Vallejo and Bancroft, a moment in which the project of history proved subordinate to the projections of both men's egos. Bancroft was left "speechless with astonishment," knowing, as he later wrote, that Vallejo's papers "would forever place my [MY] library beyond the power of man to equal." Vallejo, by giving hundreds of official documents as well as by composing a massive historical and personal narrative, expected to place himself in a position of such high esteem that his papers and "Recuerdos" would exemplify and authorize an unimpeachable history of California, the Californios, and the name Vallejo. As he wrote in a letter to the *Sonoma Democrat* the following week, he had given his papers not because he had given in to Bancroft's and Cerruti's prevarications or praises but because after viewing "thousands of manuscripts, some of them bearing the signatures of Columbus, Isabel the Catholic, Phillip II, and various others preeminent during the fifteenth century, I was exceedingly pleased" (ibid., 395). One must imagine, then, that Vallejo's ego, repeatedly lacerated by events of the preceding twenty years, would finally be restored to its rightful preeminence, both by his gift of significant documents and by the narrative history of his own accomplishments in the formation of California, which was part of the legacy of Columbus, Isabel and Phillip II, and those ancestors like Ignacio Vallejo, his own father, who had colonized California during the late eighteenth century.

II

General Cerruti and I go on writing and collecting documents for the history and since our arrival [in Monterey] have written over one hundred pages. We have many venerable documents, which I have not yet looked over, for this dictating and narrating reminiscences stupefies the memory.
—Vallejo letter to Bancroft, January 6, 1875

For nearly two years, between April 1874 and November 1875, Vallejo worked steadfastly with Cerruti on his memoirs, the two often writing while traveling between Sonoma, Santa Clara, San José, and Monterey collecting Spanish colonial and Mexican California documents, encouraging other Californios to dictate their personal narratives as well as contribute their papers. On November 16, 1875, Vallejo's "Recuerdos históricos y personales tocante a la alta California"[4] was formally presented to Bancroft. When completed, the "Recuerdos históricos y personales" comprised five volumes, nearly one thousand pages of social, political, ethnographic, familial, and personal history of Alta California from 1769, the year San Francisco Bay was charted by Gaspar de Portolá, to 1850, the year California was admitted to the Union.

As the personal and historical narrative of a man in his sixties relating the social and cultural history of California with a clear view of its social formation, its transition from Spanish to Mexican rule, and its radical sociopolitical transformation under the American regime, Vallejo's "Recuerdos" fuses his own story with the larger social history of his times. Autobiography, the life story of the individual, is here consciously combined with territorial and cultural history. Since in his estimation, he and California were conterminous, his narration of California history was regarded as the narration of his own history and vice versa. History and autobiography, therefore, meet in the narrative as a kind of auto-historiographics, with individual subjectivity involved at every turn in the process of reconstructing social history. The "Recuerdos históricos y personales," as the title suggests, establishes a reading position for auto-historiography: the narrative serves history by telling the story of Mexican California and, because Vallejo's signature is everywhere present in the narrative, autobiographical consciousness interpolates the writing of that history. The "Recuerdos históricos y personales" much like Thomas Jefferson's *Notes on the State of Virginia* narratively imbricates self-representation and national history. In such an integrative, and audacious, auto-historiographic discourse, the relations between self and history are narratively and ideologically fastened. Unlike Jefferson, however, who, given the success of the nation he helped form, remains squarely centered in his own esteem, one sees in Vallejo a gradual rift between the pre-1848 self, who had consolidated his influence in the state, and the 1875 self, who, because of constant displacement from the social and political realm, is alienated from the state and even from himself.

Vallejo's "Recuerdos," therefore, raises a number of questions about the ideological relationship between autobiography and historiography, between Vallejo's public bios and the private, even secret, life he reveals in letters to his wife and children, between Vallejo, who wrote his "Recuerdos" to refute the historians, and Bancroft, the imperial historian who authorized himself to have "all these scattered chapters of history [the Californio narratives] brought into one grand whole,"[5] which he, of course, would write. Vallejo is crucial for us because he is a bundle of contradictions both within the narrative and, as I have already suggested, outside of it. Vallejo's memoirs, characterized by detached and yet intimate narration of social and political events of Spanish and then Mexican California, never disengages itself from the post-1848 world in which it is narratorially situated. Because Vallejo could not draw away from the dispossessions of the present, from its opening pages to the last paragraph, comparisons between life and manners in the earlier period and those during the American period are interpolated in such a pervasive manner that Vallejo's memory constantly imbricates past/present.

As his memoirs show, Vallejo was the prime example of the social, economic, and political entrepreneur in nineteenth-century Mexican California whose inverse fortunes measurably reflect the shifting socioeconomic politics of his time. From his youth always quick to take the main chance, Vallejo parlayed his soldiering under the Mexican regime into ascending rank and ever-expanding property ownership. By his twentieth birthday in 1827, he had been appointed *alférez* (second lieutenant) at the Presidio of San Francisco and had also become a member of the *diputación* (legislative body). By 1833, he had been assigned by Governor José Figueroa to travel into the interior where he was to establish a settlement that would become Sonoma. And two years before turning thirty, Vallejo had been appointed comandante-general de la alta California by Juan Alvarado, the new governor of California and his nephew. After 1836, as Bancroft notes, Vallejo "was the most independent and in some respects the most powerful man in California."[6] By the early 1840s, then, with Francisca and six of their sixteen children who would be raised in Sonoma, Vallejo built an estate in northern California that began with no inherited deeds and eventually grew into 175,000 acres of land, thousands of cattle and horses, luxurious homes and furnishings, scores of ranch hands and servants, a library filled with the classics, history, and science, a carriage delivered from Paris, and, for a few years after 1848, enough money to provide the best schooling for his children on the East Coast as well as to make generous loans to family and friends, even to casual acquaintances, without worry about repayment. By the time he composed his "Recuerdos" in the mid-1870s, his estate had been stripped to the acreage surrounding his home in Sonoma, and he had lost his wealth to lawyers, venture capitalists, and other "ingrates," with the result that he was literally left roaming San Francisco and the Sonoma countryside asking old friends for small loans.

The unceasing interplay between a socially and materially powerful past and his dispossession in the present establishes a narrative sequencing that opens to synchronic social analysis even though the "Recuerdos" is strictly chronological in structure. That is, it is in those synchronic spaces, in those narrative moments when memory, by an odd reversal of the usual logic of remembering, dredges up the present while recalling the past that Vallejo, surprised by delight and pain, voices complex response to historical events in which he was agential rather than just an inhabitant: "Recuerdos personales y históricos"—the historical and personal as imbrications of each other, memory as recognition of subjectivity grounded within a sequence of events directly tied to the formation of Mexican California and the formation of individual power until 1846, nearly all lost by 1875. The "Recuerdos" constitutes a eulogy to a social and cultural subjectivity stranded in the past over and against a colonized subjectivity accommodating and acquiescent toward an American social formation that had exploited and displaced him. As self-historicizing narrative, it is everywhere nostalgic for the past and everywhere deeply vexed, nearly despondent, spiritually poisoned by his economic and social situation in the 1870s. Maintaining a balance between private bitterness and public calm was necessary to survival in both realms. As he wrote to Platon in 1874,

> There are very exceptional situations in life which are not in the reach of all. . . . Mine for instance—an accumulation of bitterness and vexation in every sense, weary of struggling against Fate for a long time now, despairing sometimes of life itself in a sea of difficulties which embitter it at every instant; exasperated always; the soul uneasy and the heart hardened, disgusted at many men (almost against humanity). With unavoidable debts which Honor, Duty, and Society demand, I have been held in anxiety, hellish, frightful and therefore unusual. Nevertheless, I have been able to endure and resist with a certain studied calm all the tempest of censure with outward sang-froid, with an austere philosophy, if you will, but in reality, burning in an abysmal inferno of griefs that have poisoned my blood.[7]

The "Recuerdos" must be situated immediately between Vallejo's private anguish and his public "sang-froid." He presents himself as a man alternately ebullient toward Americans and embittered toward los americanos, self-deceiving about American socioeconomics yet angry about the dislocations he was suffering at the moment of writing. Understanding the contending and contradictory forces that shaped his responses to the world in which he found himself trapped after 1846 may help us to understand the contradictions between the ever-optimistic, dignified public persona he created and the private darkness and anger he harbored. Vallejo, moreover, may help us to understand the competing social forces that have made a virtue of contradictory responses; a virtue, I say, because such necessary contradictions between public and private sentiments, between intra- and intercultural experience, may be seen as establishing a negotiatory consciousness for Mexican Americans like Vallejo—with Juan Seguín before him and Cleofas Jaramillo after him—which has enabled their (our) survival in North America during the last century and a half.

The confounding situation in which Vallejo found himself by the 1870s while he was composing the "Recuerdos" does much to explain why it is such a contradictory, ambivalent, even schizophrenic text. Contradiction emerges from the competing and confounding pressures exerted in the social domain. On the one hand, the narrative describes Vallejo's expansive pre-American renaissance world, a world filled with music, literature, travel, good friendship, and good conversation; on the other, it discloses a way of life contracting after 1848, disappearing as he grows older and increasingly dispossessed. And although mediated by class consciousness and ethnocentric snobbery, the "Recuerdos" repeatedly discloses the disintegration of Vallejo's social power, patriarchal authority, and cultural domain. By virtue of Vallejo's social displacement, therefore, the "Recuerdos" is pushed into an antithetical relation with such American autobiographies as Benjamin Franklin's *Autobiography* which tend to celebrate the conjuncture between the progress of the American nation and that of the American individual. As a narrative of dispossession it is set against the classic American autobiography, the discursive mode of which generally celebrates the formation of an American character successfully and happily negotiating the social sphere. Unlike the Franklinian autobiographical text that charts the rise of the individual from poverty and obscurity to wealth and enduring fame, the "Recuerdos" is a history of the individual's fall from power and his loss of wealth. For Californios like Vallejo, the competing pressures to trade Mexican cultural citizenship for American national identity are confounded by external social and cultural forces that simultaneously preclude the individual's full integration into American society and yet distance the Mexican subject from his or her own culture by denigrating native language, history, and communal affiliation. The autobiographical act, therefore, becomes a tense ritual of gathering and sorting the relics of the communal past, narratively reifying the cultural legacy while rearranging the national one, proclaiming a desire to become American but doing so in a language and discourse of opposition.

Although Vallejo says at the beginning of the narrative that he is offering his history at the behest of Bancroft, there can be little doubt that he considered his "Recuerdos" a form of prior emendation of Bancroft's historical project. As we have seen, Vallejo was at first reluctant to cooperate in the project, refusing to turn over his vast collection of personal and official papers and feigning disinclination in composing his memoirs. And Vallejo had some ten years earlier composed hundreds of pages of his own historical memoirs when the entire manuscript was lost in the fire that destroyed his home in Petaluma in 1867. Unable to regain the energy to initiate such a vast undertaking on his own, his willingness to collaborate with Bancroft on a similar project provided the impetus by which he might startle memory and recommence the "Recuerdos." It was not until after Cerruti surreptitiously gained his trust that Vallejo, equally capable of being surreptitious, relented and began collaborating on his "Recuerdos"—and even then only because he believed that the history of California could not be written without him, neither written without input of his knowledge nor written without citing his role as a principal in that history. As he originally wrote to Cerruti in mock humble declaration, the name Vallejo was "connected in such a close manner with the history of upper California, since its founding . . . that its omission in such a history would be like the omission of periods, commas and accentuations in a beautifully written discourse."[8] Given Bancroft's proclaimed intention of completing the definitive history of California, Vallejo's own discourse provided a means for one of the dispossessed elite to prescribe the Bancroft project. By restoring the details of the past, Vallejo would provide the historiographic and ideological structure upon which Bancroft's *History of California* would be constituted. Cognizant of the sociocultural stakes involved in the formation of California historiography, Vallejo worked on his history with remarkable energy, unflagging resolve, and uncompromising independence.

That Vallejo was adamant about retaining personal control of the narrative is noted by Bancroft in *Literary Industries*, in which he recalls Vallejo's remark to Cerruti, who was in a hurry to get the project under way.

> I should take you for a Yankee rather than an Italian. Do you expect me to write history on horseback. I do not approve of this method. I am willing to relate all I can remember, but I wish it clearly understood that it must be in my own way, and at my own time. I will not be hurried or dictated to. It is my history, not yours, I propose to tell. . . . If I give my story it must be worthy of the cause and of me. (393)

Unwilling to be hurried, Vallejo spent the next two years relating and organizing his personal history as well as traveling with Cerruti to gather other narratives and official and familial papers from people he had known during his lifetime whose company and conversation would strengthen his memoirs. In fact, he often worked on his "Recuerdos" in the homes of those Californios in Monterey or Santa Barbara with whom he had inhabited another world. These fading Californios talked for long hours, sharing memories, looking through old documents, collaborating on their personal narratives. The zest in his correspondence during this period suggests that he was happy again visiting old friends, happy in his writing and researches, satisfied that what he was doing would have genuine historical significance. In December 1874, he wrote to Platon from Monterey, saying, "My historical works continue 'their majestic march.' There have been written already 900 pages subject to correction, rectification, amending and augmenting and I have reached only the year 1836" (Emparan 1968 : 125). Then, in another letter to Platon late the next summer, August 1875, Vallejo writes,

> I think I'll have to give the last stroke of the brush to the history of California in Vallejo. . . . The fifth [volume] is started but we have reached the time of 1844 in which the events are very complicated, deeds are multiplied of which many persons who still live were witnesses and they are anxiously awaiting the publication of my work, some purely for curiosity and some to criticize it with all their force and others await it with envy. . . . Be that as it may, the history will come out and it will be as you've heard me say many times, the truth impartially written so it can serve posterity as a guide. (Ibid., 129)

Vallejo's assiduous management of the "Recuerdos" throughout its collaborative production with Cerruti indicates just how important maintaining autonomy over all aspects of his memoirs was to him. Although it would be accurate to say that most of the dictated personal narratives collected from the Californios were externally supervised by Bancroft's assistants (Thomas Savage, Enrique Cerruti, Vincente Gomez), in the case of the "Recuerdos," the management of the narrative project was not only supervised but constantly corrected, rectified, amended, and augmented by Vallejo himself. He simply refused to surrender authorial autonomy over the production of his narrative, Cerruti's transcription and editorial organization of the manuscript notwithstanding. Moreover, there are many indications that Vallejo wished to manage not only the production of his own narrative but those of his compatriots throughout California. There is a sense, in fact, that in a strategic act of prior usurpation, Vallejo actually regarded himself the master narrator of that history of California which Bancroft would begin publishing ten years later.

Although the task he took upon himself was onerous for a man of his age and depleted spirits, laboring to collect hundreds of Spanish and Mexican Californian documents and encouraging and cajoling scores of Californios into dictating their memoirs was both something he loved doing and something that, he believed, must be done for the posterity of those who, like himself, had little more than their papers and their memories to will to the future. Vallejo knew, quite simply, that the history of Mexican California and the future representation of his people were at stake. While visiting María Teresa de la Guerra (de Hartnell), for instance, Vallejo discovered that Duflot de Mofras, a Frenchman traveling in California, had abused her hospitality and then written a very negative travel account of Californio social and cultural manners. Vallejo encouraged Doña Teresa to dictate her memoirs as well as to give her papers to Bancroft, both of which might be used as a defense against de Mofras's narrative. An angry revisionist impulse discloses itself in a letter to Platon: "As for de Mofras I will hunt him down as I would a bear. . . . I'll put a rope around his neck and I won't lose my temper when he falls, so shall others fall who have based their writings on the calumnies of the accursed Frenchman." Vallejo's excursions were no less than warfare waged within the text of California history accruing during the 1860s and 1870s. The Californios, who had lost the war and with it their lands and social position, must not lose their papers or their memories of a way of life increasingly maligned by others. The intensity and purpose with which Vallejo and other prominent Californios worked to compose their memoirs disclose both a recognition and a fear that their history was being distorted and maligned, their people not only dispossessed but silenced by the American social and discursive regime. As he had written in a letter to Anastacio Carrillo, Vallejo was afraid that unless they represented themselves textually, they would "disappear, ignored of the whole world." Without their recuerdos históricos y personales marked in ink, experience and memory would as much as vanish into a mass unmarked grave.

III

> I am writing these lines in the same room where I slept the night of May 26, 1836, that is to say some twenty-nine years ago! So many memories! Some pleasant, others unpleasant crowding my imagination at this moment.
> —Mariano G. Vallejo, "Recuerdos históricos y personales"

However angry he may have been about the calumny perpetrated by writers such as de Mofras, the composition of the "Recuerdos" was by no means all bile or revenge. Pleasant memories of his youth in Monterey filled the "Recuerdos," before unpleasant reminders of loss crowded them out. His earliest personal recollections are of his father, Ignacio Vallejo (b. 1748), a sergeant in Monterey when Mariano was a small child. As part of the genealogy he constructs for himself, Vallejo includes a portion of the elder Vallejo's own autobiographical notes, which describes his escape from a seminary in his native Mexico where his parents had sent him against his will to become a priest. Just before he is to take his vows, he rides off with some friends; they hide in the hills surrounding Jalostitlán, Jalisco, and then make their way to the province of California where they enlist in the militia in 1773. As Ignacio Vallejo notes, he served in seven of the eight missions founded by Fray Junípero Serra and was present at the founding of San Francisco in 1776. By relating his father's story, Vallejo situates himself genealogically in upper California from its earliest European colonization, thereby historicizing his own prerogative as an authority on the foundation of California and conflating the individual (autobiography) with the state (history). Indeed, the narrative operates as both autobiography and history when Vallejo anecdotally traces the formations of his own political ideals to incidents in which he remembers himself with his father in early California. In one story, little Mariano is making rounds with his father at the Presidio in Monterey one night when Governor Vincente Sola, one of many governors imposed on the

Californios, appears. The two men talk casually for a few moments, and, just as casually, Sola draws a cigarette expecting a light from Sergeant Vallejo. The soldier lights his own cigarette only and continues talking. The governor bristles but says nothing. The boy looks on, pride mixed with fear. The scene, complete with dialogue and background commentary on Sola, operates as a tribute to his father, but it also anticipates Vallejo's own opposition, years later, to the casual impositions of governors appointed by the central Mexican government without regard for local needs or talent.

There are numerous other socially symbolic anecdotes drawn from childhood experience that mark the development of political idealism and the formation of native bonds with other boys who would grow to be California's governing elite. Along with Juan Bautista Alvarado, Jesús Pico, and José Antonio Estudillo, all of them prominent men by the 1830s, Vallejo recalls that when they were about ten years old, they rebelled against an autocratic teacher by leaving the "gatera" (cat door) open in the schoolroom, allowing a flock of chickens to roost over his papers, spill ink over his desk, and leave droppings throughout the room (Vallejo 1875, 1 : 15, 252–254). On another occasion, Vallejo and some of his young friends, among them Juan Bandini, later one of the most influential men in California, are dining with a Mexican officer who is condescending and arrogant toward what he regards as ignorant provincials. After he retires for the night, they steal into his room, doctor a bucket of water above his head, then fix his bunk so that when he moves in his sleep he will get a drenching. Their prank is intended to chastise him for treating them like subordinates. The trick works, and over a reconciling drink later that night, as he dries water off his face, he promises to treat them with greater respect (Ibid., 2 : 25).

Among the more personal and intimate chapters is Vallejo's moving account of the troubles surrounding his wedding to Francisca Benicia Carrillo. In 1830, when Vallejo was twenty-three, he asked for Francisca's hand, but the wedding was delayed for nearly two years because in accordance with the regulations of the Mexican Republic, he was required to apply for a marriage permit, which took some seventeen months to arrange. He describes the wedding ceremony in detail, remarking on the custom of placing the *arras* (thirteen gold coins offered by the groom to his bride as a symbol of his intention to provide material security) on a plate with the nuptial rings, which Francisca, instead of keeping against unfortunate times, gives to the church. A sumptuous banquet and dance are held

at the home of his padrino, Juan Bandini. Governor Echeandia de-
livers a toast, which Vallejo ostensibly remembers and quotes at
length over forty years later:

> Tengo aun presente el bridis del señor Echeandia, y creo opor-
> tuno reproducirlo, pues aunque desde entonces han trascurrido
> cuarenta y tres años todavía lo recuerdo con placer, pues me trae
> a la memoria los días mas felices de mi existencia. (Ibid., 2:190)

> [I still recall Mr. Echeandia's toast, and I wish to reproduce it
> here, since, although forty three years have gone by, I still re-
> member it with pleasure because it brings to memory the hap-
> piest days of my life.]

Memories of such earlier days will increasingly be set against
the disappointments of the 1870s. In fact, Vallejo's memoirs often
get stuck, not in the past but in the increasingly shabby present. Of
this wedding day, however, there is remarkable concentration on the
event itself as well as on his young bride's integrity and vivacious-
ness, not to mention her patience with his military career. For no
sooner are the newlyweds toasted than Governor Echeandia informs
Vallejo that he must leave immediately after the wedding dance on
a military campaign. Instead of leaving the festivities for a brief hon-
eymoon, the newlyweds remain at the dance in deference to established custom. As the chapter ends, Vallejo directs a lyrically playful
appeal to the reader eliciting sympathy for his difficult situation of
long years past:

> Lector amigo! no te inspira lástima la situación en que me halle
> entonces? por compasión! por simpatía! deja el libro y détente a
> considerar! transpórtate mentalmente a aquellos tiempos, a
> aquellos momentos . . . veinte y cuatro años de edad! lleno de
> ilusiónes! un alma ardiente de fuego voraz! salud a prueba del
> tiempo, de las enfermedades y de las epidemas! . . . omnipo-
> tente . . . el cielo abierto . . . la diosa de la dicha lista a recibírme
> en sus brazos amorosos, pero ahí! (Ibid., 2:193–194)

> [Dear reader! Aren't you moved to pity by the situation in which
> I found myself? For pity sake! For sympathy sake! Put this book
> aside and consider a moment! Transport yourself imaginatively
> to those days, to those moments . . . twenty-four years of age
> and full of illusions, my soul a raging fire, my health a strong
> proof of fitness against sickness and epidemics! . . . omnipo-
> tent . . . the sky open to me . . . and the goddess of happiness
> ready to receive me in her loving arms, but then!]

The passage ends abruptly with a dramatic flourish as the young groom embraces his bride; then, struck by her radiant beauty and afraid that he will be powerless to leave should he hesitate another moment, he extemporizes a lover's verse, leaps on his horse and gallops away to duty:

Francisca	Francisca
Ven y estrechemos; no apartes	Come and let us embrace; do not take
Ya tus brazos de mi cuello,	Your arms from around my neck,
No ocultes el rostro bello,	Do not hide your lovely face
Tímida huyendo de mí.	Timidly fleeing from me.
Oprimanse nuestros labios	Let us crush our lips together
En un beso eterno, ardiente	In an eternal kiss, passionate
Y trascurran dulcemente	And let pass sweet and
Lentas las horas así.	Slow the hours.

Vino ella a mi llamamiento; la ví acercarse radiamente de belleza y amor: ya poco distaba del lugar en donde yo estaba, cuando se me occurio que si me detenía por mas tiempo quizas podría faltarme valor para volverme a despedir: de un salto me puse sobre la silla, piqué las espuelas a los hijares de mí caballeria, y en un instante estaba al abrigo de toda tentación.

Sic transit gloria mundi! (Ibid., 2–194–195)

[She came at my beckoning; I saw her approach radiant with beauty and love; she came nearer and nearer, and then I realized that if I waited another moment I would lose my courage and never leave: I leaped into the saddle, kicked my spurs into the side of my mount, and in an instant I was sheltered from all temptation.]

The lavish prose in this section discloses Vallejo's ease with—and in—the past. And unlike other chapters that are more historiographic and political, here we read an autobiographically affectionate recollection of the beginnings of his familial life in 1832. Forty years later, when he was composing the "Recuerdos," Francisca remained in Sonoma with the younger children, worrying about her husband's increasingly troubled state of mind over their present circumstances. In one of her own letters to Platon, she compliments her husband's strength yet voices concern about his moodiness: "Your Papa is in the midst of many, many difficulties about money, with the care of the family and thousands of other things, but even yet conserves a strength of life. . . . But sometimes I see him sad and thoughtful. . . . He gets annoyed and in a bad humor, many times ending in hopelessness."[9]

For Vallejo, writing the past offered a kind of comic relief against the financial disasters and social disillusionments of the 1870s. Sexual scandal, political intrigue, inept and corrupt officials, book banning by the clergy in 1836 open narrative space for laughter about social relations in a world Vallejo could only recover in memory and memoir. The headings for chapter 44 alone give evidence of an extraordinary milieu among Vallejo's coterie for that year:

> Governor Mariano Chico throws off his mask and tramples upon the rights of the people. The Missionary fathers oppose the circulation of books containing liberal ideas. Excommunication of Don José Castro, Juan B. Alvarado and M. G. Vallejo, accused of having forbidden books in their possession. The City of Monterey dresses up to celebrate the return of the excommunicated youths to the bosom of the Church. The wife of F. Villa, blinded by jealousy, murders her husband. A public prostitute is the concubine of Governor Chico. President Santa Anna is taken prisoner by the Texans. Don José María Castanares seduces Doña Alfonsa Gonzales de Herrera. Comisário Herrera discovers the love affair of his unfaithful spouse. Governor Chico takes the adultress into his home and in company with her attends a tight-rope dancer entertainment. (Ibid., 3:97)

Such sensational headings make considerable appeal to a reader less interested in History than in the quotidian lives and comic, tangled stories that frame history. Of course, in the act of satirizing the figures of the past, Vallejo establishes authority over History as discourse, and because he participated in events that year, he reconstructs his authority over history as social event. Governor Chico, for instance, was, like the earlier Governor Sola, one of scores of officials imposed by the central government whom Vallejo and other *jefes políticos* of California were conspiring to subvert. Because from all accounts he was such a rogue, Chico made their job easy. In addition to his delight at recalling Chico's corruption in office and immorality in private life, Vallejo relishes the seriocomic excommunication of the three friends for reading "Rousseau, Voltaire and several other books of anti-Catholic feeling" that inspired "liberal ideas and any knowledge of the rights of free men." Like a popular historical journalist, he records the story of the unfortunate woman who discovered her husband's infidelity, killed him in a jealous rage, and was then dragged from her hiding place and shot by "un populacho en masa" (a mob). Vallejo takes pleasure in dramatically remembering events in a form reminiscent of an eighteenth-century comedy of manners, caricaturing political figures as he does Governor Chico and satirizing the clergy for their narrow-mindedness.

The chapter is not entirely anecdotal, however. The youthful battle for knowledge is intended to advertise Vallejo's own intellectually inquisitive nature, his habit of reading classical literature along with history and philosophy, and his early development of a republican idealism he believed was the very embodiment of Rousseauian social ideals. Vallejo's seriocomic episode with the clergy in 1836 was easily reconciled when the three young men were granted permission to read material forbidden to "people of little intelligence," but the experience created a lasting skepticism about the church's antiintellectual, antiliberal positions with which he had not been reconciled in 1875. Vallejo charges the clergy with willfully trying to keep the people of California in intellectual and political ignorance: "The reverend missionary fathers were extremely opposed to the circulation among us of books which had a tendency to inspire in our youth liberal ideas and any knowledge of the rights of free men" (ibid., 3:90). He also believed that Mexican Californians might have been better equipped to deal with the political and social ills they faced after 1848 had circulation of such books granted them deeper knowledge of the rights of free men in American society. Once again, the social dislocations of the present mediated, and usually soured, his memories of the past.

It was as though images crowded out of the past of their own volition, locking into counterpoint with Vallejo's and the Californios' declining authority, growing desperation, and sad longing for the past. While in Monterey in 1875, he was working on volume 3 in a home he had visited four decades earlier. Suddenly there is startling narrative collapse of time and experience, the past washing over the present as he witnesses himself writing about the year 1836 in the same room where he slept in 1836: "Estoy escribiendo estas líneas en el mismo cuarto en que dormí la noche del 26 de mayo de 1836, es decir cerca de treinta y nueve años pasados! cuantos recuerdos! gratos unos y ingratos otros se presentan a mi inmajinación en este momento" (ibid., 3:91). [I am writing these lines in the same room where I slept the night of May 26, 1836, that is to say some thirty-nine years ago! So many memories! Some pleasing, others unpleasant crowding my imagination in this moment.] This reads as an intellectual and physical moment of profound reflexivity in which writing and location reproduce a nearly hallucinatory presence of voices and people in the room of the past. Indeed the more he rewrote the past, the more he felt stranded in the present.

Against his grieving for the past, one is startled by those incongruous statements in the "Recuerdos" where he seems nothing less than obsequious toward the Americans, as in the reconstructed speech of 1846 which advocated annexation by the United States, "el país mas libre del Universo" (the freest country in the universe). Such utterances, however, suggest that Vallejo had one eye on his present material circumstances and another on the world he had lost; that is, crucial sections of the text correspond to the public mask Vallejo had assumed when he realized that the American usurpation was inevitable, but those narrative moments, I believe, are subverted by his tendency to compare again and again the coherence of California life before the Americanization with the confusion, moral decay, poverty, and general unhappiness after. Comparisons between life before the arrival of the Americans and that after remain sharply contrasted in the "Recuerdos" as well as in his letters to Francisca and Platon. On January 11, 1877, he disclosed his anguish to his wife: "What a difference between the present time and those that preceded the usurpation by the Americans. If the Californios could all gather together to breathe a lament, it would reach Heaven as a moving sigh which would cause fear and consternation in the Universe. What misery!"[10]

As the "Recuerdos históricos y personales" unfolds, Vallejo's anguish turns to anger, his language from a tone of loss to one of sarcasm. Vexed by the social and discursive ill-treatment his people were receiving, he elaborately counterpositioned examples of early Californio social manners against what he regarded as Yankee-induced moral and political corruption throughout California. And rather than just rail against the past, he documents his opposition to pervasive nineteenth-century representations of the Californios as the illiterate, culturally backward, socially and morally degenerate inhabitants of a progressive, right-minded, visionary American society. As early as the second volume, while describing the work of the Deputación Provincial, the governing body of California, he pointedly compares the integrity of the members and proceedings of the Mexican assembly with the corrupt dealings of the American assembly in 1874, where corruption went all the way up to President Ulysses S. Grant.

How different were the deputies of Alta California in 1827 from the members of the legislature in 1874! The former held it a great honor to represent their constituents and considered the offer of money for services rendered in that august body as an affront, while the latter, as we all know, not only collect up to the last cent which the law allows them, but even have recourse to infamy and perjury, in order to enrich themselves at the expense of the nation. . . . It's a shame to say it, but General Grant, as president of the great American nation, by his fiat sanctioned the laws which I have cited and profited hugely from the immense sums which, without his consent, could not have been filched from the national chests. I cannot conceal that I experience a real pang in reciting such feats, but in justice to the land which gave me birth, in justice to the great and illustrious men of my native country whom American writers have atrociously besmirched, for the purpose of making comparison advantageous to the new mandatories and to the injury of the illustrious men who governed the country before it became a part of the powerful union of the United States of America, I feel impelled to seek retaliation, not as has been done by the flatterers of Fremont, Sutter and the Catholic clergy, entering the forbidden field of lying and defamation, but by citing facts which are public knowledge, deeds which the American press itself has censured, facts the unfortunate results of which we all see as self evident and the dismal consequences of which are the cause of difficulties which oppress workers and farmers. (Ibid., 2:67–68)

The passage functions simultaneously, then, as a history of the Mexican period and a historicized critique of the contemporary American period. Rather than provide a description of the workings of the Mexican assembly in 1827, as Bancroft might expect given his own needs, Vallejo figures the assemblymen of the Mexican period as ideal governors whose motives are vested entirely in the public good, whereas American assemblymen are figured as self-serving and corrupt, passing laws designed to make them rich, lying whenever it suits their ends, selling their votes to the highest bidder. Then, there is the audacious move to implicate the president of the United States, a move that figures the president as standing at the head of corruption, deceit, and thievery. Vallejo clarifies his motive for writing in this vindicatory register: he is justly retaliating against those "American writers"—historians, travelers, and journalists—who have repeatedly degraded the "illustrious men," he says, "of my native country." Not content to refute anti-Mexican writers alone, Vallejo, as a former Mexican assemblyman himself, exposes the most illustrious of American public figures—the president. But there is a cunning rhetorical reversal: unlike those writers who have resorted to "lying and defamation" in flattering "Frémont and Sutter," two men who were, in his estimation, largely responsible for the formation of unethical political and economic structures in post-1848 California, Vallejo resorts only to "facts which are public knowledge." The very mention of the names Sutter and Frémont, as part of his claim of methods he will *not* resort to in his writings, brings their names into the circle of corruption and disrepute. Here and elsewhere Vallejo strategically names his enemies in the narrative, not by censuring them outright but by ironizing their presence within statements that, as in the passage cited, voice his loyalty to his "native country" and those "illustrious men" who are being degraded and despoiled at the very moment he is writing his memoirs. This is the same Vallejo, then, who in public created the appearance of an "illustrious" Californio who had gladly traded Mexican citizenship and loyalty to his "native country" for American citizenship.

Toward the end of the "Recuerdos," as the chronological division between the Mexican and American period fuses, Vallejo increasingly joins political critique with commentary on the ill-effects of American social manners on the social structure in post-1848 California society. The breakdown in parent-child relations, for example, is directly attributed to the radical shift in social structures.

> Anteriormente a la llegada de los americanos, nuestros hijos cuando nos encontraban en la calle, se acercaban respetuosos y teniendo su sombrero en las manos decían, 'Señor Padre, he salido de su casa con ánimo de ir con fulano a dar un paseo? Me permite usted que continua dividiéndome?' . . . En la actualidad, los niños dicen a los padres, 'Cómo te va Papá?' 'A dónde vas?' Pero nosotros, cuando saludábamos a nuestros padres, decíamos 'Cómo está usted, Señor Padre? Que le ofrece?'[11]

> [Before the arrival of the Americans, whenever we encountered our children in the street, they would respectfully draw near and with hat in hand would say, 'Dear Father, I have just left your house eager to go with so-and-so for a walk. May I have your permission to continue?' . . . Nowadays, children tell their fathers, 'How you doing, Dad? Where you off to?' However,

when we greeted our fathers, we asked, 'How do you do, honored father? May I do anything for you?']

Unlike children in pre-1848 Mexican society who addressed their parents and elders in the formal and respectful "usted," youth exposed to American social mores call out to their parents in the "tú," as though speaking to casual acquaintances. This postoccupation generation had lost more than respect for their elders; in Vallejo's estimation, they had lost their birthright. Their situation was truly unfortunate, their disaffection and lawlessness the result of unjust laws, crooked judges, and juries.

> La mayor parte de los jovenes que con tanta injusticia habián sido despojados, sediéntos de venganza, se dirijieron a engrosar las filas de Joaquín Murieta y bajo las ordenas de ese temido bandido pudieron desquitar parte de los agravios que la raza norte americana les había inferido. (MS, vol. 5, 237)

> [Most of the young who had been so unjustly despoiled, thirsty for vengeance, filled the ranks of Joaquín Murieta, and under his leadership were able to revenge some of the insults that the North American people had inflicted upon them.][12]

For most of these youth such desperation ended badly; some ended up in San Quentin, and, as Vallejo writes, "Some received passports to the other world through the conveyance of Judge Lynch." And yet, it seemed to Vallejo, worse than death by lynching was the travail of insanity, madness, and dementia brought on by the trauma of social rupture and dislocation.

> Cosa extraña, el hospicio de dementes tambien recibió como huéspedes a algunos Californios, cosa que causó mucha extrañeza entre todos nosotros que hemos nacidos en este país, pues . . . nunca se había visto locos entre nosotros. (MS, vol. 5, 238)

> [And strangely, the insane asylum has also received as guests some Californios, a fact which caused much wonder among those of us born in this land, because we had never seen insane people among us.][13]

By the end of the "Recuerdos" when he criticizes American derogation of Spanish language and Mexican culture—German and French were promoted emphatically in the schools in San Francisco in the 1870s, while Spanish was snubbed in the classroom altogether[14]—one can see that Vallejo has been engaged in subverting the English language by composing some one thousand pages of historiographic autobiography in his native tongue. His mannered prose, his intellectual eloquence are, as much as his unrelenting sociopolitical referentiality, fully intended to be the instruments of a counterdiscourse to a prevailing ethnocentric historiography rather than a show of one Mexicano's exception to the rule. While composing the "Recuerdos," Vallejo was acutely conscious of his self-assumed role as a guardian of the conquereds' version of their own history. Textual self-representation in a form that would inscribe itself on the public domain motivated Vallejo to relate such an exhaustive historiographic, personal narrative. Notwithstanding the egoistic claim that the history of California could not be written without the Vallejo name at its center, especially his name, Vallejo's version of history was more than a narrative monument to himself. It was, by his own reckoning, staunchly revisionist. As he wrote to Platon in December 1874,

> I shall not stop moistening my pen in the blood of our unfounded detractors. . . . You know I am not vindictive but I am and I was born hispano. To contradict those who slander is not vengeance, it is regaining a loss. . . . It pleases me to believe that there should be a hell with lakes of fire, hot lead and legions of demons with red-hot pincers to pull out the tongues of slanderers.[15]

Vallejo's verbal refutation of those "detractors" who had degraded the Mexican Californios constitutes a troubled and unremitting sociocultural struggle for the ownership of history and self-representation in late nineteenth-century California. No longer exercising influence in state matters and his once economically powerful voice fast turning into embarrassed pleas for loans from those Americans who were quickly assuming title to his properties, Vallejo had words alone with which to "contradict those who slander." Since, like the other prominent Californios, Vallejo had fallen from institutional position, language was the last vestige of social power at his disposal. Indeed, all that Vallejo had left of his once formidable institutional power was a verbal eloquence that, masked by the public persona he had carefully constructed over the years as an amiable man, a man whose word was good even if his property titles were not, might be used to confrontational ends. As one Californio wrote in a letter to Vallejo, "If you succeed in having published one quarter part of the evil that the Yankees inflicted upon us, you will effect a miracle."[16] Vallejo's inclusion of scores of letters, long legal documents (including the entire Mexican Constitution of 1824), political poems and lampoons, his own public speeches as well as those of numerous other Californios, all constitute a narrative strategy devised to challenge and revise an anti-Mexicano historiography already hardening in 1875. Such a documentational autobiographical mode resists silencing, while conferring official, even legal, authority to the voice that at once socially contextualizes and legitimizes self-representation; as though to say "Bancroft, or you, faceless/nameless americano can ignore, diminish, or dismiss the 'me' who resides outside of the text, but you cannot ignore, diminish, or dismiss the textual 'ME' residing within the documentational narrative."

IV

> I wish that if what I have written for him is considered in his estimation all fabricated by me, to return to me what I have written.
> —Vallejo, letter of August 1886

> General Vallejo is in his 83rd year. He lives in a little house near old Sonoma, the scene of his princely hospitality before California was a State. He is no longer strong physically nor independent financially. He is a broken old man, infirm and almost entirely helpless. Once immensely rich, he is now extremely poor. From a position of affluence, he has come to one of hard poverty.
> —Napa newspaper, 1890

In the fifteen intervening years between the formal presentation of his "Recuerdos históricos y personales" and his eighty-third year, Mariano Vallejo's fortunes spiraled downward without surcease. Shortly after finishing his narrative and his historical researches, Vallejo returned to Sonoma, to boredom and depression. "I am feeling like hell," he wrote to Francisca, who was away visiting daughters, "cannot read, which for me is something terrible. I am able to write with great trouble and not being able to read or write makes me feel like a fool." His younger brother Salvador, fellow settler, soldier, and Bear Flag prisoner, passed away on February 7, 1876, at sixty-three. The same year, on October 9, Enrique Cerruti, who had lost money on a mining venture, committed suicide in Sonoma. Later the same month, Vallejo himself lost another large sum of money when the Vallejo Savings and Commercial Bank failed.[17] In 1878, he saw his own material and physical situation represented in a photograph of his once beautiful home in Petaluma, now in ruins. "I compare that old relic with myself and the comparison is an ex-

Mariano Guadalupe Vallejo at his Lachryma Montis home in Sonoma, California, ca. 1880s. Photograph courtesy of The Bancroft Library, University of California, Berkeley.

tant one; ruins and dilapidation. What a difference between then and now. Then Youth, strength and riches, now Age, weakness and poverty."

Another decade elapsed with more private grief and a good deal of public sangfroid. The year 1886 was a particularly confounding one in which the seventy-nine-year-old Vallejo experienced with unremitting force the contradictions between public tribute and private disappointment. In January, he wrote to his son-in-law, John Frisbie, for a loan, which Frisbie "was pained" to deny except for a check of $50. In February, he was taken to court over a $1,500 note he believed had been long forgiven. "I am sorry to state that I am not able at such short notice to fulfill my obligation," Vallejo was to plead. In May, he received a letter from Edwin Sherman, chairman of the Associated Veterans of the Mexican War, asking if, as "an American citizen and as one of the members of the first Constitutional Convention," he would be present in Monterey to celebrate the fortieth anniversary of the "raising of the American flag" over California; he reluctantly but graciously accepted. There he raised the flags of Spain and Mexico and then gave a brief speech on the roles of those two nations in the formation of California: "I am commissioned by you today to raise those two flags in sign of respect to your predecessors, I accept with pleasure . . . for I was born on this piece of land and reared under the ensigns of Spain and Mexico, the two, which I salute with all the fervor of my soul." The conquered general maintained his dignity and upheld the dignity of his native culture, even in the face of another patronizing tribute to the dispossessed Californios.

During the summer of 1886, volume 5 of the *History of California* appeared, and Vallejo was appalled by what he read. Describing events immediately preceding the American conquest, Bancroft commented on a meeting that Vallejo said had taken place in Monterey in April 1846, in which the Californios gathered to discuss the impending crisis with the Americans. In a "desire to be strictly accurate," Bancroft wrote, "all that has been said of this meeting, including the eloquent speeches so literally quoted, I believe to be purely imaginary. No such meeting was ever held, and no speeches were ever made."[18] Vallejo, who had been eagerly reading Bancroft's *History* as quickly as it appeared, was stunned. He had sometimes commented on Bancroft's mistakes in preceding volumes with such marginalia as "Que absurdo!" Yet in general, he believed he had been successful in helping Bancroft produce an informative and fair account of Mexican California. The historian had relied heavily on Vallejo's "Recuerdos," as well as on his "Documentos," but with casual aplomb he dismissed a central event in Vallejo's narrative as a figment of an old man's imagination. Vallejo felt humiliated and demeaned.

At issue was a significant summit meeting composed of the Californio elite—among them, Governor Pío Pico, José Castro, Juan Alvarado, and Vallejo—who discussed the growing American presence throughout the territory. In volume 5 of his own "Recuerdos," Vallejo recalled the debate of April 1846 between the Californios over such matters as Mexico's neglect of the province and the consequent threat to California posed by the Americans, as well as by France and Britain, which had both expressed imperial interest in California. As Vallejo remembers, the delegates discussed California's troubles and proposed various alternatives: José Castro in favor of annexation by France because it was a Catholic country, Rafael Gonzáles for a "government that is sovereign and free" not only from the United States or France but also from Mexico; other delegates favored England as a protectorate, and Victor Prudon, Juan Bandini, and Vallejo spoke in favor of annexation by the United States.

As he was in the habit of doing throughout the "Recuerdos," Vallejo reconstituted the entire speech, the gist of which celebrated the United States as the freest country in the world, a country peopled by industrious citizens, a republic rather than a monarchy, and, most important, a constitutional republic that would guarantee their political autonomy and full representation in the Congress and Senate (5:82–83). Vallejo's narrative of the event provided an insider's account of a troubling meeting, a meeting during which the confusions set off by the encroachments against Californio society seemed to be developing quickly from many sides.

To have shared the secret meeting with an eminent historian signified the extent to which Vallejo trusted the process in which he had been engaged for two years with Cerruti. The idea had been to get the history of Mexican California right. Bancroft had convinced Vallejo in 1875 that his contribution to the *History of California* would be unimpeachable, but, without warning or justification, it seemed to Vallejo, Bancroft now nullified his version of a crucial historical event and by extension called into question Vallejo's general narrative veracity. "I am very sure that General Vallejo's memory has been greatly aided by his imagination" (5:63), Bancroft wrote within the text for all the world to see. In the appended "Pioneer Register and Index," he went on to note that although Vallejo's narrative was "not only the most extensive but the most fascinating of its class," it was, nevertheless, "like the works of Bandini, Osío, Alvarado, Pico and the rest . . . a strange mixture of fact and fancy" (5:759). The Historian had spoken. Vallejo must have stared at the pages before him, stunned and humiliated. The work to which he had committed himself for two years was in a moment called into public question, marked as a document to be corrected, a parcel of fascinating anecdotes, a picturesque mélange of "fact and fancy"— in short, a historical fiction.

As I have indicated more than once, Vallejo's narrative is indeed imaginatively written, his recollections of the past dramatized by characterization, dialogue, playful and yet serious sociopolitical language. Certainly by his own reckoning, nevertheless, the "Recuerdos" was documentationally responsible. Even if one cannot claim unimpeachable historical veracity for Vallejo's narrative, one must be troubled by the politics of narrative hegemony, the show of power displayed so adamantly by Bancroft on the very face of a powerful public discourse like the *History of California*. In a letter to W. F. Swasey (1886), who had been present at the April 1846 meeting and who had corroborated Vallejo's recollection of the meeting, Vallejo wrote, "Mr. Bancroft calls it a 'myth' and a creation of my own imagination. . . . [He] is certainly very ungrateful. . . . I wish that if what I have written for him is considered in his estimation all fabricated by me, to return to me what I have written and then Mr. Bancroft will be at liberty to select such a person as he may consider more trustworthy and whose assertions may not be considered as 'myths' or lies."[19] Vallejo's letter to Swasey is, as near as I can survey, his only comment about the Bancroft slight. There is no record of him having written to Bancroft directly. Nor does it seem that Platon, his closest confidant, received any correspondence from his disillusioned old father. Vallejo, for whom the slight was painful and humiliating, remained silent, or rather, silenced on the issue.

Vallejo and the scores of other Californios who composed their *historias, memorias,* and *reminicencias* were as much as gagged, if not altogether silenced. One realizes this to be the case upon seeing that the hundred or so personal narratives, comprising thousands of pages of life history, are smothered by the weight of Bancroft's massive historical project, set into footnotes below the main narrative, revised and in many cases discounted by Bancroft. Although Vallejo initially hoped to have his "Recuerdos históricos y personales" published, he eventually offered his five-volume manuscript to Bancroft, "confident," as he wrote in a letter, "that you will present us a complete and impartial history of California."[20] It was another Californio mistake, since the Anglo-American historian proved to be as imperialistic as the land grabbers. Vallejo might spend two years composing his recollections and collecting innumerable documents, but Bancroft regarded Vallejo's entire narrative of nearly one thousand pages and Vallejo's historical researches as his property to be used or not as he saw fit. He says as much in *Literary Industries:* "It was understood from the first that this history was for my sole use, not to be printed unless I should so elect, and this was not at all probable."[21] The five-volume "Recuerdos históricos y personales tocante a la alta California" was not returned. Nor was there any reason it should have been. As was the case with his land, the "Recuerdos" and some ten thousand manuscripts, bound into thirty-six large volumes, had been deeded away to Bancroft. Along with the rest of the Californio narratives and documents, Bancroft laid Vallejo's "Recuerdos históricos y personales" to rest in his library where it would be well cared for, safe, and suppressed.

The year 1886 closed with Vallejo dispossessed of thousands of invaluable documents and a carefully supervised narrative but still hedging his luck against his economic fate, trying once again, one last time, to file a land claim suit. In November, he filed an action to recover a portion of the San Francisco Presidio Reservation, a tract of 371 acres. In the brief, Vallejo's attorney argued that the land had been granted to him by the Mexican government in 1844, while also criticizing the harsh treatment of Vallejo and his family by U.S. military officers in 1846. "He felt that the military officers had treated him with the greatest disrespect; no leniency had been extended to him, nor was it their desire to deal justly with him; he thought the methods adopted by the U.S. law agents were calculated not to further justice but to defeat it by dilatory and expensive litigation."[22] Despite Vallejo's plea, the case dragged on through four years and was dismissed outright on October 22, 1890. Yet another claim had closed in futility. A few months before his death, a Napa newspaper editorial, pleading on Vallejo's behalf, asked that the U.S. government grant "relief" to Vallejo for "his kindness to immigrants and his noble conduct." Vallejo, the editorial pressed, was "a broken old man, infirm and almost entirely helpless. Once immensely rich, he is now extremely poor." A government pension would symbolize the country's gratitude to Vallejo, who, before the Bear Flaggers seized him as an enemy general, had welcomed Americans into his home, had given many American families grants of land, and had spoken on behalf of annexation to the United States before his own compatriots. Public relief never came, and Mariano Vallejo died on January 18, 1890.

4
"Yo sola aprendí"

Autobiographical Agency
Against Testimonial Expectation in
California Women's Personal Narrative

LAS MUJERES

> Under my direction and responsibility, Domingo Romero took care of changing the liquid. Luis the soap-maker had charge of the soap-house, but I directed everything.
>
> —Eulalia Pérez, "Una vieja y sus recuerdos"[1]

> I was already teaching young girls to read and catechism from the time I was staying in Doña Tomasa Lugo's home. Afterwards I did the same in Doña Josefa Sal's home. After becoming a widow, this lady opened a school where girls could learn to read, pray, and such things. As she had an orchard that took much of her time, I had almost exclusive responsibility for the school. There were also girls whose parents particularly sought me out for instruction. . . . Many other girls also learned their first letters and such with me.
>
> —Apolinaria Lorenzana, "Memorias de la Beata"

> Of [the Californio] officers, few offered their services when the hour came to defend the country against foreign invasion. The greater part performed no more service that the figurehead of a ship.
>
> —María de las Angustias de la Guerra, "Ocurrencias en California"

LOS HOMBRES PRE-1848

> The women of California were always noteworthy for their excellent conduct as daughters, sisters, wives and mothers. They were virtuous and industrious, and devoted to their family duties.
>
> —José María Amador, "Memorias sobre la história de California"[2]

> We taught our girls to be good housewives in every branch of their business; our wives and daughters superintended the cooking and every other operation performed in the house, the result of the training was cleanliness, good living and economy.
>
> —Salvador Vallejo, "Notas históricos sobre California"[3]

LOS HOMBRES POST-1848

> In the last twenty years [from 1850 to the 1870s] it appears that the sole pur-
> pose of young women's education is to prepare them to cut a figure at the thea-
> ters and dances, little worrying that in the administration of the domestic
> sphere they are dolls incapable of directing the management of their homes;
> and such is the fear that young men have of falling into the hands of foolish
> and vain women that many of the children and grandchildren of my old
> friends-at-arms have traveled to Sonoma with the sole object of asking me
> whether or not they should marry so-and-so or so-and-so.
> —Mariano G. Vallejo, "Recuerdos históricos y personales tocante a la alta
> California"[4]

Epigraphic fragments only—but statements that immediately divide the terrain of expectation between men's representation as patriarchal demand and women's self-representation as the assertion
of authority and knowledge in the public life of California: los hom-
bres remembering the good old days when women remained cheerfully ensconced in the home (or, so men believed), chagrined with
post-1848 women who, Vallejo charged, had abandoned the home for
the theaters and dance halls; las mujeres remembering patriarchal
constraint and their own strategies for circumventing concealment
in the home, speaking openly in the 1870s about men's bumbling in
the public domain and their inability to save California from the
American invasion.

I

In the 1870s, a group of women spoke their memories of early California life to Bancroft's oral historians, Enrique Cerruti and Thomas
Savage. They discussed the significant political and social events of
the day, but they also spoke adamantly about their own lives, their
will to authority and presence. Yet of the nearly one hundred Californio narratives collected by Bancroft, fewer than fifteen were
(re)collected from women. Why? The answer, as always, is obvious:
women have always been unequally represented when it comes to
recording experience about the public domain. When Bancroft was
collecting personal narratives for his *History of California*
(1884–1889) and for *California Pastoral* (1888), he was chiefly interested in supplementing the political history of California, which
meant that men who held office, rancheros, military officials, soldiers, or traders were called on to record their *recuerdos*. Women's

narratives were considered merely supplemental to men's; indeed, even when they were considered "reliable and fascinating," as Bancroft called "Mrs. A. Ord's" (Angustias de la Guerra's), or curiosities, such as that of "Eulalia Pérez, Widow Mariné, the famous centenarian of San Gabriel," Bancroft referred only briefly to them in *History of California* and *California Pastoral*. More often than not they were slipped into lower case (caste, I want to say), or entirely excised. But weren't women equally part of the public history of the region? Weren't they as much pioneers as the men? Weren't their memories of pre-American California worth significant incorporation into the historiography of the period?

The fact is that women's narratives—and the social knowledge they contained—were remanded to the margin of the margin by Bancroft. Yet they evince remarkable perspicuity on political events and the social structures of pre-American California. Indeed, women sustained their voices, speaking against the patriarchal orchestration of history in clear, often defiant registers that spoke their own presence—and difference—in historical discourse. Feminine signature and authority were sustained even though women were expected to be self-subordinating when it came to telling their life stories: signature and self-authority evaded the testimonial expectation that women discuss home and family only, or that when they did comment on political events, their husbands, brothers, and fathers were to be foregrounded. Subjectivity was situated, therefore, not in the home or in patronymic affiliation, not even in the memory of home or husband, but in a woman's life in the public realm, in the spoken recovery of an authority measuring personal accomplishment, political acuity and agency, self-taught literacy, and heroism against the threat of foreign invasion.

Recovering women's narratives from the Bancroft collection requires, first of all, restoring their presence on the page, bringing the names and narrative titles up from the footnotes, dislodging these disembodied women's voices from Bancroft's master list of "Authorities Quoted in the *History of California*," culturally reclaiming those whose names were concealed behind the names of their American husbands: Hartnell, Ord, Fitch et al. The twelve women whose lives were collected during the 1870s by Bancroft's field assistants are Apolinaria Lorenzana, "Memorias"; Catarina Avila (de Ríos), "Recuerdos"; María Inocente Pico (de Avila), "Cosas de California"; Josefa Carillo (de Fitch), "Narración de una Californiana"; Teresa de la Guerra (de Hartnell), "Narrativa de una matrona de California"; María de las Angustias de la Guerra (de Ord), "Ocurrencias en California"; Felipa Osuña, "Recuerdos del pasado"; María Amparo Ruiz (de Burton), "Biographical Sketch"; Rosalía Vallejo (de Leese), "History of the 'Osos'"; Eulalia Pérez, "Una vieja y sus recuerdos"; Dorotea Valdez, "Reminiscences"; Juana Machado (de Ridington), "Los tiempos pasados de la alta California." Like the men's narratives, only a few have been translated and published: Angustias de la Guerra's as *Occurrences in Hispanic California*, Juana Machado's as "Times Gone By in Alta California,"[5] and a truncated version of Eulalia Pérez's as "An Old Woman and Her Recollections."[6] Scattered references to the women's narratives may be found in parts of Bancroft's *History of California* and *California Pastoral* where the daughters of the elite landowning class recall the significant social and political events of the pre-American period or where women who worked in the missions reconstructed their daily lives within the mission economy. In the main, however, their voices are reduced to whispers in Bancroft's work; most remain silenced in the Bancroft library archives.

Because there are so few available to us in published form and because most have been remanded to archival silence, central to the recovery of women's narratives is a consideration of the patriarcho-discursive constraints placed upon Mexican women in California, which account for various modes of subordination against which women figure themselves. Although it appears that Bancroft wished to elicit information on domestic "customs and manners" from the women, the lengthy *California Pastoral* chapter, "Woman and Her Sphere," relies almost entirely on documentary evidence (judicial and state papers) written by men, upon narratives by Californio men, and, often upon statements about California women recorded by American and English men. Indeed, there is in the entire chapter not one direct evidenciary reference drawn from the women's narratives. In another chapter, "Food, Dress, Dwellings, and Domestic Routine," men like José del Carmen Lugo ("Vida de un ranchero") and Antonio Coronel ("Cosas de California") are routinely called on to (re)dress the women of California: "Lugo places upon women of this period short skirts fastened about the waist" (378) and "Coronel, in 1835, describes the underskirts of the women as elaborately and tastefully embroidered" (392). So, as it turns out, not only must Bancroft have thought that women's historical consciousness and sociopolitical knowledge were not worth incorporating into his commentary on women's experience in pre-American California but they presumably could not even be trusted to remember what they wore. More likely, of course, they were not interested in what they wore forty years earlier, at least not as the only topic memory should regather.

By the 1870s, nostalgia for coherence in the social and domestic sphere generated reverence for the family in those many Californio narratives that reconstruct the powerful public identities the patriarchs enjoyed before they lost their land to the Americans and their families to a social economy in which, the fathers muttered, children did as they pleased. Juan Bautista Alvarado, José María Amador, Manuel Castro, Pío Pico, Antonio María Osío, and Mariano and Salvador Vallejo, along with scores of other once prominent Californios, collaborated on narratives that reconstructed the period from the late eighteenth to the mid-nineteenth century, an era during which they ruled over a vast expanse of geography—native people as well as their own families. Aristocratic, socially elitist, manipulative, and exploitative, the world these men made for themselves and their families was one predicated upon their unquestioned authority as fathers and husbands. In such a reified world, patriarchal authority, the fathers believed, gave coherence and purpose to the family, as well as to the larger social community.

One of the most influential of these patriarchs was Mariano Vallejo, whose "Recuerdos históricos y personales tocante a la alta California," as I have indicated, comprises nearly one thousand manuscript pages of personal, familial, social, and cultural history. Vallejo's narrative, of course, discloses a deeply embedded patriarchal consciousness in which wives, daughters, and sisters are remembered as virtuous and obedient before 1848, recalcitrant and foolish after. Respect for, obedience to, honor of, deference toward the patriarch were, for Vallejo, signs of familial and general social well-being before Americanization; after the displacement of the patriarch, the children fell away from the code of behavior and the patriarchal world collapsed. Once, young men greeted their fathers in the street with respectful address. Young women, once prided—by husbands or fathers—for their ability to administer the domestic affairs of home and family, were, after 1848, interested only in making an impression at the theater and at dances and were, Vallejo charges, "muñecas incapaces de dirigir el manejo de sus casas" (dolls incapable of directing the management of their homes). As Vallejo's epigraph crows, he had been approached by many men, young and old, seeking advice on what to do with these recalcitrant women. There were more *solteronas* (old maids) than ever after

1850, he insisted, because men were reluctant to marry, afraid that they would be ruined and dishonored by these "mujeres necias y vanidosas" (foolish and vain women). (4:336–337)

Reading the women's narratives against the grain of such patriarchal presumption is necessary principally because the gap between women's representation by men and women's self-representation is not only disparate but often directly at odds: men remembering wives, daughters, sisters as domestically devout, cheerfully obedient, and unconcerned about men's political and business dealings before 1848, then as "necias y vanidosas" after; women, however, seldom seating themselves in the domestic sphere but remembering rather their work in the world or, even though confined to the home, describing themselves as more prescient than men at reading the signs of American conquest in the early 1840s, more cognizant of the ways in which political factiousness and fiscal mismanagement throughout California made the country easy prey for the Americans.

Of course, men also engaged in the typical argument over women's chastity: she was represented as sexual outlaw, in some versions, and as pure in mind and action in others. Whereas the Mexican patriarch reconstituted "his" women as ideal maternal and domestic creatures (at least before 1848), for American and other foreign men the Mexican woman was the riddle of sexual promise and denunciation (even before 1848). By 1840, Dana had represented California women's sexuality as promiscuously rampant and dangerous: "The women have . . . a good deal of beauty, and their morality, of course, is none the best. . . . If the women have but little virtue, the jealousy of their husbands is extreme, and their revenge deadly and almost certain."[7] In contrast, Alfred Robinson, who married Ana María de la Guerra, upheld the virtue of Californianas: "There are few places in the world, where, in proportion to the number of inhabitants, can be found more chastity, industrious habits, and correct deportment, than among the women of this place."[8] As Antonia I. Castañeda argues, the representation of women's morality manifests "the polarities of 'good' and 'bad' women applied to women generally."[9] But in the case of Californianas, the "simplistic dichotomous portrayal" was complicated by ideological and hegemonic projections, not to mention personal stakes. In refuting Dana's representation, Robinson and other American men like William Davis were upholding their own reputations for marrying Mexican women. "The former [Dana's 'bad' women]," Castañeda continues, "set the precedent for pejorative stereotypes of Mexicanas in the North American mind. The latter [Robinson, Davis] effectively separated elite women from the history, gave them a new history, and thus made them acceptable to Americans."[10] As Castañeda suggests, women, prevented from speaking their own versions of history, were provided patriarchal master narratives by both Californio and American historians.

So, it comes as no surprise that when Bancroft sent his men to collect their life stories, women like de la Guerra, a member of the elite class, and Eulalia Pérez, a working-class woman, were not asked to describe women's morality or to corroborate or refute tales of sexual improprieties in Californio society—much less were they asked about their own deportment. Nevertheless, Bancroft's representation of women in *California Pastoral* constitutes them as objects of desire and derision. And, ironically but not surprisingly, what he has to say about the women is reconstructed not from their own but from men's accounts. Bancroft's "Woman and Her Sphere" is voyeuristic, presenting a documentary exhibition of domestic infelicities and infidelities, on occasion describing women's separations from drunk and abusive husbands but more usually husbands' dissolutions from unfaithful wives, and of these immoral women, case after case of sexual innuendo, salacious anecdotes about sexually troubled marriages, concubinage, prostitution of wives, illicit intercourse, and the punishments meted out to transgressors. In *California Pastoral*, Bancroft exhibits one group of cases from "actual life" on the harsh "legal discipline" imposed on women who ran to freedom; they were all recaptured and ordered by the courts (men) to return home where they were to remain contrite and quiet. One woman, María de la Nueves, left her husband and refused to return, "whereupon she was put in prison, there to learn obedience," and another, the (unnamed) wife of José Madriaga, "repelling all of his advances," was asked by him if she had made a "vow of chastity, and was answered no. He proposed that they should confess to the priest, . . . but she refused to confess, or have anything to do with the priest. That night she ran away" (307).

The longest passages in *California Pastoral*, however, are saved for observations—innuendo and hearsay really—by foreigners commenting with stern authority on California women's morals: "'I hear from the most unexceptionable authority,' writes Sir James Douglas . . . 'that the ladies in California are not in general very refined or delicate in their conversation . . . indulging in broad remarks which would make modest women blush. It is also said that many, even of the respectable classes, prostitute their wives for hire; that is they wink at the familiarity of a wealthy neighbor who pays handsomely for his entertainment'" (322). The chapter closes with a last(ing) vivid example of a scandalous sexual liaison, unspeakable except in a history of pastoral Mexican California: in 1830, a soldier in Monterey "was holding illicit relations with a woman and her daughter at the same time, and the latter was pregnant by him. . . . The result of the trial was that the soldier was made to marry the pregnant woman. The man and woman, from the day of the first publication of the banns, were compelled to kneel near the presbytery, in full sight of the public, bound together by the neck with a thick hempen rope, and having before them a washtub filled with green grass, representing the manger of a stable, to signify that the man and woman had been living like beasts." But, of course, the irony for Bancroft—an irony possible only in Mexican California, presumably—was that despite public shame, the couple "afterward lived together happily, and had a numerous family. Their descendents live in California, and flourish to this day." This patronizing tone pervades Bancroft's orchestration of anecdotes, cases, and tales of sexual transgression, as of a private joke between himself and his readers, as though the social mores and sexual manners of the Californios were the material of humorous and suggestive reading for Americans far removed, in 1888, from pastoral California but not removed from Mexican Americans of that period who still represented sexual improprieties that Americans might gawk at with secret desire.[11]

In the course of the entire chapter, however, we do not hear from the women themselves. Maybe Bancroft's interlocutors, Savage and Cerruti, were too squeamish about asking de la Guerra what she thought of Sir James Douglas's imputation of the moral character of elite women and their fishmongering husbands, or too timid to ask Pérez and Lorenzana whether they had seen, or even heard of, women judicially reprimanded for refusing sex to their husbands, running away from unhappy marriages, or being publicly shamed for illicit sexual intercourse. Yet reading the personal narratives of these and other women, one hardly gets the impression they would have been reluctant—much less squeamish—about discussing women's desires, erotic or otherwise. There is complete silence on such issues. Indeed, the California women seem to have no voice at all in those concerns burning in men's narratives. On the contrary, the women whose lives we must read back into presence articulate resentment about, and resistance to, those patriarchal obsessions suggested by Bancroft's textual museum of statements about women's dress, domestic duties, marital duplicities, and sexual license.

If for men like Vallejo, the good old days of patriarchal authority evoke memories of harmonious filial, marital, and social relations, or if for Bancroft and other men, the "problem" of woman's morality is a phallic obsession, the women's personal narratives provide a markedly distinct description, especially of personal, communal, and gender-related experience. While there is a general affirmation of pre-American society, women's subjectivity is strongly grounded in female affiliations that, by the affectionate and valorous recollection of female agency and self-sufficiency, expose those constraints placed on women within the Mexican patriarchy. Many narratives are by women from prominent families whose reminiscences were recorded primarily because of their relationship to certain influential men; yet although the women may begin their *memorias* speaking about their husbands, almost invariably the men get lost in the narratives. A few of the most memorable narratives were left by lower-class women who made a claim on independence and self-sufficiency, who rose to positions of authority over men, or who adamantly chose not to marry at all. Despite class differences, therefore, husbands are generally banished from all the women's narratives. Women commented on gender-related issues, but even when asked to remember their lives vis-à-vis men, women invariably appropriated the testimonial moment to narrate their own experiences. In fact, women have much to say about their own work and those political events from which they were officially barred. Dorotea Valdez's "Reminiscences" (1875), for example, opens with her saying that she has witnessed "every event which has transpired since that time [her birth in 1793], but being a woman [I] was denied the privilege of mixing in politics and business." Valdez goes on to argue that she is a reliable witness on state affairs: "My education has been very limited, but my memory is good, and being aware of the fact that you [Cerruti] are the emissary of a learned man [Bancroft] bent . . . on writing a reliable history of this country, I will with great pleasure give you the benefit of my recollections." So, while it would appear that exclusion from the business of state would redirect memory back to the "woman's sphere," such was not usually the case. Valdez and other women indeed felt they could give Bancroft the benefit of their recollections not on what they wore or where they danced but rather the benefit of a memory sound on the political history of their country.

Memory, contrary to my own earlier reading of the women's narratives,[12] therefore, was not summarily pointed back toward women's domestic activities. Or rather let me say that women refused to speak on the domestic sphere alone. Women lived in the public sphere and, as much as the men, participated in the settling of the province, experienced the public turmoil of numerous civil antagonisms between Mexican-appointed governors and the Californio patricians, and rose against the American conquest with determined opposition. The point of convergence where obligatory oral history turned toward a consciously individuated narrative, which we think of as autobiographical, was also strongly marked by collective feminine subjectivity in which wives, sisters, and daughters gave witness to each other's historical presence. Women reconstituted themselves in relation to other women whose own presence substantiated their own: Apolinaria Lorenzana remembers Eulalia Pérez, just as Juana Machado de Ridington remembers Apolinaria Lorenzana. In fact, Machado tells us more about why Lorenzana was called "la Beata," the blessed, than she herself does, and even though blind, indigent, and, as she thought, forgotten, Lorenzana was beloved and highly regarded by Angustias de la Guerra, who suggested to Savage that he seek her out and collect her personal narrative. So although there are too few women's narratives, those few we do have disclose a remarkable identificatory matrix of sympathy and affection between women. Remembering herself in the public domain amid other women, rather than just in the "woman's sphere," cleared narrative space necessary for reconstituting a woman's own historical subjectivity. What we see is that women refused to distinguish the domestic space of the "woman's sphere" in a way that makes private/public a strict binary opposition; rather, domestic space provides the vantage point from which history is witnessed as well as the strategic space from which women act upon history.

It was precisely in a woman's appropriation of subjectivity in the male realm that testimony directed by Bancroft's fieldworkers (all men) became genuinely autobiographical: *reminiscencias* in which women steal male authority when speaking about affairs of state but do so without mimicking patriarchal tonality or passively subordinating their own estimation of state matters; *memorias* in which women constitute themselves as historical agents rather than as muñecas confined to the domestic sphere; *recuerdos* in which women remember their own and other women's presence of mind in the face of patriarchal bumbling when the Americans invaded California. In each of the narratives I have encountered, therefore, a distinctly individual, yet collectively gendered, autograph and will to historical presence emerges which cannot be dismissed.

II

The Lieutenant and his people came into my bedroom without saying a word. He had a pistol in one hand and a candle in the other. He looked under my bed

but found nothing. Then he came near me holding the pistol and candle to my face and said that he was hunting for a man who was said to be hidden in my house. . . . Then he said he was rather tired and that he regretted having had to bother me, because he supposed that I was rather frightened, and would like a chair to sit down. I answered that I was not frightened by anything and that he could go to his house, because no one could rest in my room who was not a member of my family or a friend.
  —María de las Angustias de la Guerra, "Ocurrencias en California"

Doña Angustia, he said, I had made famous by my praises of her beauty and dancing, and I should have from her a royal reception. . . . In due time I paid my respects to Doña Angustia and . . . I could hardly believe that after twenty-four years there would still be so much of the enchanting woman about her.
  —Richard Henry Dana, Jr., "Twenty-Four Years After,"
               in *Two Years Before the Mast*

Strange, I want to say, but entirely predictable that Dana's representation of Angustias de la Guerra—his Doña Angustia—should remain so insistently fixed on her as a beautiful and enchanting socialite, while in her own narrative she figures herself as a woman of fearless presence of mind and socially knowledgeable conviction and agency. Yet as his companion told him, Dana's praise of her "beauty and dancing" had settled her—along with Vallejo and other prominent Californios—as a courtly presence of the past in a book that sold ten thousand copies in its first year.

When Dana first saw her at her sister Teresa's wedding dance in 1836, he and Angustias de la Guerra were both twenty-one years old. However, she had already been married for five years and was hardly the coquette we are presented in his recollection of her lavish dancing and girlish breaking of *cascarones* (eggs filled with cologne or other essences) over the head of her favorite uncle.[13] When twenty-four years later he returned to California, Dana called on the de la Guerra family in Santa Barbara, "walked about the place, . . . ate the old dinner" of "frijoles, native olives and grapes, [and] native wines" and recalled the "gay scene . . . where Don Juan Bandini and Doña Angustia danced" so many years earlier (Dana 1869:350). Whereas San Francisco had undergone a profound transformation (a "city of one hundred thousand inhabitants"), with teeming streets that disoriented and startled Dana in 1854 ("I could scarcely keep my hold on reality at all, or the genuineness of anything"), Santa Barbara, a small town at the curving edge of the Pacific, was in Dana's estimation "still a lifeless Mexican town" rather than "part of the enterprising Yankee nation." The town and its Mexican(American) inhabitants retained an aura of pastoral memory for Dana, "the same repose in the golden sunlight and glorious climate" as in the past.

Dana's nostalgia for an earlier, less hectic moment phrases itself during a moment on the beach at Santa Barbara where he mused on a world lost. "How softening is the effect of time," he writes of his feelings in 1859, "I almost feel as if I were lamenting the passing away of something loving and dear" (ibid., 352). Angustias de la Guerra and nearly all the other old Californios who Dana names in his retrospective retain this imaginary repose of a historical moment softened by time: "still so much of the enchanting woman," a courtly inhabitant of a "still lifeless Mexican town," among other ghostly presences throughout California which under the spell of Dana's nostalgia were figured in images of enduring feminine beauty ("The wife of Don Juan, who was a beautiful young girl when we were on the coast . . . was with him, and still handsome" (353), or, in the case of the men, calcified "relics of another age," specimens of pastoral entropy arrayed against the "enterprising Yankee nation." Mexican(American)s—women or men—textually reified as "spared pillars of the past" (359), forever decaying statuary to be refigured after Dana in the narrative romanticization of a Spanish Arcadia, discursively reopened and popularized in Helen Hunt Jackson's enormously successful and generative mission romance *Ramona* (1884), Bancroft's own *California Pastoral* (1890), and Gertrude Atherton's romances of the Old California aristocracy and its sad (but dehistoricized) demise: *The Doomswoman* (1892), *A Daughter of the Vine* (1899), and *The Splendid Idle Forties* (1902).

But in 1878, when, in the fullness of maturity, Doña María de las Angustias dictated her personal memoirs to Savage, the "effect of time" had neither softened nor induced a lamenting nostalgia for the "passing away of something loving and dear." The impending death of her brother José Antonio distressed her, Savage notes, yet her "Ocurrencias en California" is astonishingly fresh, emotionally and intellectually reserved, adamantly precise on social and political events in pre-American California, unrelenting in its implicit renunciation of the image Dana dooms her to as the apotheosis of the blithe, enchanting Mexican California woman, beautiful even as an old woman, more engaging in light social conversation than to be worried about as a woman who harbored old resentments or who might display a keen political, and politicized, intellect. Although Savage mentions in his introductory notes that he "had hoped to obtain from her much information on manners and customs of the Californians," de la Guerra's narrative fixes squarely upon political figures and events. Her "distressed situation," he writes, brought the interview to an abrupt close (an issue to which I will return) but not

María de las Angustias de la Guerra, ca. 1870s. Photograph courtesy of The Bancroft Library. University of California, Berkeley.

before she had completed what Bancroft considered among the most impressive personal narratives in his archive. We cannot know what she would have said about the social customs and manners of her people; however, given the higher seriousness of her account of political events, it is unlikely that we should have witnessed a narrative split in mood or intention, or an articulation swerving away from the perspicacious political history we read in "Ocurrencias en California" (1878), where her re-vision of the past spares no time for Dana's "repose in the golden sunlight" of memory.

One can understand why Bancroft would say that de la Guerra's "Ocurrencias" was "one of the most accurate and fascinating narratives in [his] collection."[14] What he rightly meant was that her narrative provided a highly detailed and precise account of political and social events from the time she was about three years old (1818) through the American invasion of Monterey and Santa Barbara in the 1840s: page after page reconstructs political events, historicizes crucial figures and contending factions, witnesses and recalls not only scores of names but scores of official titles for scores of public figures from her early childhood, through her adult years as a mother with a newborn child, harboring a Mexican soldier from the Americans. Of a revolt in 1836 against Governor Nicolás Gutiérrez, for example, she discloses the entire conspiratorial list, including members of her own family: "I remember that my brother José Antonio and Ramón Estrada with several other leading men of Monterey went to Santa Cruz and other places in the north, probably to promote the revolt. . . . District Judge Luís del Castillo Negrete, though not required to leave California, did so voluntarily. His brother, Don Francisco, who had been Secretary of government under Chico and Gutiérrez, also left. The authors of this revolt were Don Juan Bautista Alvarado, Don José Castro, Don Angel Ramírez, administrator of customs, Attorney Cosme Peña, and others. Among those who supported the movement with their influence, and even with military service, were the three Vallejo brothers, Captain Hinckley, and my brother, José Antonio." Nearly every page of de la Guerra's narrative provides this kind of rich detail, accurate chronology, episodic clarity, and logic.

Yet her perspicacity opens a crucial issue about woman's place in the social domain that may doom her in another way—to the role of ventriloquist for a patriarchal history of California. That is to say, her account constitutes the very assertion of social knowledge, grounded in experience and presence in the event, which women were not expected to bring to the personal narratives collected by Bancroft. But according to Bancroft and other patriarchal authorities, de la Guerra was not just any woman: she was the daughter of, sister of, wife of prominent political figures during the Spanish and Mexican period. In the manuscript Introduction, Savage implies that in addition to being "well known as a lady of intelligence," because de la Guerra was the daughter of wealthy and influential Santa Barbara scion José de la Guerra y Norriega, sister to two of the most influential men in pre- and post-1848 California,[15] and then wife of Manuel Jimeno Casarín, an influential official during the Mexican period, she had such "connections and position" as to enable her to "inform herself upon Governmental affairs, prior to the transfer of this country to the United States" (3). Her description of "Governmental affairs," an exclusive male domain in the California *diputación*, appears as a substitution for her (deceased) husband's official description of affairs of state. From the outset, therefore, she is identified as an authority by virtue of her "connections and position" in the patriarchal group who governed California. But this very authorization, the granting of license to speak in the public realm about crucial political events to which she was a reliable witness, threatens to de-gender, or rather to masculinize, her narrative. That is, María de las Angustias de la Guerra would assume a surrogate male voice for her father and husband who had been dead for decades when Savage appeared at her door, trusting her for a useful narrative because she was a woman who, as he says, "bears a good name for veracity"—a "good name" however, not her own but echoing her father's (de la Guerra y Norriega), her husband's (Manuel Jimeno Casarín), and ending with a final confirmatory stamp of the American "Dr. James D. Ord." Hence, the names she "bears" for men license her "veracity."

Nevertheless, having suggested that she assumes masculine authority in narrating significant political events, I would argue that she may also be said to critique male experience in the narration of those events in ways that countermand patriarchal self-investiture. Once again, as I have suggested, she moves beyond testimonial compliance to figure herself and other women in her sphere as agents within, rather than passive witnesses of, important events. First of all, although she has been singled out by Savage for her knowledge through "connection and positions" vis-à-vis prominent men, she bears witness to history as an insider, only rarely attributing her knowledge to men. Only once does she mention that Casarín, her long dead first husband, "told" her "about" an occurrence, and, as is the case with all the women's narratives, she does not name him; rather, describing a mutiny in 1829, she refers to a Padre José Joaquin Jimeno, a mission priest whose "brother later became my husband, who told me about this occurrence" (18). And although it is possible that her two brothers, Pablo and José Antonio, related many of the events she narrates, she persistently offers testimony as though her knowledge of governmental affairs originated in her own experience. In short, she offers very few footnotes bearing men's authorizing versions in her text of the past. This expropriation of public knowledge quickly turns toward recovering a distinctly gendered feminine perspective through which she articulates a powerful critique of the political cowardice and short-sightedness of the men who controlled the social sphere. Of course, as a beneficiary of the Spanish Mexican landholding class and a member of one of the leading Californio families, de la Guerra generally ratifies patriarchal concerns over land, wealth, and political and social status; this is as one would expect, since in reaffirming male class prerogatives, she reaffirms her own privilege. However, when we reidentify the voice and concerns of de la Guerra, her affirmation of women's social power in the public sphere is clarified through an orchestration of scenes in which Californianas are remembered as not only witnesses to but at the very center of action in those social and political events she otherwise fills with men's names and offices. Although men are mentioned by the scores, women are remembered as heroic. In fact, she often names the very men she aims to undermine by repeated instantiations of female agency. Prominent men often buttress a narrative of women either shoring up their cowardice or correcting their limitations; these include her father, husband, and brothers who are either absent during a crisis or, as they imply, constrained by office.

From the beginning, she represents herself and other women as poised in the midst of social upheaval. She was only three in 1818 when the pirate Bouchard's raid on Santa Barbara sent families scurrying for safety into the interior; although others were terrified, she recalls her wonder at riding through the pouring rain. "I remember that the day of departure was very rainy. I rode in a cart, into which the rain poured from every side" (6). Although a socially privileged young girl, she fashions herself as subversive, defiant of political and social injustice, willing to risk her position to help political prisoners. She was fifteen when she carried concealed notes from her father to a Padre Martínez who had been charged with conspiracy against Governor Echeandia. "I told my father I would go to where the padre was and arrange to give him the paper. . . . On giving the handkerchief to the padre, I touched his hand with one finger and slipped the paper into it. . . . All of this happened in the presence of the officer, who had gone in with me, without his notice" (18). Of the revolt against the corrupt Governor Mariano Chico (alluded to already as the comic miscreant in Vallejo's "Recuerdos"), she recalls the pivotal roles she and other women played in deposing this arrogant buffoon. When Chico has the beloved mission prefect, Padre Durán, jailed for insubordination and then threatens to exile him, the twenty-one-year-old de la Guerra acts as an emissary once again for her father who wished to warn the priest but "didn't know how." She makes her way through the guard and informs Padre Durán of his impending doom. "He responded laughingly, 'Tell the patriarch that those who suffer persecution for justice are fortunate because theirs is the Kingdom of Heaven. He should not take care of this'" (41). But the matter is left neither to the patriarch nor to fate. Rather, the pueblo stages an intricate scheme for saving the padre from exile in which women play the principal roles in a drama of social subversion.

> They took [Padre Durán] to the beach in his cart. When they arrived at the beach all of the women of the pueblo were already there. . . . When the padre arrived at the beach, Don José Antonio Aguirre, owner of the ship and of course an intimate friend of his, invited the padre to alight from his cart and go aboard the boat which was waiting for him. Then all the women surrounded the cart so that the padre couldn't leave.
>
> Sr. Aguirre appeared angry and ordered them to withdraw. One woman took a stick to use on Aguirre. All of the women commenced to moan and cry. At this the padres who were brothers of my husband, who were hidden in the thicket nearby, and others who had run to the place from the pueblo, declared that what the women wanted had to be done, and that they would support them at any cost. The people took the cart back to the Mission with the padre in it, and all accompanied him there.
>
> Thus we have the pueblo of Santa Barbara in open revolt against Chico's authority. (41)

Soon after this, Governor Chico, opposed throughout the province, left for Mexico "threatening to return at once to punish the disobedient Californians." But as de la Guerra says with finality, "I do not know whether or not the government approved of his actions. It is certain, however, that he never came back" (41).

Before reading de la Guerra's account of the incident in Santa Barbara, I never knew that women had indeed stood in the front ranks of political agitation in Californio society. I wanted to know more about these resolute foremothers, but there was little to be learned from Bancroft or other historians of the period. Had de la Guerra not spoken for herself, or had she failed to represent other women as politically conscious, women's work in the social realm would have evaporated into those images of the cheerful and obedient wives and daughters we see in the men's narratives, Bancroft's included. True, Bancroft does credit women in the Santa Barbara incident: "When an attempt was made to put the padre prefecto on board a vessel, the people of the town rose en masse, women in the front ranks, and prevented the local authorities from executing Chico's orders." And he does mention "Mrs. Ord's" version in a footnote.[16] Yet even though women are mentioned as occupying "the front ranks" in the uprising, the phrase they occupy in the sentence is flattened out, put into subordinate rank somewhere in the middle, parsed into the action of the town en masse, with no elaboration, except in the lowercase note that, although more detailed, distances women's activity from the main text. De la Guerra's instantiation of recurrent feminine agency, on the contrary, offers a representation of political presence that has continuity and accruing force; that is, women are repeatedly represented as courageous, politically decisive, unswerving in principle. All at once we see that women's political consciousness and activity was not only alive but crucial to the formation of the social realm. Such political work in the social world, however, would be forgotten or suppressed unless narrated and saved by women like de la Guerra. Her "Ocurrencias" marks women's political agency in this and two other scenes of social conflict, these not about troublesome Mexican officials but about the foreigners from the North, los americanos.

On October 18, 1842, some four years before the Bear Flaggers took Vallejo prisoner in Sonoma, the United States exposed its imperialist intentions when, as de la Guerra remembers, "Commodore Jones of the U.S. Navy arrived . . . in Monterey Bay [and] stated that war had been declared between his country and Mexico" (52). Jones sent 150 marines and sailors ashore two days later to capture the town, which like Sonoma in 1846, was neither armed for nor expected a major assault. The Californios, who the night before had decided that armed resistance would be foolish, capitulated and then had to listen to one of the first of many proclamations liberating them from Mexico, this one by Jones himself: "Inhabitants of California! You have only to remain at your homes in pursuit of peaceful vocations to insure security of life, liberty, and property from the consequences of an unjust war, into which Mexico has plunged you. Those stars and stripes, infallible emblems of civil liberty now float triumphantly before you, and henceforth and forever will give protection and security to you, to your children, and to unborn countless thousands."[17] The next day, Jones, realizing he had jumped the gun, rolled up his proclamation and to the astonishment of the Californians, as de la Guerra tells it, 'called Capt. Silva of the artillery and informed him that a mistake had been made, . . . that he was convinced he was in error and desired to return the post and property and raise again the Mexican flag and salute." After lowering the American flag, the occupying force returned to ship, "the Mexican flag was hoisted and saluted by the Commodore with 21 guns," and things returned to normal. At least as far as the Americans were concerned. De la Guerra's wry and openly sarcastic account of the American "mistake" discloses her resentment of American presumptuousness. She was one Mexican who would not stand docile before American demands. When one of Jones's men appears at her door demanding the key to the Custom House she was thought to be hiding for her brother Pablo, customs officer at the time, she is unflushed: "I refused to deliver it, saying I did not have it. He threatened to knock the Custom House door down, and I replied that he could do as he pleased" (53).[18]

De la Guerra's defiance of Jones's impudence is increasingly figured in forcefully gendered commentary against what she regarded as the failure on the part of Californio officials (read: men) to assert themselves forcefully and directly against American imperial gestures. When referring to the early incursions of American "adventurers" surveying California, for example, she seizes the moment to issue an unexpected but sustained critique of the men's handling of the American threat. Describing events of the early 1840s, she says that it was obvious, at least to the women, that the Americans in the territory were up to no good. When she and Adelaida Estrada (de Spence) make their suspicions about Charles Gillespie known to Manuel Castro, a commanding officer, they are chastised. "Castro told us that we were thinking ill of an invalid gentleman, accusing all the women in general of thinking ill of others, much more than the men. We answered that almost always we more often hit the mark." She and Adelaida were right on the mark: Gillespie was an American agent who was instrumental in staging the Bear Flag uprising in Sonoma (June 6, 1846), which, as I have shown, threw open the war between Mexico and the United States. As de la Guerra recalls, "Gillespie remained at Monterey only a short while and then went to join Frémont. . . . The capture of Sonoma immediately followed" (59).

In a related part of the narrative, she charges that California's officials had made the conquest of California easy for the Americans: there was constant fighting between "the people of the north and the south, and between both against the Mexicans," and "the worst cancer of all was the plundering which was carried on generally. There had been such looting of the resources of the government that the treasury chest was 'scuttled'"(59). This is contrary, of course, to Vallejo's version of governmental affairs. Then there is her withering comment on the military command: "Of these officers, few offered their services when the hour came to defend the country against foreign invasion. The greater part performed no more service than the figurehead of a ship" (59). In fact, Castro is the object of eternal ridicule in de la Guerra's narrative. "Castro was not addicted to expose his interesting person to bullets. He preferred to settle things for the best, or at least temporarily, in any manner that would not risk his hide" (58). Her scathing remarks about Castro and other officers are then immediately and aggressively countermanded by the dramatization of her own determined struggle against the Americans in which she describes an incident at the outbreak of the war in which a Mexican soldier, José Antonio Chávez, fleeing for his life from the American troops, was concealed in her home, this at a time when her husband was away and she had just delivered a child.

The scene is astonishing for its description of the strategies arrayed against the Americans by de la Guerra, who, true to her name, deployed such gendered guerrilla tactics as cross-dressing and trading on male assumptions of domestic powerlessness. Her first challenge was to transport Chávez, who had suffered a dislocated ankle, from the "little home of an old Mexican soldier" to her larger house where he would be more secure. Her plan was marvelously ingenious. "The son-in-law of the soldier was a Portuguese of small stature, and as Chávez was also small, the two together would make one man of large stature. The Portuguese carried Chávez sitting on his shoulders covered with a Spanish shawl and a felt hat which I had provided. Thus they passed the guards of the Yankees and arrived at my house without being discovered" (62). Although the Americans invade her home and rouse her and the family out of bed, she never flinches in her resolve to hide Chávez, who is lying under a pile of blankets upon which her infant, Carolina, is sleeping. There is a frightening moment when one of the soldiers enters her room, but her account once again sustains ironic nuance. "He came near me holding the pistol and candle to my face and said that he was hunting for a man who was said to be hidden in my house. I asked him if he had found him, and he said he had not. It pleased me greatly because I had not told any lies." When the invader apologizes for frightening her and asks for a chair to sit down, saying he is "rather tired," she sneers. "I answered that I was not frightened by anything and that he could go to his house to rest, because no one could rest in my room who was not a member of my family or a friend." Finally, in an astonishing and powerful affirmation of women's control of the situation, de la Guerra describes Chávez being secreted safely out of her home and out of Monterey two days later, "dressed as a woman." Indeed, throughout her account of the resistance, women are figured as the principal agents: María de la Torre, a neighbor, Manuela and Carolina, her daughters, and various maids are complicit in the concealment of Chávez. The women's presence of mind (de la Guerra commanding the domestic battlefield) and undaunted courage (fearless even with a gun held to her head) read as a forceful critique of men like Castro, who was not willing to expose "his interesting person to bullets." When we remember that she accomplished all of this after "having given birth to a baby girl a few days before" (61)—at a time when elite women were confined to bed for up to forty days after delivery—it is apparent that power has shifted to "the woman's sphere," to use Bancroft's telling phrase.

The Chávez account together with her criticism of certain other elements of the patriarchy constitute enunciations that mark the narrative with her own name and feminine identity, not those of either of her husbands. Such internal autobiographical enunciation is required if the personal narrative is to remain hers. Let me explain. Although *a posteriori*, Savage's introductory notes to the narrative he transcribed, as well as those to the 1956 published translation of her memoirs, all but bury her identity under the weight of men's names and position. Savage writes, "Mrs. Ord (née Angustias de la Guerra, and whose first husband was Don Manuel Jimeno Casarín, secretary of State, Senior member of the Assembly, and several times Governor pro tem, of Cal. & c) is well known as a lady of intelligence." Even more glaring is the English translation in which the editors write, "The historical manuscript, Ord (Angustias de la Guerra), *Ocurrencias en California* was related to Thomas Savage by Mrs. Dr. James L. Ord for the Hubert Howe Bancroft Collection in 1878" (Foreword). María de las Angustias de la Guerra survives only parenthetically in these introductory notes, precisely because it was "her connections and position," as Savage noted, that "enabled her to inform herself upon Government affairs"—connections and position vis-à-vis influential men, obviously. And, of course, throughout Bancroft's *History of California*, she is referred to summarily as "Mrs. Ord." Yet in her entire narrative there is no mention at all of Dr. James L. Ord and only passing, usually indirect, mention of Don Manuel Jimeno Casarín. In fact, as she remembers, Casarín, along with her brothers Pablo and José Antonio, was away during the dangerous situation in which she proved her own heroism against the "foreign invaders." Such heroism and tactical audaciousness disappeared in Bancroft's *History of California*, where of the Chávez incident, like the Chico affair, all we read is that "Lieutenant Chávez was cared for secretly at some of the ranchos, and finally came to Monterey in January, where for a long time he eluded the vigilance of officials, largely by the aid of prominent ladies."[19] Ladies!

In any reestimation of women like de la Guerra it will be necessary, first of all, to reread "Ocurrencias en California" with the proper name recovered from patriarchal excess, as she does on the opening page where she claims herself in the first utterance—"Yo, María de las Angustias de la Guerra nací en San Diego el once de Junio de 1815." Then, central to the narrative constitution of female subjectivity, we must read the gendered and culturally politicized presence she marks in staunch voice throughout a personal narrative that is all but muted in Bancroft's *History of California*. Finally, we must retrieve the mature and socially intelligent self-representation she constitutes for herself in "Ocurrencias en California" over and against Dana's (in)famous representation of her as an enduringly enchanting socialite.

III

> In 1876 an old woman was sent to the Centennial Exposition. She was 135 years old and believed to be the oldest living human being. They had the baptismal records at San Gabriel Mission to prove it. When she returned after the unheard of trip to Philadelphia, there was a reception committee to do her honor. She would not ride in the carriage provided, but insisted on getting into an old carreta drawn by oxen and thus have a real comfortable drive home, after the exhausting Pullmans and soft spring buggies in the East. So she sat flat on the bottom of the old cart and was hauled in state to San Gabriel to her little adobe hut near the big tunas. I think the old lady's name was Eulalia Perris.
> —"The Remarks of Major Frederick R. Burnham," 1926[20]

> In June of the year 1876 my sister María Antonia . . . wanted to make some money by capitalizing on my mother for six weeks, exhibiting her in San Francisco for $5,000 in Woodward Gardens, and afterwards taking her to the exposition in Philadelphia.
> Fortunately, she had already been taken secretly to Los Angeles.
> —María del Rosario (de White), December 10, 1877

The truth is that the anecdotes and arguments about her as a curiosity of old age are more impressive than the narrative Eulalia Pérez (not Perris) dictated in 1877. This should not be surprising. After all, how much should a woman her age be expected to remember? And how well? The thirty-three page "Una vieja y sus recuerdos" provides a cursory outline of her life, focusing on her work in the mission system, then ends with her playfully boasting that when she was a girl she "was very fond of dancing, and was considered the best dancer in the country" (MS, 20). But aside from her casual remark, "I do not remember the date of my birth," she says little about her age. Maybe Pérez privately delighted in the public acclaim her reputed age brought her. As the epigraphs above show, her status as an object of curiosity, a living museum piece, fascinated and troubled people. If María del Rosario says that she was rescued to Los Angeles to be spared such public indignity and exploitation by another sister, we should believe her; after all, her mother was living with her in 1877 when Savage visited. Yet Burnham's anecdote is deliciously vivid. After riding in "exhausting Pullmans and soft spring buggies," stubborn old woman that she was, she refused to ride in a carriage, choosing instead a carreta where she could stretch out. Although her daughter's story seems the more likely of the two, Burnham's version opens toward a disclosure of personality apparent in her *recuerdos*. That is, while it is almost impossible that she would have made such an extensive trip just the year previous without mentioning it in her narrative, she represents herself throughout "Una vieja y sus recuerdos" as the same sure-minded woman we see in Burnham's anecdote.

When Savage visited San Isidro Ranch where Pérez was living with her daughter, he found an equally sure and self-sufficient *anciana*. In his introduction to the narrative, he mused on her evident and astonishing age. "She is certainly a very ancient person; there can be no doubt that she is a centenarian. The accompanying photograph gives a very correct idea of her as I found her." (See "accompanying photograph" here.) Although he must have been surprised by her age and frail appearance, Savage remarked that she was neither "feeble nor helpless." She still did needlework and walked about on her own. Savage, as one witness of her independence, was impressed by her calm self-sufficiency.

> She sat by me upon a chair yesterday; but her usual seat is on the floor, and when flies or mosquitoes annoy her, she slaps & kills them with her slipper on the floor. When wishing to rise, she places both palms of her hands on the ground before her,

Eulalia Pérez, reputedly 139 years old. Photograph courtesy of The Bancroft Library. University of California, Berkeley.

and lifts herself first on four feet (so to speak) and then with a jerk put herself on her two feet—for this she needs no assistance. After that she goes about the house without difficulty. She did it in my presence yesterday, and saying that she felt chilled, walked out and sat on the stoop to sun herself a while—then came back and resumed her former seat.

I was assured that with support, and occasional rest on a chair taken with her, she walked to her granddaughter's house, distant five hundred yards or more. (MS, 1–2)

The body's own narrative of unrelenting will. Whereas in introductory commentary on his other subjects Savage tends toward formal and detached biographical notations (the kind of biochronological notes Bancroft copied into his "Pioneer Register and Index"), in the Pérez narrative Savage's usual disinterest was transformed by an old woman's strength of will unencumbered by a frail body. His description is not only vivid but vivified by the image of the old woman slapping flies, lifting herself without help, taking a chair for occasional rests when she walked long distances. And whereas he expressed impatience and no small aggravation at having to wait on his other subjects, when she interrupts the dictation to walk out into the warm sun, he simply waits for her to return in her own good time.

Her story was worth waiting for, however, not just because she was "a very ancient person" but because, despite her age, "her memory is remarkably fresh on some things," especially on the fourteen years she worked in the mission system. "Una vieja y sus recuerdos" is the acronical story of a woman reputedly 139 years of age when she related her life's work as *partera* (midwife), *cocinera principal* (head cook), and *llavera* (keeper of the keys) as well as *dueña* (supervisor) of various shops at San Gabriel mission in the first half of the nineteenth century. Pérez's precise if brief recollections of the daily life of San Gabriel mission were pertinent to a history of the Spanish/Mexican period: the entirely self-sufficient production system of the mission, its proselytization and exploitation of Native Americans, its ecclesiastical and material concerns, and its demise in the 1830s, when the missions were secularized, was information of the kind that Bancroft had ordered Savage to collect. As Bancroft noted in *California Pastoral*, Pérez, "who lived many years in the missions" (226),[21] proved a reliable source on the mission system, especially on the training of Indians. However, he says nothing of the remarkable appropriation of authority she succeeded in wresting during the course of her life there. Her narrative indeed provides valuable ethnographic information, but the story it tells—once we listen—is rather about herself than about the mission system. She may have been a curiosity by virtue of her advanced age and a storehouse of information for reconstructing mission operations, yet rather than settling the question of her age or subordinating herself to a catalog of information, Pérez reconstructs the self-empowering process whereby, some seventy years earlier, she appropriated authority within the mission system that, as she makes quite clear in her recollections, granted her power over numerous men. What for Bancroft, therefore, was a narrative from which information about the operations of the mission system might be elicited was for Pérez an opportunity to describe how, alone with five children, she brought the male-dominated world in which she lived into compliance with her own will to be self-sufficient. Relating her long experience as *mayordoma* (superintendent) of the San Gabriel mission during the 1820s and 1830s provided narrative space for reconstituting the significance of her life—for herself.

Although she does not remember the day she was born, she does remember marrying at fifteen Miguel Guillén, a soldier, who, along with the Presidio commandant, refused to let her leave San Diego to visit her family in Los Angeles. When Guillén died in 1818, she was left a widow with six children and no work to support them, so she made her way to San Gabriel where Padre José Sánchez gave her lodging. After being there a short time, she had to compete for a job as cook against two other women who had long been working in the mission. Pérez wins the contest, she remembers, by preparing a menu of "sopas, diversidad de rellenos, postres" (soups, various stuffed turnovers, desserts and other delicacies) that so impresses the judges—the prefect general and three other men—that one, she recalls, "pondered awhile, saying for many years he hadn't eaten the way he'd eaten that day—that he doubted they ate any better at the King's table" (MS trans., 7). Remembering the event long decades later, however, Pérez does not gloat over her victory, saying that she proved herself so as to support her children and to gain self-sufficiency, not because she wished to supplant the other women, both of whom she liked and respected. One of these women, María Ignacia Amador, is remembered with special fondness: "Sabía cocinar, coser, leer y escribir, y cuidar enfermos—era buena curandera, y enseñaba a leer y escribir a algunos niños en su casa" (she "knew how to cook, sew, read and write, and take care of the sick—she was a good healer and taught a few children to read and write in her home") (MS trans., 5). Soon after her appointment as head cook, she was charged with supervising the kitchen and within a year was entrusted with the keys for the mission storehouses and production workshops, which meant supervisory authority over the entire mission factory. As her description of mission operations indicates, her supervisory capacity positioned her, first, on equal footing with men who were initially her supervisors, and, ultimately, warranted her position as their overseer.

> They put under my charge everything having to do with clothing. I cut and fitted, and my five daughters sewed-up the pieces. . . . Besides this, I had to attend to the soap-house, which was very large, to the wine-presses, and to the olive-crushers that produced oil, which I worked myself. Under my direction and responsibility, Domingo Romero took care of changing the liquid.
>
> Luis the Soap-maker had charge of the soap-house, but I directed everything.
>
> I handled the distribution of leather, calf-skin, chamois, sheepskin, Morocco leather, fine scarlet, nails, silk, etc.—everything having to do with the making of saddles, shoes and what was needed for the belt- and shoe-making shops.
>
> Every week I delivered supplies for the troops and Spanish-speaking servants. These consisted of beans, corn, lentils, candles, soap and lard. To carry out this distribution, they placed at my disposal an Indian servant named Lucio . . .
>
> When it was necessary, some of my daughters did what I could not find time to do. Generally, the one who was always at my side was my daughter María del Rosario.

Pérez's steady and pervasive acquisition of supervisory position marks her detailed inventory of the mission manufactory with a seal bearing her name: everything produced and distributed during her "many years in the missions" (Bancroft) was overseen by her or, more significantly, made by her own hands or those of her daughters. And notice how she draws a tight circle of authority centered in the "women's sphere" of her own family; when she does not have the time to do something, she simply turns authority over to her daughters, especially, it seems, to María del Rosario, who remains at her side even to the day Savage takes her narrative. María del Rosario, in turn, appends a note to the narrative attesting to its general accuracy but more important, speaking to the intimacy of their relationship over a span of many years: "From the time I was seven or

eight years old, I used to go around with my mother in all her tasks."
Indeed, María del Rosario moves through the various rooms of the
narrative, a companion and confidante to her mother. Such strong
attachment to her daughters and her manifold responsibilities satisfied and sufficed Pérez such that she was altogether disinterested
in ever marrying again, even when Padre Sánchez prevailed on her
to do so. "Yo no quería casarme," she resolutely remembers; she did
marry, but only at the pleading of Padre Sánchez, the mission prefect, who had taken her in when she was a homeless widow with six
children and whom she considered a parent: "No me hallaba con
ánimo para negarle nada cuando él había sido para mí y todo mi
familia, como padre y madre" (I didn't have the heart to refuse him
anything, because he had been like a father and mother to me and
my children). She may accede to Padre Sánchez's pleas out of a sense
of filial obligation, and she may marry, but she says almost nothing
about her husband, whom she glancingly refers to as Mariné (his last
name), and of whom she remembers "que tenía alguna fortuna en
dinero, pero nunca me dió possesión de la caja" (that "he had some
wealth, but never turned over the cash-box to me"). Perhaps most
telling of her feelings for him, she says, "When I married him I was
a woman well along in years, but very strong and active, with hardly
any gray hairs. Nevertheless, I didn't bear him any children." If they
were married in about 1832, she would have been at least sixty, presumably well past her childbearing years, but that is not the point:
she suggests that she was still sexually capable, so if she bore him
no children it must have been his fault, not hers. At any rate, from
separate evidence it appears that they separated after a few years,
and while she does not say anything about their differences, she
charges him with keeping the land granted to her by Padre Sánchez
prior to their marriage.[22]

Pérez's narrative concludes with an unexpected break to her
love of dancing when she was a girl, with a recitation of fragmented
song verse from such dances as "El Caballo" (The Horse), "La Zo-
rrita" (The Little Fox), and "Las Pollitas" (The Chicks). She is probably responding to Savage's injunction from Bancroft to collect material on "manners and customs," but notice once again that rather
than simply imparting ethnographic information, she turns the
question to her own ends, quite literally turning an obligatory recollection into a self-affirming moment: "Once in Santa Barbara, la
Chepa Rodríguez and I were dancing together. Chepa had the reputation of being a great dancer. We danced the *jarabe,* and she got

tired and went off to sit down, leaving me still dancing. Also I won out over another lady, a famous dancer, and a challenge was sent clear up to Monterey to send someone down to compete with me in dancing, and no one came." This abrupt revisitation of girlhood, although narratively disjointed, provides a final affirmation of self-esteem and self-assurance manifest from her early years, through mature adulthood as a hardworking and self-sufficient mother of five daughters, to her last years as an old but tough and independent woman of 104 rather than 136 years of age.

However, much like de la Guerra, Pérez was burdened at the end of her life with the dead weight of men's names. Savage introduces her as the "widow, first of Miguel Antonio Guillén, and next of Juan Mariné," but, like de la Guerra, her own immediate autobiographical utterance is an act of toponymic self-identification that disburdens her of the patronym: "Yo Eulalia Pérez, nací en el presidio de Loreto en la Baja California." Neither the names Guillén nor Mariné, her two husbands, are noted here or anywhere else in her narrative, except where she concedes her brief marital phases with them; not being present in the text, theirs are names without substance. Pérez's reappropriation of her given name thus constitutes an act of self-volition, the willing into textual permanence of her own personality and experience. Once again we discover a narrative in which a woman stakes her claim to autonomy otherwise than as wife or domestic, although she was twice married and worked as a mission domestic for much of her life. It is as though women like Angustias de la Guerra and Eulalia Pérez realized that their identities were in danger of being lost behind those of the men with whom they lived, by whom they were censored, accorded adjunct status, effaced. Their response, decades later, to the threat of obscurity was literally to seize the opportunity for reconstituting their own lives through the Bancroft oral history project, where in narrating the past they rediscovered areas of long evaporated personal experience that affixed memory with identitarian constancy. Once marked by the symbolic, and real, constraints of the patronym, woman's self-naming opens narrative terrain for recuperating experience dislodged from a husband's name, however much experience may have resided inside of marriage.

Yet, de la Guerra's and Pérez's location of a distinct identity outside of relationships with husbands points to a particularly critical issue in many women's narratives: women reveal no little resentment about the constraints imposed on them by marriage—no matter how long their husbands have been dead. The common custom of marrying girls at a young age—between thirteen and fifteen—is described in many women's narratives where it surfaces with startling regret and resentment when other momentous life experiences seem forgotten. The entire arrangement, from betrothal at an early age to the actual wedding ceremony, was discussed and effected almost exclusively between the fathers, with mothers executing the patriarchal dictate on their daughters. María Inocente Pico de Avila, a member of the wealthy and influential Pico family in Los Angeles, defers to her husband's life early in her narrative, "Cosas de California" (1876), commenting on his family genealogy, education, military career, and resistance to the American forces. Her husband may be foregrounded in the narrative, but when remembering their marriage, she suddenly recalls that like other girls she was only beginning to read, write, and do arithmetic when taken from school to begin preparation for her primary role in life as his wife. As she remembers,

> Muchas niñas no concluían ni esos pocas estudios, porque las quitaban sus madres de la escuela casi siempre para casarlas, porque había la mala costumbre de casar las niñas muy jovencitas, cuando la pedían. Yo estuve en la escuela sólo hasta los 14 años; después me llevó mi madre al rancho para enseñarme a trabajar, y a los 15 años y ocho meses me casé." (MS, 20)

> [Because of the terrible custom of having to marry while very young, many girls never even finished these few studies because their mothers nearly always took them out of school to marry them off when they were called for. I only stayed in school until my fourteenth year; then my mother took me to the ranch to prepare me to work, and at fifteen years and eight months of age I was married.]

In the men's narratives, as one might expect, the primacy of marriage and the shaping of domestic consciousness in women were regarded as central to the maintenance of the social order. In his "Notas históricos sobre California" (1874), Salvador Vallejo, brother of Mariano, remembers that "we [the patriarchs, of course, with mothers as the enforcers of male dictates] taught our girls to be good housewives in every branch of their business; our wives and daughters superintended the cooking and every other operation performed in the house, the result of the training was cleanliness, good living and economy" (MS, 99). The women's narratives expose such domestic training and early marriage as forms of sexual coercion (read: child abuse) and social control. Read against Vallejo's smug pronouncement, Pico de Avila's forceful denunciation of "la mala costumbre de casar a las niñas muy jovencitas" ("mala" additionally signifying "hateful," "evil," "malign") is decisively antipatriarchal. The autobiographical enunciations of the California women, almost without exception, show that they were conscious of the constraining sociosexual function of early marriage, or, for that matter, marriage at any age, as Pérez's opposition to marriage in her late fifties indicates. For many women, especially those of the landowning classes like Pico de Avila, having their schooling abruptly terminated, or being denied a lettered education altogether because of gender, meant having a vital part of the self closed off, stunted. Pérez may not have had much schooling, and she may have been largely unlettered, but, as her *recuerdos* demonstrates, she was hardly the kind of woman who would allow herself to be suppressed by such constraints.

IV

> On my visit to San Diego this year [1878], many of the native Californians there of both sexes spoke of [Apolinaria Lorenzana] in the highest terms of praise. She was known by many as Apolinaria la Cuna (the foundling) & by most as la Beata (the pious). She appears to be a good old soul, cheerful and resigned to her sad fate, for in her old age and stone blind she is a charge on the county and on her friends, having by some means or other lost all her property. She was loath to speak on this subject, assuring me that she didn't want even to think of it.
> —Thomas Savage, Introduction to "Memorias de la Beata"

> Desde muy niñita, ántes de venir de México, me habían enseñado a leer. . . . Ya cuando era mujercita en California, yo sola aprendí a escribir, valiéndome para ello de los libros que veía—imitaba las letras en cualquier papel que lograba conseguir—tales como cajillas de cigarros vacías, o cualquier papel blanco que hallaba tirado. Así logré aprender bastante para hacerme entender por escrito cuando necesitaba algo.

> [When I was a very young girl, before coming from Mexico, I had been taught to read. . . . And so when I was a young woman in California, I taught myself to write, and encouraged by the books I saw, I imitated letters on any piece of paper I could find—such as empty cigarette packets, or any sheet of blank paper I found discarded. In that manner I learned enough to make myself understood in writing when I needed something.]
> —Apolinaria Lorenzana, "Memorias de la Beata" (1878)

So Apolinaria Lorenzana remarks in her account of her life as a nurse and teacher in the California mission system of nineteenth-century California. She was in her late seventies when she collaborated on her memorias, feeble in body and therefore discouraged because she felt like a burden to the people around her, poor, dispossessed of land that she had acquired independently during a lifetime of work and service, completely blind. The world she had known was receding into a past as unrecoverable as her sight. Still, during the late winter of 1878, she was scrawling her mark upon history, *scrawling* I say because at the end of the narrative transcribed by Savage she literally sealed her life on the last page in a nearly illegible marking of her initials. For an old woman who had completely lost her eyesight, this act of will signified a final utterance of personal identity, a veritable signature of her experience as a self-sufficient woman. The marking of her initials stands as exemplar of the will to presence marked in this small group of women's narratives.

Just after her seventh birthday, Lorenzana migrated from Mexico along with a group of families, her single mother, and a group of orphaned children to Monterey, California, where, she remembers, the foundlings were distributed among families "como perritos" (like puppies). She was with her mother; so, she was one of the lucky ones. But not for long. Like many of the young women who arrived in California alone, her mother met and married one of the Presidio soldiers and for some reason returned to Mexico without little Apolinaria. Lorenzana does not say much about this rupture in her childhood, except that her mother died soon thereafter in Mexico—"tal vez del sentimiento de haberme dejado a mí" ("undoubtedly from grief over having left me"), she imagines. She never saw her mother again and like the other orphans was left to fend for herself. Over a period of seven years, like the other "perritos," she was passed between several families, mostly to soldiers' homes in San Diego where she worked for her food and keep.

Although the searing displacements of childhood are apparent in her words, she discloses an intellectual precocity and, perhaps because of her own displacement, a kindred spirit with the sick and needy that marked her life as a mission nurse and teacher. As she says, she had learned to read even before immigrating from Mexico, and so, during the difficult years between many residences, rather than just survive from hand to mouth, she taught herself to write on scraps of paper as she walked the countryside. "Así logré aprender bastante para hacerme entender por escrito cuando necesitaba algo." Teaching herself to write on scraps of paper was, of course, a means of communicating her needs in the world, as well as a strategy for winning independence, but she was never acquisitive in her learning. She not only proudly describes how she taught herself to write but how, like the young Frederick Douglass, she shared her knowledge with other young women who were eager to learn in a society that, as the story of María Pico de Avila shows, generally discouraged women's intellectual development.

> Ya desde que estaba en casa de Doña Tomasa Lugo había empezado a enseñar a leer y la doctrina a algunas niñas. Después hice lo mismo en la casa de Doña Josefa Sal. Esta Señora después que enviudó abrió una escuela para enseñar a las niñas a leer, rezar, y otras cosas. Como ella tenía una huerta que le ocupaba mucho la atención, yo tenía a mi cargo casi exclusivamente la escuela. También habían algunas niñas que sus padres me las habían encomendado a mí particularmente.
>
> Enseñé a las tres hijas que entonces tenía el Alférez Don Ignacio Martínez: María Antonia, Juana, y Encarnación, la madre era Doña Martina Arellanes. También enseñé una sobrina de Doña Tomasa Lugo, que se llamaba Bernarda Ruiz y vive aún aquí en Santa Barbara. Muchas otras aprendieron las primeras letras, y cosas conmigo. (MS, 5)

> [I was already teaching young girls to read and recite their catechism from the time I was staying in Doña Tomasa Lugo's home. Afterwards I did the same in Doña Josefa Sal's home. After becoming a widow, this lady opened a school where girls learned to read, recite their prayers, and such things. Since she had an orchard that took up much of her time, I had almost exclusive responsibility for the school. There were also girls whose parents particularly sought me out for instruction.
>
> I taught Ensign Don Ignacio Martinez's three daughters: María Antonia, Juana, and Encarnación, whose mother was Doña Martina Arellanes. And I also taught Doña Tomasa Lugo's niece, a girl named Bernarda Ruiz who yet lives here in Santa Barbara. Many other girls also learned their first letters and other such things with me.]

As she points out, she did not exclude boys from lessons: "Enseñaba a leer a los niños de uno y otro sexo que sus padres me pedián que le enseñase" (I taught children of either sex to read at the request of their parents) (MS, 42).

Before she was thirty years old, then, she had established herself as a loving and beloved nurse, teacher, and, like Pérez, mayordoma for the San Diego mission. As Juana Machado recalls in her own memoirs, "Tiempos pasados en la alta California," rather than marrying, Doña Apolinaria "dedicated herself to the service of the church. . . . There in the mission she taught girls, whose parents asked the favor, to read and write. . . . She went by the name of Doña Apolinaria la Cuna (the foundling). She was godmother to a large number of children, of whites as well as Indians."[23] As for not taking a husband, Lorenzana has this to say:

> Cuando era muchacha, hubo un jóven que se empeñé mucho en que yo me casará con él. No me llamaba la inclinación al estado del matrimonio (a pesar de conocer los méritos de una institución tan santa), y rehusé su oferta. Entónces me dijo que pues no quería yo casarme con él, se iba para México. En efecto, se fue. (MS, 43)

> [When I was girl, there was a young man who often entreated me to marry him. But I did not feel inclined toward matrimony (knowing full well the requirements of that sacred institution), and so I refused his offer. He then told me that since I wouldn't marry him, he was leaving for Mexico.Well, so he left.]

Notice Lorenzana's ironized doctrinal evasion: it is not so much that she does not like the poor young man; rather, she dares not enter into the sacramental gravity of matrimony lightly. Lorenzana says no more about the matter. Nowhere in her narrative does she express the least regret that she had no husband or children; never does she complain of having been lonely. Lorenzana simply chose independence and service to the young and sick. Indeed, as Machado indicates, because of her teaching and general care of children, she was highly regarded, enough so that she had well over one hundred godchildren, an honor bestowed much more typically on men, especially *ricos*, than women, especially *solteronas*.

Much like Eulalia Pérez, whom she met in San Diego about 1808 and for whom she was also "madrina de dos hijas y un hijo," she describes her many responsibilities in the mission system, from overseeing the infirmary to instructing the neophytes in sewing to boarding cargo ships for supplies to making overland journeys along the coastal mission chain. She also points out, however, that in addition to her mission duties, she actively oversaw the ranchos she obtained from the government in 1833–34 (officially granted 1840)[24] and another she bought outright. "En aquel tiempo tenía yo todavía mis tres ranchos; uno que yo había comprado llamado Capistrano de

Secuá, que estaba situado entre medio de mis otros dos ranchos, y
que me lo vendió mi compadre Juan López. Los otros dos me los
había dado el gobierno años antes" (MS, 28). (At that time I still had
my three ranches; one that I had purchased called Capistrano de
Secuá, which was situated between my other two ranches that my
compadre Juan López sold to me.) One of these ranchos, Santa Clara
de Jamacha, provides the site for the anguishing account of Doña
María de los Angeles, whose own neighboring ranch was over-
whelmed by an Indian revolt, her husband and the other men killed,
the houses burned to the ground, her two daughters taken captive,
she escaping with her two sons. While Lorenzana is nursing the
traumatized woman, Doña María tells her story: while her husband,
Anastacio, and the ranch mayordomo, Camacho, defend the house,
she and the children flee and hide in an orchard but are apprehended.
The Indians, Doña María cries, were more merciful to them than to
the men, but they take her two daughters Tomasa (18 years) and
Ramona (10 years) captive, ordering her to leave immediately with
the two boys if they expect to live. Ramona clings to her mother's
skirt, crying, refusing to let go, but is dragged away. Lorenzana's presentation of the mother's inconsolable grief at losing her daughters
is gripping. "La desgraciada madre no hablaba ni lloraba, la congoja
la tenía abrumada. Traté de consolarla, y de hacerle tomar algún
alimento, pero estaba inconsolable. . . . Doña María de los Angeles
el resto de su vida estuvo sufriendo mortalmente, sin consolarse
nunca—al fin sucumbío bajo el peso de sus podertos (MS, 36, 41).
("The miserable mother neither spoke nor cried, for the anguish had
crushed her. I tried to console her, tried getting her to eat, but she
was inconsolable . . . and for the rest of her life Doña María suffered
deeply, unconsoledly—until at last she died under the weight of her
grief.)

One notices here and throughout the "Memorias de la Beata"
just how much Lorenzana's narrative is woman-centered. She gives
substance to women, makes their desire to learn, their illnesses as
well as their griefs, real, memorable, and painful. Such feminine
filiations developed and matured during her long career of service to
women, from their infancy to adulthood, through multiple generations: she was often *partera* (midwife) at a child's birth, *madrina*
(godmother) at baptism and confirmation, and, after helping raise a
girl, saw her to the marriage altar, then helped birth her children.
One of these girls, she recalls, "Tuve á mi cargo, cuidándola desde
que tenía dos o tres años, una niña, cuya madre era mi ahijada de
bautismo y de matrimonio, y despues fui madrina de tres hijos de

ella. Esa niña que fue la primera que tuvo, la enseñé a leer, rezar, coser, y demás a su debido tiempo se casó, y hoy es madre de familia" (MS, 43). (I had in my charge, caring for her from the time she was two or three years old, a girl, whose mother was my goddaughter in both baptism and marriage and for whose three children I was also godmother. That girl, who was my first charge, I taught to read, pray, sew, among other things, and when the time came she married and is now the mother of her own family.) Such intergenerational affiliation secures Lorenzana's recollection of herself as a woman whose work has been conducted within an intimate familiocultural matrix; indeed, her nurturing of this female lineage confers the very intimacy, continuity, and knowledge that constitute the matrix of cultural subjectivity in enduring female relationships.

In her late seventies, Lorenzana retains a strong sense of kinship for and respect within the California community. As Savage points out in his prefatory remarks to the "Memorias," "Many of the native Californians of both sexes spoke of her in the highest terms of praise, . . . as la Beata (the pious)." Machado was one of these natives. "I knew Señora Apolinaria Lorenzana whom everyone called La Beata."[25] The degree to which she was esteemed—revered as a living saint—discloses the profound gift of affection conferred upon her by the community for her charity and service. Yet nowhere in the narrative does she herself make pretense to piety or saintliness; rather, toward the end of the "Memorias," she represents herself as being very much in the world, very much distracted and troubled by material dislocation, very old and frail, a burden to others.

On the whole, the narrative discloses a sense of positive individual achievement put to social use. However, her material worries do disclose a sociopsychological split in the narrative, like that witnessed in the conflict between Vallejo's public sangfroid and his private resentment, a bifurcation between her description of service to the sick and young over and against her anger about the loss of her ranchos to unscrupulous Americans after 1850. Although she would like to focus on her career as teacher and nurse, she cannot keep her memories focused on the matrix of loving relationships she has established with scores of children without reminding herself that the world they all occupied has been broken by the new social order. In her own words, "Me presumo que si fuera a San Diego, estaría bien recibida, pero como estoy lejos y ciega, y aquellas gentes no están en muy buenas circunstancias, aquí me hallo pobre y desvalida, con escasa salud." (I believe that if I went to San Diego I

would be well received, but as I am far removed and blind, and those
people [my old friends] aren't in very good circumstances, I find
myself here, poor and destitute, my health broken.) Her anguish,
she says, is not merely the result of age, blindness, and infirmity.
Rather, like many Californios, women and men both, she felt displaced, dispossessed of her land, and hence confused, embittered,
resentful toward a nation that had made her a stranger in her own
country. For remember, here was a woman who was not only independent but a woman of independent means. During the many years
she worked in the mission, she had been keen enough to acquire
three separate ranches of her own. Two of these had been granted to
her by the government, a privilege seldom extended to women. The
other, situated between the two, she purchased outright. Although
Savage notes that she "was loath to speak on this subject, assuring
me that she didn't want even to think of it" (Preface), she does say
enough to convey a strong sense that she maintained a proprietary
interest in her land, never intended to sell it, and was quite clear
about the fact that she was swindled, although like many other
Mexican Californians, she was not sure precisely how. Someone
she remembers as "Mr. Forster," who had agreed to oversee one of
the ranches, apparently rented it to a "Captain Magruder" who arrived in California in 1846, but not only was she never paid for use
of the land, she never saw her American "friend" Forster again and,
of course, ended up losing the ranch to Magruder—this after she
twice made it clear to him that she had no interest in selling. At this
point in the narrative, startled by a twenty-five-year-old nightmare,
she says,

> Es una história larga y no quiero ni hablar de ella. Los otros dos
> ranchos me los quitaron de algún modo. Así es que despues de
> haber trabajado tantos años, de haber poseido bienes, de que no
> me desposié por vento ni de otro modo, me encuentro de la
> mayor pobreza, viviendo de favor de Dios y de los que me dan
> un bocado de comer. (MS, 30)

> [It is a long story and I don't even want to discuss it. The other
> two ranches they somehow took from me. So, that's the way it
> turns out, that after working so many years, after having ac-
> quired an estate, which I certainly didn't dispose of by selling or
> by any other means, here I find myself in the greatest poverty,
> living only by the grace of God and through the charity of those
> who give me a mouthful to eat.]

Lorenzana discloses little self-pity over her fragile condition, her loss of sight, or her poverty, as such; yet her "Memorias" is suffused at this juncture with a troubled memory of the American conquest and its particular material consequences for her. Where there is evidence of dispiritedness underlying her narrative, it takes the form of sociocultural displacement present in a majority of the Californio narratives, the women's and men's both. She more than once emphatically mentions the *tristeza*, or sadness, she and other Californios felt during the 1840s when Americans were invading the country: "Yo estaba muy triste por la toma del país por los americanos, y no quería por eso volver a San Diego." During the course of the conquest in 1846–47, she recalls leaving San Diego for the north, followed by one of the priests who could not bear to be left behind: "Entonces el Padre [Oliva] me dijo, 'pues, si tú te vas a San Juan, yo también voy allá—que haré yo solo en San Diego?' Fuimos primero a Santa Margarita, y lo quedamos allí algunos días. Le dije al Padre que se quedase allí, y yo me iba a San Juan Capistrano. Yo estaba encalavernada con la cosa de los Americanos—me sé giré me figuraba yo—si por irme yo, se irían los Americanos también" (MS, 20). (Then Padre Oliva entreated me, 'Well, if you are going to San Juan, I am coming too—what will I do in San Diego by myself?' First we went to Santa Margarita, and stayed there a few days. I told the Padre to remain there, that I was going to San Juan Capistrano. I felt run aground by the situation with the Americans—and I figured that if I traveled alone, by my leaving, the Americans would also leave.) Although it was wishful thinking at best to believe that absenting herself would have the effect of making the Americans disappear, she nevertheless imaginatively appropriates responsibility for their troubling presence, suggestive of reaching an imaginary resolution of the psychological disequilibrium caused by that presence. Of course, the Americans did not disappear, so she and Padre Oliva continue the journey north, their movement constantly impeded by the war between "los Californios contra los Americanos" (22), forced to remain in San Luis Rey for some two months, during which time many terrifying stories about the hostilities circulate in the mission. Padre Oliva died in January 1847, the same month, she remembers, that Commodore Stockton and General Kearny entered Los Angeles. By the end of the 1850s, she had lost all of three of her ranchos. By the 1870s, she had been taken to Santa Barbara where she was living in the home of Señora Noriega, as a ward of the county. She was once again a foundling.

Like nearly all of the Californios of her generation, she found herself in the 1870s not only near the end of her life but also at the end of a way of life. Dispossessed of her land like so many others, she had little to show for a career of hard work and nurturing affection for so many children, nothing but her words steeped in memory's revisitation of a life she had built for herself. The matrix of loving relationships remains intact in ghostly outline, buttressed against her literal displacement from San Diego, her built home and the seat of that matrix, to Santa Barbara, her rest home and the location of symbolic dematrization as a ward of the county. Whereas Pérez never mentions her age, or says anything about the frail body she lifts in a sudden jerk from all fours, Lorenzana's frailty and broken health are measurable within the narrative itself, measurable as the gauge of her sadness and the material dislocation underlying her poverty, the shame and anger she must have felt for having to relying on "the grace of God and . . . the charity of those who give me a mouthful to eat." Anguish apparent in some sections, repressed in others, Apolinara Lorenzana literally inscribed her initials on the final page of the "Memorias" not only as a hedge against her own death but, it seems to me, as a gesture of defiance against an impending threat of historical and cultural death.

Apolinaria Lorenzana's initials marked to the narrative "Memorias," 1878. Photograph courtesy of The Bancroft Library, University of California, Berkeley.

V

The women's narratives should remind us of just how tenuous life in post-1848 Californio society must have been for people who were trying to give purpose to personal experience during a time of immense social, political, and cultural upheaval. Life in a stable social world was difficult enough for women. Their narratives make this plain. But what they also make plain in partnership with the men's narratives is that the American takeover was a trauma that entirely disrupted life for everyone—notwithstanding patriarchal constraints, gender misrelations, social class stratification. As Lorenzana said more than one hundred years ago, it is a long and troubling story the way Mexican Californios in the latter part of the nineteenth century were dispossessed of their land, their livelihood, their dignity, often their very voices. Bitterness, a profound sense of loss, confusion, and displacement color the women's personal narratives fully as much as the men's. They felt equally humiliated by the occupation and angry about the losses they sustained after the conquest. Some of the women were so deeply embittered by events in 1846–1848 and after, that when asked to comment on the war they spoke through clenched teeth. Lorenzana was, as Savage notes, herself "loath to speak on the subject," but she did speak. Rosalía Vallejo (de Leese), sister to Mariano and Salvador Vallejo, however, was still so angry three decades after the war that she refused to give more than a brief six-page narrative, which Bancroft dismissed as among the "least-useful of my collection." However brief, her words are decisively oppositional. Like de la Guerra, she describes her resistance against the Americans by saving a seventeen-year-old girl from being sexually assaulted by Frémont and his officers. She also remembers being forced to write a letter to a Capitán Padilla who was riding toward Sonoma with troops, enjoining him to return to San José; she says, "I consented, not for the purpose of saving my life, but being then in the family way I had no right to endanger the life of my unborn baby; moreover, I judged that a man who had gone so far would not stop at anything (Frémont told me he would burn our houses with us inside them) . . . and being desirous of saving trouble to my country women I wrote the fatal letter" (5). Her "History of the 'Osos'" (Bear Flag incident of 1846) then ends with these words: "Those hated men inspired me with such a large dose of hate against their race, that though twenty eight years have elapsed since that time, I have not yet forgotten the insults they heaped upon me, and not being desirous of coming in contact with them I have abstained from learning their language." Rosalía Vallejo also forbade her children to speak the language of *los extranjeros* in her presence in the years after 1848.

Yes, I know, her words here are presented in English, the language of *los extranjeros*—but neither by her choice nor mine. For some reason, Cerruti transcribed the document in English, even though Rosalía Vallejo's narrative, like the majority of the Californio narratives, was dictated in Spanish. As I have argued in my comments on Vallejo's "Recuerdos históricos y personales tocante a la alta California," the issue of language is crucial to both recovering and reading the Californio personal narratives. On the one hand, we must valorize the language of our literary production by sustaining Spanish as the voice in which our *antepasados* (ancestors) daily spoke and in which they encoded oppositional articulations about their divided status in the new American social economy. On the other, for those of us recovering these articulations, the presentation of the narratives in translation is requisite if we expect to effect socioliterary change within that still-divisive economy. As you know by now, I have freely interspersed Spanish with English translations, or for the sake of convenience (as we always say) I have provided English translations alone. But a warning is in order here, a warning that bears significantly on translation and meaning: very few of the narratives have been translated, but even those few texts that have been will require careful rereading as there is evidence of mistranslation that subverts intent. I raise this issue here because it is directly gender related.

To elaborate. De la Guerra's narrative, one of the handful that have been published in English translation, gives the impression at a crucial juncture that women were not troubled by the American occupation, a notion that has been firmly fixed in the American imagination because Mexican women like her married American men. In Francis Price and William Ellison's translation, *Occurrences in California*, de la Guerra is *made* to say that "the conquest of California did not bother the Californians, least of all the women" (59) when what she *did* say was "la toma del país no nos gustó nada a los Californios, y menos a las mujeres"—which should be translated as "the taking of the country did not please the Californios at all, and least of all the women." Precisely because so few of the California personal narratives have been translated and published, the Price and Ellison mistranslation has led to a perpetuation of the image of

Mexican women as mindlessly disloyal to their cultural homeland. The effect of such careless translation (or was it preconception that made for mistranslation?) has been damaging. Even David J. Weber, one of the leading historians of the Mexican borderlands, carelessly echoes the English translation when he writes that "there were members of the aristocracy who openly welcomed American conquest. Such a one was Angustias de la Guerra. . . . The sixty-two-year-old wife of Dr. James L. Ord professed to speak for the women of California."[26] In his widely read documentary anthology, *Foreigners in Their Native Land*, Weber then proceeded to publish just that paragraph in which de la Guerra damns herself and her Californiana sisters to historical ridicule for their alleged complicity with the American invaders. Yet contrary to the Price and Ellison mistranslation—and Weber's misreading—of her comments on the women's reception of the American occupation, de la Guerra and other California women did *not* welcome the American conquest or the transformation of their native land. "Ocurrencias en California" therefore, must be read as an oppositional narrative.

Moreover, although Bancroft supposedly solicited women's personal narratives to provide general information on the "women's sphere," the women made the testimonies individually and culturally self-reflective. In each of the narratives I have discussed here, a substantive individual identity emerges which warrants autobiographical legitimacy. The women's narratives are contextualized by the sociopolitical and gendered experience that constituted a historical subjectivity in which cultural difference marked opposition to Bancroft's project of eliciting merely supplemental information from women. In that respect, the narratives must be seen as the products of a dialectical process. That is, since the narratives were being collected by men who represented the occupying culture, it is reasonable to assume that Mexican women were engaged in a power struggle within the interview process itself. Angustias de la Guerra is sought out for interview because she was related to influential men through whom she had apparently informed "herself upon Governmental affairs," yet by the end of the narrative process she has expropriated the narrative to inscribe her own life. And even though at the moment she gives her narrative she is "Mrs. Dr. James L. Ord," she does not ratify the American occupation as perhaps the interviewer expected. Eulalia Pérez was initially approached for interview, I cannot help but think, because she was a curiosity—a woman, the story had it, who was 139 years old; she does not relate her life story, however, as a wonder of longevity but as a story of self-reliance. Although Apolinaria Lorenzana is remembered as "la Beata"—in fact, it was Savage who titled her narrative "Memorias de la Beata" (a title she would not have ratified)—her own memory fixes not on her piety but on her work in the world, teaching girls to read and write, sustaining numerous responsibilities in the San Diego mission, and running her three ranches. In each of these narratives there is evidence of evasion, redirected narrative reflection on the past, and a reconstituting of the "self" that proceeds beyond interrogatory expectations.

As for the intracultural dialects of gender present in the narratives, while it may be inaccurate to make a generalizing claim that women's narratives roundly criticize the patriarchal system, they did provide a stunning and open-throated critique of patriarchal domination within California Mexican culture that placed constraints on their intellectual development, excluded them from the networks of sociopolitical hierarchy, and sought to domesticate their desire for self-sufficiency. Hence, intracultural and gender-related commentary of a critical bent is more manifest in the women's narratives than in the men's, where patriarchal customs are self-servingly remembered. Again and again one reads narratives by women who were articulate, intellectually inquisitive, "self" conscious, who undoubtedly were capable of fully independent living, as demonstrated by Eulalia Pérez and Apolinaria Lorenzana, who resisted in various fashion men's attempts to keep them domestically contained.

Patriarchal and testimonial forms of containment, therefore, often provided the necessary impulse to reconstruct individual identity and personal experience in a genuinely self-empowering manner. María de las Angustias de la Guerra reconstructs her own heroism against the insolent *americano* soldiers and thereby levels a critique of Californio men; Eulalia Pérez marks in strong voice her consciously planned appropriation of authority in an otherwise male domain; María Inocente Pico de Avila gives tribute to her husband but also remembers being yanked out of school to undergo domestic "training" for him; Apolinaria Lorenzana re-creates her life not only as nurse and teacher but as property owner who had to contend with Americans who swindled her out of her ranchos. In each of the narratives I have read, women push beyond testimonial expectations to discover or invent the narrative space required for reconsidering their lives within a male-controlled domain, for reassessing the social transformation that affected them as much as their male counterparts, and, ultimately, for celebrating their own lives. Given the substance of such women's personal narratives, Chicano males even now need to reconsider how our own patriarchal nostalgia for a more familially harmonious and socially coherent cultural past is often reconstituted at the expense of women's lives and history.

5
Leaving a "clean and honorable name"
Rafael Chacón's "Memorias"

> I have done this work to please my children, who often have urged me to undertake it for their sakes.
> —Rafael Chacón, "Memorias" (1912)

I

As the family story has it, during the composition of his "Memorias" the seventy-year-old Rafael Sotero Chacón sent handwritten drafts to his nephew, Felipe Chacón, a prominent journalist[1] in Las Vegas, New Mexico, who reviewed them, read them aloud to his children after supper (as one of these children, Vera, remembers), and then returned the manuscript with comments to the old patriarch who was living in a small house in Trinidad, Colorado, with Juanita, his wife and compañera of many years. When the "Memorias" was completed after six years of writing—Chacón seals the date as "August 8th, 1912"—his son, Eusebio, a lawyer and the author of two novelas,[2] had three copies made, one of which he kept, another of which he gave to a daughter, and the last of which Juanita gave to Felipe after Chacón's funeral in 1925.

This genealogical elaboration is necessary not simply for introducing an author and the history of his text but because the narrative's long journey toward public reading remains troubled by lost origins, tangled lines of descent, truncated versions, and a recent reconstruction in which Rafael Chacón's gift to his children is misplaced once again in a recently published version of the "Memorias." The original Spanish manuscript, as well as two of the typescripts, disappeared. Somehow the first two chapters, translated and typed as the "Memoirs," found their way into the Historical Collections Library at the University of Colorado, but "records do not cite a source for the document," nor is there a clear date of receipt.[3] Felipe's typescript, fortunately, was preserved by one of the daughters, Herminia Chacón de Gonzales, who had listened to versions of the

"Memorias" as a child. Her copy remained preserved within the family until Vera Chacón de Padilla, another of Felipe's listener-daughters, undertook to see the manuscript into print as it appears Rafael wished. Chacón's narrative bequest to his family has had a long journey through family lines until its recent extrafamilial and defamiliarized textual appearance in 1986. For all practical purposes, the "Memorias" that Rafael Chacón wrote to "please [his] children" remained with his children until Jacqueline Dorgan Meketa, working from Vera Padilla's copy, "built" the bio-auto-graphical text entitled *Legacy of Honor: The Life of Rafael Chacón, A Nineteenth-Century New Mexican.*[4]

Perhaps Chacón's "Memorias" still belongs to the family, where it remains in the only Spanish typescript copy. For as Meketa freely acknowledges in the introduction to her book, rather than "do the obligatory research, editing, and annotation, and then publish the memoirs pretty much as written by Chacón, allowing them to stand on their own" (5), she decided to "develop a book around the memoirs" (6). The term "around" signals an immediate danger to Chacón's authorial status, not to mention a threat to the narrative proper, which, in Meketa's version, assumes a different form altogether. Meketa, for example, markedly restructured the narrative: Chacón's first chapter, "My Birth and Childhood," is reorganized into the first three chapters of Meketa's text, his detailed chapter headings are cut, and the narrative is resequenced rather considerably. The entire Chacón narrative is framed by a substantial and, I might add, an informative and intelligent introduction and epilogue. Meketa also provides contextualizing chapter headnotes and inserts supplemental material—"oral interview transcripts, personal correspondence, military letters and reports, newspaper articles, military service and pension records, and eyewitness accounts" (5–6)—directly into Chacón's text "to bridge an ambiguous gap between two events not clearly defined; the desire to flesh out several interesting but brief accounts with minutiae that would humanize events, such as Chacón's wedding, and allow the readers to imagine the festivities as though they were present; and last, but by no means least, to authenticate and support some of Chacón's statements" (6). This long, multiphrased sentence on her reconstructive method illustrates just how easily Chacón's text gets displaced by the editor's insertions.

To be just, Meketa's insertions do much to historicize Chacón's "Memorias." Her exhaustive background notes on the Civil War in New Mexico, for example, are invaluable for understanding the role

Nuevomexicano[5] soldiers played in that crucial event as well as the scapegoating and general ill-treatment they received at the hands of Anglo officers. As Meketa points out, her guiding motive was "to reach the many lay historians and nonspecialist members of the reading public interested in New Mexico's past rather than create a strictly academic work . . . familiar only to professionals" (6). However, Meketa's text is much more academic in appearance than it might have been had she followed her "original plan" and published "the memoirs pretty much as written by Chacón." *Legacy of Honor* has all the trappings of an "academic" book, complete with a table of contents, maps and illustrations, two Appendices, substantial discussion notes, a bibliography, and an index—*and* it is published by a university press. As it turns out, Chacón's "Memorias" is transformed from autobiographical to biographical narrative, and his life history is subordinated to the historiographic project of reconstructing New Mexico's nineteenth-century territorial period.

To cite only one of numerous examples of ethnosubject reconstruction, I refer to Krupat's introductory remarks on the textual evolution of Sam Blowsnake's personal narrative.[6] As Krupat has shown, the construction (and reconstruction) of Native American personal narrative has often resulted in the displacement, sometimes the multidisciplinary fracture, of the subject of the narrative.[7] Paul Radin, one of the pioneers of ethnography, took Blowsnake's own written syllabary autobiography—edited by Radin and published as *The Autobiography of a Winnebago Indian* in 1920 as a relatively short narrative—and substantially reconstructed it for republication in 1926 as *Crashing Thunder: The Autobiography of an American Indian.* In the 1926 version, Radin inserted numerous myth and origin stories, ceremonial speeches, and other personal narrative and speech fragments at strategic moments in Blowsnake's text to culturally contextualize the tribal events Blowsnake rather casually mentions. The interpolated product, as Radin points out in his preface to the 1926 edition, results in a "considerably enlarged" narrative aimed at a "wider audience" (Radin 1983 : xxiii).

Yet the narrative logic of the original version is disrupted, the speaking voice muted by repeated anthropological insertions, the autobiographical subject subordinated to a "larger" project of constructing a "scientific" Native American representative. The autobiographical narrator, Sam Blowsnake, who should remain in the narrative foreground, is so thoroughly reconstructed by the editor that he is actually displaced from his own story. That is, Sam Blowsnake, the subject name of the 1920 text in which he was identified primarily as "S.B.," is completely erased, to be replaced with an even more Indian-sounding name—Crashing Thunder. Personal narrative, however mediated, is transformed into biography, or anthropological cultural document, or historiographic narrative, or some such rhetorical collocation. What we have before us in such a reconstructed text is an example of the way an editor decides that the cultural Other needs contextualizing, needs to be situated in his or her own history, needs to be explained into reality for a "wider [read: white] audience." On the one hand, the result of such textual construction is useful because the speaker is culturally contextualized for an otherwise ignorant and often ethnocentric audience; on the other hand, such contextualization, when externally manipulated, robs the individual autobiographer (what theorists, in an equally nullifying move, call the "I-speaking subject") of voice, turning it to service as a cultural representation, the object of an audience's curiosity about a tribal group, as in the case of Blowsnake, or about Mexican Americans, as in the case of Chacón.

As for Meketa's reconstruction of the Chacón narrative, one must be fair enough to say that without her work the narrative may not have appeared for many years, or may have been altogether concealed within the Chacón family archive. Recovering and restoring a narrative that has been dormant for three quarters of a century is a remarkable undertaking. Making it widely public is also a way of restoring Rafael Chacón's status as a Hispano whose life story figures importantly into nineteenth-century territorial New Mexican military, intercultural, and political history. Without the historical information Meketa includes, Chacón's tight-lipped description of the discriminatory, even hostile treatment he and other Nuevomexicano soldiers experienced in the Union army during and after the Civil War would remain unenforced. As Meketa says, Chacón "used considerable restraint" in his handling of the subject of "prejudice displayed against Hispanos in the military." She, therefore, incorporated several of his military letters and "the experiences and opinions of some of his contemporaries" in a move to concretize "the breadth and scope of the ugly and ubiquitous problem" (7) he and his fellow Hispanos faced.

Meketa's historicizing comments, scathing as they are, reveal by contrast much about Chacón's own narrative confrontation with events occurring forty years earlier that had confounded, angered, and embittered him. Although he has bad memories about that period, he remains rhetorically reserved, describing events succinctly and presenting documents that speak for themselves rather than resorting to emotional display. Meketa writes Chacón's restrained enunciations back into the text, but she foregrounds them in a manner that undermines restraint. That is, she says what he would not, or chose not to, say. So, even though her advocacy is narratively disruptive, it proceeds from a politicized sensibility, from a position intended, for instance, to call historiography about U.S. military affairs into question. By situating Chacón within a socially discursive matrix, she rehistoricizes a period that had been troublesome and painful for Mexican Americans.

Meketa's interpolative narrative, however, creates a bind for Chacón: he is biographically expanded and made to function as a heroic character in Meketa's historical narrative. Like the Native American subject, he is given more, and different, presence in the bio-text than he made for himself in the "Memorias." The result is that we perhaps know more about him than he wished us to know. For example, in addition to the Chacón letters and military documents that Meketa inserts into the Civil War period, she collates diary entries Chacón wrote as a military scout "for his commanding officer" (227) in August and September 1863. The entries not only supplement the "Memorias," as Meketa points out, but correct faulty memory, since the events did not take place in June as Chacón reconstructs the experience some "forty-four years after the fact."

Is it the case, then, that incorporating Chacón's words from the earlier period supplements and even supersedes an old man's failing memory? Perhaps, but such an editorial move violates a principal autobiographical choice: perhaps Chacón did not wish to disclose the details of past experience fully; perhaps he did not think it necessary, or in his best social or cultural or historical interest, to provide a prolix description of his campaigns against the Navajo, his sickness and bouts of severe rheumatism, or the continual struggle with Anglo-American soldiers who had no more regard for the Nuevomexicano troopers than for the Indians these latter were ordered to battle. It does seem reasonable, therefore, to assume that Chacón was saying all he wanted to say; after all, he did work on his "Memorias" for some six years when he was still intellectually vigorous. Chacón's failure to say more about his career in the army, however, opens space for Meketa to expand the memoirs in the direction of bio-history. As she says, "The decision to insert the editor and the translator's own words included the necessity to bridge an ambiguous gap between events not clearly defined" (6). Given her editorial "desire to flesh out several interesting but brief accounts with minutiae that would humanize events" (6), Meketa provides the necessary corrective details for the following gaps in the memoirs: "Chacón and his men were surely involved in more skirmishes and scouts than are recorded in the memoirs" (237); "This brief account of his days in Santa Fe leaves volumes unsaid" (243); "although Chacón does not emphasize it, the racial slurs, prejudicial attitudes, and lack of respect continued" (246); "Once again Chacón, perhaps mellowed by the passage of the years, fails to mention in the memoirs that upon his return from Arizona he was ill, discouraged, and probably angry" (258). In supplementing Chacón's memoirs, Meketa gives us a version of Rafael Chacón that in the process of thickening the biographical subject, eventually so disperses Chacón's own narrative that the autobiographer himself is displaced.

The "Memorias" must be restored to its original voice and published in Spanish, with English translation, if we are to read Chacón as he represented himself. In the meantime, Chacón has assumed enormous historical stature and representational responsibility in the text that has been developed around the old man's own carefully constructed memoirs. Since the Spanish longhand version of the "Memorias" remains in family keeping, we will, for the present, have to read him through *Legacy of Honor.* Although I read Chacón contextually, my own historicizing of his discursive and sociocultural situation is intended not to supplant or resettle but to reinstate the subject of Chacón's narrative, allowing Chacón to speak for himself and following what I take to be the more native logic of his "Memorias" as a genealogical narrative of culture and family rather than a historical account offering, as the book jacket claims: "new insights into events in New Mexico history during the Mexican and early territorial periods, especially the Civil War." What we read of Chacón's life from his own words in the early chapters on his childhood before 1846 discloses his nostalgia for pre-American social and cultural practices that constituted the epistemological ground of subjectivity and memory. In the middle sections Chacón describes the culturally strategic accommodation to national transformation through service in the American army, which he and other Nuevomexicanos joined after 1848 to secure their beloved homeland for their families and their posterity. These middle chapters, moreover, are less an old soldier's vain reminiscences of his glory days in the field than vivid and sometimes startling recollections of Chacón's desire to return to domestic life in the face of Anglo-American hostility in the military, severe rheumatism and privation during long scouts, and, more than anything, loneliness for his wife, Juanita, and their small children. And since he composed his autobiography for the children whose lives, he believed, were being modified by social transformation, the closing section of Chacón's "Memorias" articulates a genealogical desire to secure the family name against historical dispersal, with Rafael Chacón acting as family scribe for "a clean and honorable name."

II

> Before the arrival of the Americans, the customs of the populace of New Mexico were very sane and sober.
>
> —Rafael Chacón, "Memorias"

Although Chacón's "Memorias" opens typically enough with reference to his birth in Santa Fe in 1833, the narrative poses the central autobiographical concern within pages when, in recalling a local political uprising in New Mexico when he was a child, he acknowledges the problematics of memory. "Our memory is frail," he writes, "more so when so many years have gone by, in the course of which we have experienced so many changes; for this reason it is not possible for me now to recall many of the things which I fain would remember" (44). More than disclosing an understandable anxiety about the intellectual decline expected in old age, Chacón's remark poses the brooding epistemological uncertainty about recuperating vanished experience that so often troubles the autobiographer. If "our" memory is frail to begin with, and since we experience "so many changes," it becomes all but impossible to recall, much less understand, the meaning of past experience. But the inability to fully reconstruct the past to which all autobiographers are heir is for Chacón complicated by a cultural deracination that has ruptured continuity with a sociocultural habitat that both supplies and structures the forms of narrative that are to him familiar.

The autobiographical problem raised by Chacón, as it turns out, resounds throughout the narrative as the problem of occupying dissonant cultural worlds—one that structured Chacón's locus of identity, the other that disrupted the cultural environment in which his identity was situated. His anxiety about reconstructing the past may be in part associated with age and the loss of recuperative power, but there was something else in that past that also troubled memory. The sociocultural dislocation and relocation revealed throughout his narrative simultaneously provide autobiographical motive and threaten memory. As Chacón says, he was encouraged to compose his memoirs by family, friends, and historians because of his distinguished military service and the general eventfulness of his life. Territorial historians like Benjamin Read, Ralph Twitchell, and Edwin Sabin visited and corresponded with Chacón, because they knew he was, like Mariano Vallejo, Angustias de la Guerra, and Eulalia Pérez in California, an invaluable source book for their own historical projects. And as Meketa writes, "After the turn of the century . . . Chacón suddenly found himself the center of much attention among historians and writers, and after he began work on his memoirs, he was often sought out by such people. Chacón was interviewed a number of times and spent many long hours pouring over his old documents and letters and writing long descriptions and explanations to historians" (330). Chacón, therefore, began to reconstruct a life they regarded as valorous and historically significant; however, what he remembers about that life, especially his life under the new American regime, is hollowed out by images of cultural disfigurement, dissatisfaction in the U.S. Army, and nostalgia for an older cultural habitat. The story he recalls of a troubled intercultural state of affairs makes his military career appear ludicrously disjointed when compared with his recollections of the pre-American Hispano society into which he was born.

Chacón's situation, nevertheless, was typical of the nineteenth-century Mexican(American) autobiographer for whom cultural discontinuity transformed personal narrative into a cultural document describing the profound historical break that unsettled collective discourse and in so doing destabilized the cultural subject. This is to argue that memory—how we remember and what we choose to remember, since we cannot or do not wish to remember everything—is intimately tied to a culturally organized discursive habitat. On the one hand, Chacón wrote from the standpoint of a retired, honorable American officer recalling his military exploits in the 1850s and 1860s; on the other, the social disequilibrium he experienced in the military gave voice to a discontented persona who, rather than celebrating his military career and American citizenship, strove instead to reconstitute a home and family apart from Anglo-American culture. Relocating himself within a prior cultural economy required a profound autobiographical feat: he must restore a world the American army tried to destroy.

Let me continue with the epigraph on the "arrival of the Americans," the logic of which I elided. After questioning the ground of memory, Chacón says, "But at the moment of penning these fragments of ancient songs, their swing and rhythm come back to my mind like a wail of the past, and I live once more under the paternal roof, and my thoughts again survey the scenes of my childhood" (44). This autobiographical "moment" startles Chacón with its haunting call upon memory. It may seem odd for songs from childhood to be remembered as "ancient songs," odd until we understand that these songs are indeed ancient because they are echoes of traditional cultural practices preceding Chacón by generations, practices that by 1900, Chacón fears, are eroded, or lost altogether. The songs he recalls in a "wail" of remembrance once functioned to situate experience within a collective habitat that preserved social events in formal verse structures. However, rather than the documentary content of the ballad, the language and nuance of the poetic form guides Chacón to a past that no longer exists, not only because he has grown old but because the cultural grid is broken. *Inditas* and *cuandos*,[8] popular songs and poetry "that saved . . . the tradition" (72) and functioned as cultural mnemonic markers, have been lost as a result, he will argue, of the American invasion.

The "fragments" of topical ballads that Chacón pens into his "Memorias" simultaneously provide a historiographically important account of a political uprising that took place in 1837 (when he was only four) and retrieve the emotive field of childhood for Chacón, thereby satisfying the autobiographical desire to restore his own presence in the past. The ballads establish a formal space for both discursive activities. Chacón's autobiographic "penning" of the popular romances of an "ancient" time reestablishes the autobiographer's relationship to a cultural past retrievable only in fragments. As he says, "I was still very young in the year 1837 to be able to have a personal recollection of the Rebellion," but the songs and tales the event generated, and which his father and family members related, provide the material of early experience he retrieves sixty years later. It is not ultimately the event's historical significance that matters to Chacón—although the event is important to the history of his own formation as well as to the production of the text he is encouraged to compose—but rather the memory of childhood, family, and home in a geocultural locale that by 1906 appears in ghostly outline under the reconfigured map of the American West.

Before he remembers the dispersive effects of the American conquest, or perhaps as a prelude to that signal event, Chacón describes his preparation as a cadet at the Mexican Military Academy in Chihuahua. In 1844, when he was only eleven, he trudged hundreds of miles by wagon to Chihuahua where he would become the youngest of a group of New Mexican boys sent at the order of Governor Ar-

mijo, who as the commanding general of New Mexico had successfully led his troops against a group of Texas filibusterers riding toward Santa Fe with intentions of annexing the territory in 1841.[9]

This section of Chacón's narrative on the military preparation
for the American invasion may initially have been generated by his
desire to provide historiographic information about the events leading up to the U.S.-Mexican War, but it becomes autobiographical
discourse when the old man fixes his gaze on the child he was sixty
years earlier. He remembers himself with bemusement as a vulnerable and rather gullible boy of eleven who no sooner arrives in Chihuahua than he is cajoled into making loans to other cadets—"who
already knew the ways of the world." Sensing they have found a
sucker, they proceed to strip him piecemeal of all his money and
belongings. Chacón writes of the immature military cadet with
comic self-irony.

> After these rascals had despoiled me of the best of my belong-
> ings and of the money, they sold me a horse, on which I had the
> pleasure of riding only once; they afterwards borrowed it from
> me under some plausible pretext and that was the last I ever saw
> of the animal . . .
> When all the cash which I had loaned them had been spent,
> the gentlemen of schemes, my comrades, borrowed my trunk,
> my blankets, and my rug, and I let them have everything, re-
> maining without bedding and without anything to eat, lack-
> ing even the resources to procure for myself the necessities of
> life. (50)

Like many another naive waif whose first departure from home
proves disastrous, the young Rafael, bound by the principles of behavior learned from the *Catón*, the "manual of politeness, morals,
good manners, and etiquette" (16) introduced to children in primary
school, is incapable of believing that others could act so dishonora-
bly. But they do. None of his money, his belongings, not to mention
his horse, is ever spoken of again by his fellow cadets. As in Benjamin Franklin's autobiographical anecdotes about the perils awaiting
the young adventurer, Chacón offers his own story of the treacherous strangers he meets on the road of life. Unlike Franklin, the
young Chacón finds strength not only in his own resources but in
Catholic prayer. As the still-reverent old man remembers, "I do not
know how long I went hungry, but I do remember that one day I was
weeping bitterly when I received a letter from my father, and in it
he enjoined me that whenever things did not go well with me I

should recite the Salve Regina in honor of the Blessed Virgin Mary and go to the church to hear Mass" (50).

Immediately after reading his father's advice, and while on the way to church praying "not one but many Salves" (50), Rafael finds nine pieces of silver in the road. Not only does he happen upon the money but, like manna fallen from heaven, he also discovers "some pieces of bread as hard as rock" (51) close to a stream. For Chacón this is an emblem of God's presence and the power of prayer: "Someone had lost his money in order that I, a helpless child, without experience and in a strange land, should receive a visible proof that God watches over the needy who, with confidence and faith, pray for the protection of His Providence" (51). Indeed, as Meketa points out, Chacón's description of feasting on the river-softened bread reads like an "allegorical representation of the Catholic sacrament of Holy Communion" (360). The aged narrator enforces this orthodox interpretation of a remote event, it turns out, as an analogue to the conditions underlying his impoverishment at the moment he is writing his memoirs. His remembrance of youthful faith in God's succor sustains the aged narrator who views the vulnerable child through the filter of a narrative present in which he again finds himself the victim of selfless charity, much like Vallejo and other Californios. Although he had accumulated property and livestock in the 1880s and 1890s, he had lost everything—in no small part because, still following the dictates of the *Catón*, he had helped friends who could not repay his kindness. As he writes,

> With the destitute I was more liberal than good judgment would approve, since I signed [cosigned] large fiscal obligations and had to pay them. On writing these memoirs I have nothing, but, nevertheless, in what seems like a paradox, I lack nothing. The God, who has watched over me since I was a child on foreign soil and who later allowed me to come out of combat unharmed, watches over me every instant of my life and provides me with what is necessary to sustain the body (326).

Chacón's Christian extrapolation makes him a figure in his own allegory of model behavior: his children will find a model of Christian charity, faith, and patience in the father's text. His story of steadfast faith, moreover, is a familiar example of the nineteenth-century Hispano's deeply embedded religiocultural consciousness. However, religious orthodoxy must be sustained in the presence of social ruptures that unsettle the community's religiocultural matrix. In narratively circularizing the vital position of orthodox faith in his life, Chacón autobiographically grounds character and personality within a strong cultural configuration threatened at every turn by the "ostracism of this commercial age" (333). Desire for moral stability—both in life and in the narrative—develops as a response to the unstable social world in which he finds himself. The numerous episodes that resonate with Christian interpretation are socially immanent allegories of personal faith and exemplifications of stability in the face of commercial alienation. Chacón's religiocultural construction of a moral center, with its extensional codes of social behavior and familial relation, resides at the heart of narrative motive in the text. What he has to say about childhood never appears as the obligatory function of ego-centered memoir but rather as the socially significant function of textual self-possession. The formation of a stable personality capable of coherent responses to life's contingencies is requisite for anyone; for members of Chacón's generation, the traumatic social upheaval of the U.S. military invasion and the succeeding colonial domination intensified that normal human task. The "Memorias" records Chacón's salvaging of the personal life in the face of negative social relations that were destroying the cultural ecology that had shaped group and individual experience in New Mexico.

Chacón's remembrance of the injustices he and other Nuevomexicanos later experienced when they were mustered into the U.S. military troubles his narrative recovery of the American invasion in unexpected ways: having lived on the surface of two distinct plates of social experience—one cultural, the other national—recalling such events produces a distention of consciousness in which his own contradictory loyalties grate against each other, creating immense psychological pressure and occasions of narrative tremor. These juxtapositions work themselves into the autobiographical recollections in what is no less than a series of shocks of recognition. Having proven himself a loyal military officer in the 1860s, and in his late years having become a celebrated figure, he might very well have muted the immediate effects of the American takeover in 1846. He might have passed over the specifics altogether. But he did not. Neither did he overdramatize, or melodramatize, his people's responses.

Casting a glance back over the American conquest in August 1846, Chacón remembers that his people immediately recognized the *americanos* as an invading "enemy," who in one town "burned the public markets, the granaries, and everything that people were not able to carry away" (67). And he speaks to the issue of why the

Nuevomexicanos, under the command of General Armijo, did not battle the Americans as they were marching toward Santa Fe. In a letter to Benjamín Read at the turn of the century, Chacón sympathizes with General Armijo's dilemma and abrupt decision not to engage the enemy.

At that time I was incapable of estimating men's actions. I was a child: when I reached mature age I cast a glance back over that event and what first struck my imagination was that the conquering army came provided with everything that was necessary for the conquest. General Armijo and our poor people had no other resource than that of 'going to fight'. . . . What could Armijo do with an undisciplined army without any military training. . . . He was a dwarf against a giant. (63)

Only after he has been a member of the American "conquering army" does Chacón understand Armijo's position and his pragmatic decision not to see his people's blood spilled in a socially symbolic but futile effort against the *americanos*. It may have been the case that the Mexican army did not put up a sustained fight, but narratives like Chacón's put to rest the fabrication that Nuevomexicanos welcomed General Kearny's forces as the liberating army so often imagined in American historiography. Yet the letter to Read is less a revisionist attempt to clean up Armijo's image than a rereading of his people's traumatized response to the American invasion. As I have argued in chapter 2, for most Nuevomexicanos the fear and confusion entrenched in their memories of events during the later 1840s were so strong that even though they participated in the American regime, they never forgot the widespread resentment and fear of the Army of the West, an army that had come as friends to "absolve" them of their allegiance to Mexico and to protect them as long as they remained quiet. Remembering must have been especially painful for people like Chacón who had to reconcile his U.S. military career with his memories of villages razed by the same army only a few years earlier. The very succinctness of his description of the American conquest enforces the intense fear that Nuevomexicanos experienced as the U.S. Army made its way from town to town: "I remember that there was such terror instilled by the Americans that when a dog barked the people killed it, the burros were muzzled so they could not bray, and if the roosters crowed at daylight they killed them. Only at night were fires permitted in order that the enemy not discover the smoke from the huts" (67).

As was the case for Mexican people throughout the Southwest, the American invasion entirely disrupted normal life for the Chacón family, not to mention a way of life in New Mexico that had been in formation for over two hundred years. Chacón recalls that his own father, Albino Chacón, was sought for questioning by the military on suspicion of subversive activity and that the elder Chacón later refused to cooperate in the formation of the territorial government. Although his father was a member of the educated, landowning class and might have prospered in postoccupation society, he refused to reconcile himself to the conquest, thus ending up economically and politically ruined. Other New Mexicans not only refused to cooperate but fought where and when possible.[10] Chacón remembers the scattered guerrilla warfare against the Americans during the early months of the occupation as well as the general climate of anxiety that prevailed but chooses not to elaborate on this period. Since he was a witness at such a momentous historical transformation, one might expect him to say more, but instead, as Meketa points out, he turns "his thoughts and writing to the native people, their customs, their traditions" before the invasion. I think that Chacón says less than he might simply because by 1906 when he was writing the memoirs, he had been a U.S. citizen for over fifty years, having sealed that ambiguous bond with distinguished service in the U.S. military. To write more about the American hostilities than he does would have placed him in a split discursive situation. How could he reconstruct detailed descriptions of the invasion by an American "enemy" and still go on to record his own high-minded service in that enemy's army? Yet although there is a good deal of repression, Chacón's narrative turn to pre-American cultural life is reminiscent of that discovered in much autobiographical narrative of the period in which the colonized subject describes life before 1848 as culturally and socially coherent and yet praises the social and material advances made after 1848.

Like the Californio narratives produced during the 1870s, the New Mexican autobiographer finds himself remembering a way of life before the invasion and ensuing disruption. The world these colonized autobiographers reconstruct both delights and pains them. As I have suggested in my remarks on Vallejo and Lorenzana, narrative reconstruction that valorizes pre-American society sets itself against their sense of material and social displacement. Likewise, half a century after the conquest, Chacón's memory of childhood settles disquietingly on the fragmenting of a prior cultural epistemology that destabilizes identity in the present. Although he is a loyal citizen of the United States, he does not, or cannot, celebrate an American identity. Rather, as he remembers that his father harbored the family in a safe place "during the critical time of the invasion," the names of family and close friends all at once proliferate on the page, along with memories of pre-American planting and harvesting customs, trading and bartering practices, and the many festive occasions that extended from this collective life—dances, singing, especially extemporaneous verse contests, feast days celebrated with various Pueblo Indians, and buffalo hunts.

This section of the narrative initially appears motivated by a desire to provide an outline of village life and customs for Chacón's turn-of-the-century contemporaries; after all, he shared his broad historical experiences with members of the historical preservation societies then being organized in southern Colorado at the end of the nineteenth century.[11] Nevertheless, a culturally contextualized reading would focus rather on the way the narrative fulfills this function as a recuperatively powerful social articulation of individual presence within an enabling and coherent matrix of communal relations. Once Chacón locates himself in the social economy of the pre-American past, his narrative lights up, displaying a capacity for thick detail that appears generated by outright joy at remembering such collective events as harvesting and syrup production. I quote at length.

> During the reaping of the crops . . . it was a joy to see neighbors helping one another in the gathering of the crops. Much syrup was made. They made presses from white pine logs on which several men would climb, pressing the cane as the men worked the log back and forth. The juice from the cane would then run into a receptacle built for this purpose. The cane was then pounded with sledgehammers of oak and heavy mallets and the cane was thrown in a canoe made of stout white pine. When the cane juice came out it was put in kettles and hung on syrup racks, and under the kettles they made sort of a furnace where they had a fire and put the kindling. The men and women worked together in order to carefully watch the timing of the syrup cooking. They sang songs and had dances with much modesty, and always good order prevailed. The young people of both sexes enjoyed themselves without failing to show respect and good manners, and all was enjoyment and happiness. (75)

I commence in the middle of the passage to emphasize Chacón's apparent delight, yet repressed anguish, at reconstructing cultural practices that by 1906 had either drastically declined or vanished.

Memory reproduces the sights and sounds of childhood, when a seasonal cycle of events was an enriching collective experience. What might be read as a nostalgic and idealized cultural reminiscence, however, when reframed by Chacón's opening remarks in the paragraph, opens toward a critique of American despoliation: "Before the arrival of the Americans, the customs of the populace of New Mexico were very sane and sober. The people lived simply and very contentedly, with no ambitions that pushed them into vice. They did the sowing in the spring, and the corn was generally planted on the fifteenth of May, the feast of San Isidro Labrador" (74). His description of seasonal consciousness and the cooperative structuring of labor that characterized Hispano rural life is told from the point of view of someone whose words measure the disintegration of the collective economy that produced him. A reader familiar with the social history of New Mexico village life may be skeptical of Chacón's revisiting of what appears as a conflict-free community. The landowning classes, it might be argued, were as influential as the seasons in keeping village peons working on schedule. Given our knowledge of class division and its abuses, coupled with a poststructuralist distrust of narratives that construct harmonious communal origins, we can hardly be expected to believe that life was ever so joyous, cooperative, morally sane, peaceful—anywhere. However, what bears analysis here is not Chacón's recuperation of what may read as a socially idyllic communal past so much as a strategic reconstruction of a pre-American community that fully integrated food production activity, religious festivities, village entertainments, and artistic enactments of various kinds. Remember that the sociocultural nostalgia here, functioning to startle and plot memory, is contained in Chacón's initial words—"Before the arrival of the Americans." Every succeeding word in this section, where native values of the pre-American rural community crowd the page, must be read against the devastating sense of a world ruined.

The fragmentation of Hispano oral poetics is figured as a rupture in the cultural epistemology of the Nuevomexicano. On recalling the extemporaneous verbal dueling that routinely took place between competing *trovadores* (troubadours) at dances, religious feast days, and various gatherings, Chacón laments the loss of an oral speech community that simultaneously sustained aesthetic tradition and an orally transmitted epistemology embedded in the community's historical, political, moral, and mythic narratives. In recalling the singing of *inditas* and *cuandos*, the autobiographer is transported to an earlier cultural locale in which the play of language was both a cultural activity of great pleasure and a linguistic event of significant social dimension. *Trovos*, duels matching repartee and the verbal improvisation of formally complex *cuandos* commemorating historical events, buffalo hunts, commendatory verse acknowledgments of loved ones, or verse *memorias* of deceased relatives were performed by well-known *poetas*. But villagers were by no means passive auditors witnessing the performances of famed *poetas trovadores*. On the contrary, they passed immediate judgment on the ability with which these *trovadores* performed a series of rhetorical feats. Verbal extemporizing was part theater, part intellectual competition between *poetas* and villagers, and part schooling in rhetoric for children who were absorbing the sociolinguistic conventions of their community.

Chacón, for example, remembers one occasion when Juan Bautista Vigil y Alaríd, one of the celebrated "improvisers in the Mexican Era" (72) and the same man who as acting governor when Kearney arrived with his troops offered the surrender statement in Santa Fe,[12] was challenged to "instantly compose, and without stopping, recite a verse that ended with the words, 'I say that there is no hell' and that at the same time he would say nothing blasphemous nor offensive to the dogmas of the Catholic religion" (73). Vigil y Alaríd was tested for his ability to extemporize in a sustained manner, following formal conventions of meter and end rhyme. Yet success was not granted to rhetorical performance alone, since the *poeta* must reverse the heretical signification of the phrase in a manner consonant with the community's religious mores. While rhetorical skill could not be dislodged from the community's ethics, such elasticity did function to invigorate the culture through a renewing play of language.

Such collective rhetorical practices constituted the means by which Mexicanos sustained their historical and cultural narratives, their religious beliefs, their medicinal practices, not to mention their sense of humor. The narratives in this storehouse of collective historical knowledge and cultural values were transmitted to succeeding generations, not through an array of static values but through an oral poetics of complex verbal codes that constituted group subjectivity. As Chacón's contemporary, the noted folklorist Aurelio M. Espinosa, wrote in 1913, such practices "constitute a kind of life philosophy, which, with the authority of tradition and experience, is ever present in the minds of the people."[13] And as a more recent folk historian, Rowena Rivera, writes, "What gave resiliency and flexibility to Spanish/Mexican colonial oral poetry was precisely its bond to the reality of the common folk. As such it was therefore always suitable to be used in any way that it was needed, so long as it adhered to the community's religious ideology, its code of ethics, its sense of aesthetics, and it own literary canons."[14] Yet as Chacón points out, this collective socioaesthetic discourse was radically altered by the American installation of a hegemonic social, cultural, and linguistic economy. Vigil y Alaríd, for instance, as I have argued in chapter 2, ended up having to apply his rhetorical skills to a document of surrender that improvised an accommodating (but covertly bitter) response to the American military takeover that, with the imposition of martial law, would silence public resentment almost entirely as well as rupture the ease with which oral poetics was practiced.

Therefore, because Chacón worries that the community has already lost touch with a crucial part of its identity at the turn of the century, the examples of fragmented verse compositions included in his memoirs do not so much represent an effort to preserve, or even recover, oral poetics as to come to terms with its loss. Rather than restore the past, he admits the breach between himself in 1906 and himself as an inhabitant of an earlier cultural discourse. The popular *romances* that "saved the tradition . . . have been forgotten or have been corrupted until they now [ca. 1900] remain completely distorted" (72). Not because he is an old man with a failing memory but because he, like other Nuevomexicanos, has been severed from everyday cultural practice, he can "only remember a very few verses of their compositions" (72). Hence, to reproduce only fragments of oral poetics proves a pathetic, disincorporated textual gesture. Espinosa, working at the same time, did reproduce these cultural artifacts for folkloric study, but when one looks at the list of over four hundred one-line "New Mexican Spanish proverbs," Chacón's anxiety about the disfiguration of cultural practices and oral discourse is made manifest. Espinosa himself expresses his own anxiety about the erosion of proverb practice: "A proverb is considered the final word on any subject, on any occasion, and in any emergency. That a few, however, are beginning to scoff at them, is evident."[15]

The brooding question about memory's frailty that underlies Chacón's reconstitution of his cultural childhood is central to the autobiographical enterprise: how can Chacón adequately describe personal experience when the cultural ecology has been stripped of the discursive equipment necessary for representing subjectivity seated in everyday practice? As it turns out, rather than reconstructing a coherent order of experience, autobiographical narrative is forced to describe fragmentation, dispersal, the subject's inability to articulate himself. Chacón suppresses his anxiety at such a juncture by moving on to other episodes of life, yet his narrative of childhood writes itself as an anguished memory of familial, cultural, and linguistic discontinuity that scars much of the text.

III

> Do not trust the Mexican troops.
> —General E. R. S. Canby, Commander
> of the Union troops in New Mexico,
> March 1886

> Obliged by circumstances always to defend themselves with weapons, in the country and in the village, like the Roman populace in Roman times, they soon raised among their sons a populace of soldiers by nature intelligent, intrepid, valiant, and lovers of their country and of their liberty. The New Mexicans, raised in the use of arms from their childhood, did not know what fear was and God grant that those in whose hands our destiny has fallen will begin someday to appreciate their beautiful qualities and their temperaments.
> —Rafael Chacón, "Memorias"

After the North American invasion, the Chacón family, along with their compatriots, was forced to make major economic and social readjustments, or surrender themselves to despair. After the family moved to El Chamizal in 1850, Chacón developed his skills as a laborer, woodcutter, trader, and pack freighter as well as buffalo hunter. What this episodic section of the narrative shows is that Chacón, like other Mexican(American)s, was racing to survive after the destabilizing effects of the American takeover. During the period from roughly 1850 to 1861, when he was enlisted as an officer in the Union army against the impending Confederate march into New Mexico, Chacón spent long periods freighting cargo between Santa Fe and various towns, went out every autumn to hunt buffalo for winter meat, joined the American army for a period of about six months in 1855 to pursue a group of Apaches and Utes, and then, immediately after fighting against those tribes, was an "Indian trader for four or five years, meeting the Cheyennes, Comanches, and Arapahoes" (106).

Chacón's narrative is replete with details about his enduring relationship with the land that comprised the map of his people's cultural geography. His description of buffalo hunting, for example, figures prominently into the "Memorias" as a metaphor for the formation of an intimate cultural discourse. Hispanos had hunted buffalo for generations and would continue to do so until the herds were killed off entirely at the end of the century. In addition to providing a stable meat source, the excursion for buffalo every October was an occasion of immense social and discursive significance. Chacón describes the buffalo hunting practices of the Nuevomexicanos less as an ethnographic tale of the Western frontier experience than as a narrative of social bonding: "On the plains, where the silence was crushing, the hunters assembled from many parties and made camp together in order to become a society. There we met kinsmen and friends, and friendships were made that lasted for life" (93). Chacón represents the hunt as an activity that produced not only food but collective events of the sort that evolved into usually comic but occasionally tragic narratives that were retold again and again in increasingly elaborate form.

The anecdotal hunt scenes that appear in "Memorias" as embryonic narratives reappear in more extensive and different narrative form in Miguel Antonio Otero's autobiography, *My Life on the Frontier* (1935), and especially in Fabiola Cabeza de Baca's autobiographical *We Fed Them Cactus* (1954), in which one of the ranch hands— El Cuate—relates story after story of the buffalo hunt to an enthralled audience of children and adults. Even in the fiction of Fray Angelico Chávez and Rudolfo Anaya, the social significance that derives from stories about life on the *llano estacado* (the central plains of New Mexico) emerges from a condition of material absence that produces an imaginative desire to reconstitute those narrative events that were lost when the buffalo were destroyed.[16] The fact that the buffalo were killed off and the *llano* fenced in has produced a narrative enterprise in Nuevomexicano autobiography and fiction that simultaneously operates to criticize the American hegemony while developing a socioideologically charged figuration of cultural presence on a landscape that will not be surrendered. Cabeza de Baca's *We Fed Them Cactus*, in fact, is "the story of the struggle of New Mexican Hispanos for existence on the Llano, the Staked Plains" (Preface). Cabeza de Baca remembers her father's intimate attachment to the *llano*: "He had taken deep roots on the Ceja [cap rock country in the llano], roots deeper than the piñon and the juniper on his land. . . . He had his children, but they could never be as close to him as the hills, the grass, the yucca and mesquite and the peace enjoyed from the land" (175). Another father, Gabriel Marez, in Anaya's *Bless Me, Ultima*, a man whose consciousness is seated in the *llano,* will not be reconciled to life in town; although he is fenced off the range, he buys a small plot of land edging the *llano* as a symbol of his refusal to surrender his claim to a traditional way of life. For Chacón just after 1900 as for Cabeza de Baca in 1954 and Anaya in 1972, the *llano* represents the homeland, a zone of cultural freedom replete with stories that sustain personal and cultural identity over time. In fact, the original Nuevomexicano story about the *llano* and the buffalo is Juan de Oñate's "Relación del descubrimiento de las vacas de cibola," a firsthand account of his first viewing of the buffalo in 1599.[17]

The autobiographically positive figuration of the homeland, therefore, allows Chacón to narratively reinforce an identity that has been constructed over a period of three hundred years. Although *Nuevo Mexico* became American territory in 1848, Hispanos did not surrender their deeply rooted conviction that they were inextricable from the land. The homeland had always to be defended from its enemies and, therefore, Chacón, "raised in the use of arms from . . . childhood" took what recourse he must and joined the American army. Yet that army, as Chacón came to realize, had little regard for New Mexico as homeland, or the Nuevomexicano as soldier.

Defending the homeland—especially in American uniform—must have been a test of will for Hispanos who found themselves socially disfranchised after centuries of permanent residence. In the collective mind, what became the Territory of New Mexico under the American regime was actually *la Nueva Mexico,* a land settled in 1598 by Juan de Oñate and a group of five hundred colonists, a land in which the oldest capital in North America, Santa Fe, was established in 1610, a land that during the succeeding two centuries and a half had become a homeland to some seventy thousand Nuevomexicanos.[18] However, some forty years after Chacón had served with distinction in the American military, his words register an unreconciled concern about the perilous position he and fellow Nuevomexicanos held in American society during the last half of the nineteenth century. Writing his memoirs after 1906 when he was in his late seventies, he remembers that "those in whose hands our destiny has fallen"—*los americanos*—refused to appreciate the Nuevomexicanos's courage, even after they had proven their "martial character" during Civil War battles fought in New Mexico and the military campaigns leveled against the Navajos and Apaches, not to mention their participation in the Spanish-American War of 1898.

Chacón's "Memorias" presents one more version of the manner in which nineteenth-century Hispanos had adapted to the American transformation—but not without experiencing what for members of his generation were confounding divisions between loyalty to the United States and their disenchantment with its common mistreatment of them in the military. Like Juan Seguín and Santiago Tafolla in Texas, Chacón adapted to life under the United States, even excelled as a military officer in the wars against the Navajos, Utes, and Apaches, as well as in the brief New Mexican Civil War battles, but as his narrative twists about on him, Chacón's memories of military duty are less about service to his adopted country than about the persistent conflict with Anglo soldiers who derogated Mexican American troopers on a daily basis. The long middle section of the narrative—the section that reconstructs his military years from 1861 to 1864—appears as a rejoinder to haunting Anglo-American voices from the past that were constant reminders of ethnocentric snobbery and outright exclusion. Yet there is great reluctance on Chacón's part to engage in revisionary writing.

Recall that in his preface, Chacón writes that he expects "no greater reward" for his labor than that his readers be supplied with "some short hours of amusement." Yet aside from some few anecdotes drawn from childhood and curious incidents from his military career, there is little that a reader can expect from the book in the way of amusement. Not that Chacón is grim, nor would he think his life tragic, but memory retrieves a life history troubled by intercultural tensions that constantly cloud his narrative. In the same short preface, he remarks that he has "gone over all the events of greater importance, from a biographical standpoint," and that having responsibly completed that documentary outline he will satisfy himself to "leave details and amplifications of historical narrative to other works of greater pretensions." He may leave amplification to others, yet because the personal life was so affected by those "events of greater importance" and because self-representation was staked in the historical narratives such "events" produced, he was forced to clarify and revise viciously ethnocentric representations of Nuevomexicano soldiers current at the time he was writing the "Memorias." Writing from the standpoint of a man whose major phase of adult life requires a version of telling that discloses the disappointments life under the American regime had imparted, like Seguín and Vallejo, Chacón documents his experience as an American citizen who is often treated like the enemy. Yet his version of the troubling military career remains strategically tight-lipped, undetailed, as I have suggested, because to elaborate means to place himself within a narrative vortex that might split him apart altogether. Chacón's is the common predicament of the colonial subject whose loyalties are split by conquest.

One must begin here by questioning the apparent contradiction: why did Chacón and other Mexicans join the U.S. military so soon after they had been the victims of American conquest? Early in the narrative he says that the family suffered materially and emotionally at the hands of the Americans; so, on the face of things, joining the conquering military appears ludicrous. After all, he describes the family situation as extremely destabilized.

> The severity of the American occupation swept away the few properties of my father. . . . My poor sisters and my mother, little accustomed to those trials, suffered the hardships of the poor like true heroines. . . . During the days of discouragement, of which there were many, my father entrusted us to the hands of God, and I have still saved a very beautiful poetic composition which gave him comfort in the sad hour. (86)

Given this disclosure of postoccupation material hardship and spiritual discouragement, it is difficult to believe that Chacón—in a sudden turn of mind—became an American patriot in 1855. Rather, his decision to muster into the military is common for people in a colonial situation who are made the instruments of their own suppression. In New Mexico, as in California and Texas, economic conditions after the conquest were so severe that thousands of men joined the army just to survive. Promised handsome cash bonuses and the prospect of steady pay, Chacón and scores of other Nuevomexicanos joined the American army. As Darlis A. Miller reveals, when the Civil War threatened to extend into the territory, Union officials "initiated plans to raise two regiments of volunteers among the territory's citizenry."[19] Only after they were given bonuses for joining, promised that their families would be cared for, and guaranteed stable pay were they willing to muster in. As Miller writes, "Despite hesitancy, approximately 2,800 residents—most of them Hispanos—had enlisted in the New Mexico volunteers by February 1862. Undoubtedly these men joined the army for mixed reasons, but for many the chief attraction was the prospect of soldier's pay and bounties" (107). The monetary inducement must have been enormously attractive to a people whose economy had been squashed less than fifteen years earlier.

Yet a more culturally autochthonous reason for mustering in was their desire to secure the homeland. Joining the American army provided the Nuevomexicanos with the military means to defend the homeland against their "ancient enemy," the Navajos,[20] and the more recent but more deeply hated enemy, "*los tejanos.*" As Chacón writes, the Texas military "invasion of 1841" aimed at extending the Texas border to Santa Fe was beaten back by New Mexican forces, but the "legacy of bitterness and hatred" that developed as a result of that incursion was fresh in the minds of New Mexicans well after 1848. Such antagonism proved exploitable in recruiting efforts in 1861 when troops were being organized for the Civil War. "The legislative assembly of New Mexico issued a manifesto which stated bluntly that the enemy was Texas and the Texans and that 'every Mexican in the Territory' must rally to the cause" (Miller 1979:120n). And Governor Henry Connelly issued a proclamation warning "the people that the territory had again been invaded by Texans and that their 'manhood' called upon them to defend their homes, their families, and the soil of their birth" (ibid., 108–109).

Nuevomexicanos had historically been "obliged by circumstances to defend themselves," and they were certainly ready to do so against the Confederates. But by the usual twist of American chauvinism, they were considered more an enemy than the Confederates, who after all were still Americans, because they had recently been (and, of course, always would be just) "Mexicans." Writing on the Confederate invasion of New Mexico in 1916, the prominent historian Ralph Emerson Twitchell pointed out that General George Canby, the commanding officer, sent "many telegrams and orders . . . to notify commanders of posts and others to place no reliance in them whatever except for certain purposes."[21] The letter (to Major Donaldson, March 7, 1862) that warned, "Do not trust the Mexican troops," was then amplified by Donaldson in a note to a General Thomas that read, "No reliance can be placed on the New Mexico Volunteers. . . . They have a traditionary fear of the Texans and will not meet them in the field" (Twitchell 1912:34). Additionally, the inspector-general in Santa Fe wrote, "No dependence whatever can be placed on the natives; they are worse than useless; they are really aides to the enemy" (Meketa 1986:180). As Twitchell notes, although the "opinion of all the officers of the regular army is unanimous," such "judgment of their qualifications as fighting men as a class, in the face of an enemy of the prowess of the Texans, is unfair." The result of this general "blackwash" was that the volunteers "were employed in garrisoning posts, or in expeditions against the hostile Apaches and Navajos" (Twitchell 1912:36). This pervasive hostility displayed toward the Nuevomexicanos and the exploitation of their services remained fixed in Chacón's mind while he wrote his memoirs. The result was a narrative recovery of the Civil War period that functions to exonerate his compañeros and himself, even though there was nothing for which they needed to be exonerated.

Chacón's most vivid memories of the Civil War period are less about valorous battle against the Confederates than about recurrent scenes in which Union soldiers and officers were openly racist to him and his compatriots. What we encounter in the "Memorias" is a description of determined soldiering on the part of the Nuevomexicano soldiers and, without having to read through any subtext, Chacón's pointed disclosure of the denigrating treatment to which he and his men were daily subjected. Yet he remains composed, saying what he must, never falling into narrative histrionics, as though to prove that even in old age he can confront the specters of the ethnocentric Anglo soldiers with the studied calm of a young officer. The entire section is marked by pride for the integrity he and his fellow New Mexicans maintained during their service to the Union. The "Mexican" soldiers, whom, he writes, "came with me in all the battles in which I fought and in everything showed valor" (127), are recalled by name in an act of textual specificity that inscribes their names upon history as "a remembrance and a recollection for their posterity" (127). Some eighty-six native Nuevomexicanos with such names as Mateo Arguello, Ramón Chávez, Isidro Durán, Encarnación Lucero, Enríquez López, José León Mora, Francisco Pacheco, Juan Romero, Remigio Sandoval, Antonio Isidoro Velásquez are listed—not very American-sounding names for a U.S. Army company, not names to be trusted. And Chacón knew his compañeros were neither trusted during their service nor respected by American military historiographers who often chose to scapegoat them. In fact, they were roundly blamed for losing the initial Civil War battle in New Mexico at Valverde in February 1862.

In his descriptions of training for their encounter with the Confederates, Chacón makes no mention of any "traditionary fear of the Texans," but he does have much to say about intercultural conflict with the Union regulars that presaged the scapegoating of Nuevomexicano troops. One story concerns a Lieutenant A. P. Damours, assigned to Chacón's company because he was bilingual. Damours was a sadistic racist who, instead of proving helpful, the aged autobiographer remembers, "always mistreated and insulted the Mexicans," "pricked their thighs with his sword," or rammed a "stick to their neck in order to make them straighten up" (131). As company captain, Chacón was charged with maintaining unity and calm among his men, which meant maintaining his own poise. "I, who was very impetuous in my youth, repressed my anger all that I could, in order to see if he would correct his ways." But when Damours continually made derogatory slurs at mess, he no longer held back.

> The next time when he began with his jokes once again at the table, I said, 'Until now I have suffered and allowed you to talk of my people, but from now and henceforth I will not allow you to return to denigrating them in my presence.' He replied that I did not have the right to keep him from speaking. . . . I repeated that in my presence he was not to do it anymore, and that if he would . . . he should know that I would stand behind my word. He was frightened and used arrogant language. Then I seized some loose boards . . . and broke them into two or three pieces. He attempted to draw out his sword but I did not give him time to use it, but I began to hit him with the boards. . . . Then, seeing me infuriated, he fled outside, dragging his sword, and ran over into the middle of a group of officers, and I went after him. . . . I explained everything and they began to laugh. (131)

Episodes of this kind—and there are a good many in this part of the narrative—adopt an accent of comic detachment from experiences that might just as easily have been remembered in bitterness or brooding self-righteousness. Chacón maintains a rhetorical mask that transforms repressed anger into comic dismissal of an old adversary. However, as he continues to detail army exploitation and ill-treatment of Mexican volunteers, his rhetorical ruse cracks now and again. As in his encounter with Damours, there was simply too much to repress. At this point, the narrative assumes a dense documentary, impersonalizing posture that endangers autobiographical coherence. Chacón (not Meketa) includes more and more correspondence—some of his own letters, many official military and judicial letters—which, it appears, he has saved for just such an occasion. Chacón's documents certify the army's failure to pay the men, its failure to reimburse him and other New Mexicans for the horses, feed, and equipment they agreed to front temporarily, and, most painfully, notes the army's general disregard for and hostile treatment of the Nuevomexicano troops.

At a crucial moment in the formation of Chicano autobiography, "self" concentration is disrupted once again by memories of social discomfort and historical misrepresentation. Chacón is forced to rewrite personal history as an argument against common and pervasive denigrations by historians and Anglo-American veterans. In 1906–1912, Chacón was himself a celebrated military figure, a hero, but rather than crow over his valorous deportment in battle, the "Memorias" turns to refuting the issue of the Nuevomexicano's service during the Civil War. At stake is the honor of the Nuevomexicanos involved in the single major Civil War battle fought at Valverde in southern New Mexico.

In brief, after bloody and often confusing skirmishes on February 21, 1862, the Confederate forces prevailed along the Rio Grande in Valverde. Narrating the movements of both armies with great precision, Chacón describes the day of battle from sunrise—"which many of us would not see set" (167)—through a daylong chronology of "flanking attacks," cannon fire, cavalry attacks, the spectacle of "blood, horses, torn and dismembered limbs, and heads separated from their bodies" to "the hour the sun went down [and] the order was given to retreat" (171). Memory is so alive to a significant day some fifty years past that, along with remembering names and ranks of a host of officers, he sketches "from memory two maps" that are copied into the "Memorias" as a cartographic warrant against historical inaccuracy. The Civil War episode concludes with Chacón pointing out that he "had had the honor to exchange the first shots with the enemy Confederates at the beginning of the campaign . . . and the honor to discharge the last shots on the enemy, already fugitives, at the end of the Texas invasion" (185).

Yet in the official report, General Canby wrote that "the battle was fought . . . with no assistance from the militia and but little from the volunteers, who would not obey orders or obeyed them too late to be of any service" (Meketa 1986:164). As Meketa points out, Canby's charges laid the foundation for all the subsequent historiography of the encounter and "fostered a rash of rumors, accusations, and exaggerations which, ever since, have clouded the true picture of that day's events and unjustly dishonored many of the native soldiers" (165). Twenty-five years later, the story, related by one Anglo veteran of the battle, had become aggressively comic.

> Before the insidious advances of the "tortilla" they were invincible; the red hot *chile colorado* had no terrors for them, and against whole batteries of cannistered beans, Caesar was nowhere. But for anything indigestible, as grape, unfermented, they retired with respectful celerity, which the demoralization of a single six-pound shot precipitated a stampede equaled only by a break of terrified buffalo. (181)

By the turn of the century, such old-fart stories were being told at meetings of Civil War veterans throughout the territory, some of which were attended by Chacón, who surely was not laughing at the ethnic jest. In a letter to Sabin in 1911, Chacón once again tries to correct things. "Personally I have always disliked to speak of matters that might be construed into self-praise. . . . But there are times, and this is one of them, when we must speak on behalf of the truth to correct all erroneous impressions given out about the Battle of Valverde. That was a bloody battle, not yet sufficiently understood" (182).

Although he valorizes his own efforts, the memoir does not distinguish Chacón from his fellow Hispanos. To his way of thinking, he was but one of many men defending their country against foreigners as they had done for centuries. Chacón's response to the ethnocentric barrage leveled at the Nuevomexicano volunteers remains strategically soldierly to the end, when he reminds his readers that defense of the homeland was a culturally ingrained reflex.

> Since the Spanish colonization this nation of *Nuevo Mexico* endured an unequal struggle against the savage nations [*naciónes bárberas*] that surrounded it, without any rudiments, without resources, without assistance of any kind from capitals of ruling countries. They have fought and died, always with the faith that it was necessary for them to defend their hearths. Obliged by circumstances always to defend themselves with weapons. (185–186)

More effective than an emotional outburst, his culturally historicizing language countermands the slandering images of "tortillas", "red hot chili," and "cannistered beans," as well as the accusations of cowardice perpetuated by many historians. Chacón's dignified rhetorical position neither denigrates the Anglos along whose side he fought nor lapses into sentimental cultural extremism. His final words on the Civil War period, however, are unsettling, divided by deep regard for his people's topographic identity and his recognition of their unfortunate subordination in a country that exploited the Nuevomexicanos during its wars without seeing "their beautiful qualities." Writing during the years before New Mexico was to become a state (1912), Chacón, like Seguín, Lorenzana, and Vallejo before him, projects an uncertain future for his posterity, a destabilized condition in a country into "whose hands our destiny has fallen."

IV

I gave him my hand, looked directly into his eyes, and he, embarrassed and
ashamed, lowered his head.
                                        —Rafael Chacón, "Memorias"

There is a daguerreotype of Rafael Chacón, seated, sword in
hand, dressed in full military regalia, facing out from the front cover
of Meketa's *Legacy of Honor*. Chacón appears robust, with well-
groomed black hair and trimmed mustaches, and with dark, intense
eyes peering into the camera and beyond. Meketa says that the
photo was probably taken in the summer of 1862 while Chacón—
about twenty-nine years old—was stationed in Santa Fe. This would
have been some four or five months after the invading Confederates
were routed from New Mexico. Chacón had reason for appearing
confident, since, as he writes in the "Memorias," he had performed
the symbolically crucial act of firing the first and last shots at the
"enemy Confederates." In 1912, Read's *Illustrated History of New
Mexico*[22] included a three-page biographical profile of Chacón drawn
primarily from the official military records as well as a wonderful
photograph of him, this time as an old man, the Chacón who was
writing his "Memorias." The photograph was, one imagines, among
those taken of septuagenarian veterans at a Golden Anniversary
celebration of the Civil War battles. The image is startling because
Chacón, once again in full military uniform and cavalry cap, is
standing at attention, with full chest and head erect, gazing intently
into the lens. Only his white mustaches, the white hair showing
below his cap, and the passage of many decades give him away.
Otherwise, his bearing is that of the 1862 daguerreotype.

The photograph of the old soldier circa 1912 shows a man strong
of body for seventy-nine, broad shouldered, direct of gaze, an officer
demanding the dignity and respect "that correspond to my rank."
The "Memorias" composed by the old man pictured in the photograph insists upon the same recognition and respect. However, the
photograph of Chacón as an old soldier raises questions about the
way Chacón was appropriated as a kind of specimen-object of the
Old West by historians. Once again, personal narrative was endangered by the objectification of a life spanning the Mexican period,
the American invasion and subsequent territorial period, and the
admission of Colorado into the Union in 1876 and New Mexico in
1912. Here, after all, was an old man who not only had lived a long,

Rafael Chacón in 1862 as a twenty-nine-year-old U. S. Army Cavalry officer. Photograph originally appeared in *Historia Ilustrada de Nuevo México* (Santa Fe: Campañia Impresora de Nuevo México, 1911).

Rafael Chacón in military dress at a Civil War Veterans Reunion ca. 1911, when Chacón was seventy-eight years old. Photograph originally appeared in *Historia Il- ustrada de Nuevo México* (Santa Fe: Campañia Impresora de Nuevo México, 1911).

eventful life but who had been a major participant in events that shaped the history of the West. Writing the past of the self, writing autobiographically, that is, was mediated by frequent requests for information by historians who were reconstructing the territorial period. The danger was that Chacón's memories, and his "Memorias," put to service by historians, would end up, like the Californio narratives, appropriated for their usefulness to regional history alone, with its individual voice overlooked.[23] Like Vallejo, he was a storehouse of information from whom historians, journalists, and historical society members were eager to elicit eyewitness narrative as well as to collect the many official documents he had saved.[24] But whereas Vallejo delighted in writing himself into the history of California, in fact, argued that the history of California could not be written without the name of Vallejo at its center, Chacón was less interested in situating himself at the center of an expansive territorial history. To be sure, he cooperated with historians by writing numerous letters and providing narratives of his years in the cavalry, but his own "Memorias" reinhabits the geography of the past less to reconstruct an image of himself as a hero in uniform than to recall for himself and his family the heartsickness he felt at being far away from them so often and so long. In fact, rather than celebrating his military service, he focuses upon confinement within a uniform.

Committing himself to paper between 1906 and 1912, Chacón confronted a past that did not square with the story under construction by the "historical societies," which, in my estimation, have always made a business of romanticizing the past. The "Memorias" does not glamorize the U.S. Cavalry the way popular pulp dime novels of the West so often did; on the contrary, his is the story of bone-hard work, constant exposure to danger, material privation, sickness, and, as if that were not enough, daily intercultural conflict. On this front, Chacón's text unsettled the popular image of the mounted cavalry trooper as a tall, blue-eyed soldier who, as it turns out, was not only a "Mexican" but a "Mexican" who usually marched rather than rode. When in the "Memorias" he does reconstitute his service in the military, it is less because he wishes to fashion himself a cavalry hero of the Old West than to dismantle romanticized narrative aggregations of the "Winning of the West" as well as to expose, once again, the ethnocentrism he and other Mexican American troopers were made to endure. While writing, therefore, he often found himself in the startling and embarrassing, certainly the embittering, position of rediscovering the truth of a past that makes the photograph of him as the proud old soldier appear circumspect, given the alienation and grief he actually experienced when he wore the uniform. The necessarily combative stance he assumes in the autobiographical narrative is one that implicitly questions the efficacy of his service in the U.S. military. Memory leads not to a romanticized reconstruction of events or to a nostalgic valorization of the Nuevomexicano's role in the American army but rather to a series of politicized rememberings of the sociocultural stresses a forty-year gap could not occlude.

Chacón autobiographically subverts a contrived image of westward expansion, exposes the ethnocentricisms of the very groups that encouraged his remembering, and seals his experience not with a vain old soldier's romanticized memory of the forty-year past but with a documentable presence in that past—the official correspondence that spoke beyond the present writing of his memoirs and beyond the written memoirs into the present of this and all subsequent readings. Again, an understated but powerful individual and cultural performance of autobiographical resistance was being enacted by a retired American soldier who was encouraged to remember his exploits and who, in remembering, recalled not so much the exploits as the exploitations. Moreover, rather than focus on life in the field, the cavalry section of the "Memorias" is primarily the story of his unceasing efforts to establish solid ground for his wife and children while military assignments were driving him farther and farther from them. The section of the narrative in which Chacón retraces the period between 1862 and 1864 outlines numerous skirmishes with Indian groups, maps his military movements throughout New Mexico and Arizona, comments on the unrelenting poor treatment of the native soldiers, and records his own bouts with debilitating rheumatism along the trail—constantly repeating his desire to finish his service and go home.

After the retreat of the Texas Confederates, the New Mexico volunteers were reorganized into a cavalry unit, and Chacón, awarded a command, continued to serve in the U.S. military. He quickly rose in rank from captain to major and from cavalry officer to commander of Fort Stanton in 1864. In fact, Chacón's service record, from all accounts, was exemplary, so exemplary that when he began to apply for resignation in early 1863, his requests were either ignored or rejected by his commanding officers. His resignation letters and the commentary surrounding them speak to his longing for family and home and his often desperate pleas to be allowed to resign. As Meketa explains, however, "It seemed as though his requests just disappeared into some sort of void at the military headquarters and that the only communications he received were further orders for more dangerous and difficult duty" (267).

As early as October 1, 1863, he addressed a letter to his commanding officer, General Carleton, in which he tendered his resignation, citing, as the major reason, a complete lack of recognition for his services. He reminds the general of his loyalty in the fight against the "Rebellion of the South" as well as against the Indians but complains that his "sacrifices have not been well considered or perhaps even forgotten" (242). Then in a brilliant rhetorical maneuver, he writes, "Observing the coolness, the indifference, the reserve of the Department in view of the undeniable acts achieved by me . . . I have believed it appropriate to tender my resignation in order that I may return to domestic life, so that my vacancy be filled by some other one of more enthusiastic patriotism and valor" (242). There can be no mistaking his anger here. The triple repetition saturates the sentence with the officer's legitimate anger over the blatant failure of the military command to recognize not just another honorable service record but an unimpeachable record of documented bravery. He has sacrificed his wife and children for the good of his adopted country, but his country has not given the slightest notice to either service or sacrifice. Chacón's final rhetorical move in the passage, that of suggesting that he will retire in order to leave a vacancy for someone of more "enthusiastic patriotism and valor," establishes both its own ironic question and answer. The vacancy he leaves cannot be filled.

Nine months later, he addressed another letter of resignation to General Carleton, this time focusing more precisely on his responsibility to his family: "Full of privation in an age when the man struggles to sustain it, my family is entirely abandoned, relying on chance, my wife is sick almost all of the time without anyone to help her and my young children are left to fate without my presence to guide them" (June 25, 1864). Yet even in this letter, before he cites family responsibilities, Chacón indicates that he has been subjected to "the most severe and active part" of numerous military campaigns and, although an officer, has had to "drive back a strong and greedy enemy" with "only a handful of men" (264). Once again, the letter speaks his distinct concerns in a manner that shows Chacón's understanding of how multiple rhetorical moves can be effected in the rather dangerous space of official correspondence. That is to say, his critique of the army's exploitation of him and his men is stated obliquely but clearly and then redirected to familial concern that domesticates the language of his resignation. As in the letter to

Carleton of 1863, lest there be any question of his patriotism, he closes by strategically offering "to sacrifice [his] life in honor of the nation . . . when the circumstance should arise" (265).

Only a month later, on July 21, 1864, Chacón's language is increasingly direct and his reasons for wishing to resign patently clear. As he writes in the "Memorias," he was finally forced to articulate a number of concerns about the persistent problem of anti-Mexican sentiment that he and other native soldiers continually endured. "My patience already almost exhausted, with a determination to take severe steps . . . I had written to the Department in the following words" (281). Chacón would no longer repress his anger and alienation at the horrible state of intercultural relations. What he had hinted at in other correspondence and reports here issues forth in unrestrained utterance.

> I have been left alienated by the same attitudes which always, since I have been in the service, have been in effect among the officers and soldiers of the regular army toward the volunteer officers and soldiers. And this is truly one of the principal reasons why I have put in my resignation many times, and the grief that I felt when it was not accepted stings me every time that I see the demeanor with which they conduct themselves, and I am well satisfied that this goes on toward all of the volunteers in this Department, and for my part I no longer want to leave such offenses in silence. (281)

He goes on to recount a personal affront as newly appointed commanding officer at Fort Stanton by Anglo soldiers who were charged with building furniture and outfitting his quarters. "The carpenters . . . made two or so regular pieces of furniture but, upon the arrival of Lieutenant Cook, the chief commissary, they turned their attention to him. . . . In only one day they outfitted the quarters of that officer with all the necessities for comfort and decency due to his official rank, and I, who have been here for twenty days, am still living without many of the necessities that correspond to my rank" (281).

The inclusion of numerous such letters in the text of the celebrated old soldier's "Memorias" must be read in light of Chacón's understated but powerfully documented undermining of that soldierly past. Imagine what the members of the Early Settler's Association of Southern Colorado—a group established by Anglos—must have thought on reading Chacón's scathing letters and commentary. Here was a (Mexican)American who insisted that in all military action he was guided by a sense of duty, honor, and patriotism and yet who, as a Mexican(American), was disrespected not only by the highest- but the lowest-ranking Anglo "regular" soldiers. Like Seguín before him, he had been duped: he had achieved the rank of captain and then major, even been appointed commandant of an outpost fort, but he was still just a "Mexican" who could not get a couple of low-ranking carpenters to furnish his commandant's quarters. The old autobiographer sifted through forty-year-old documents that might joggle and clarify memory, and what he found must have provoked the same impatience and anger he felt as a young officer of thirty who decided he would not "leave such offenses in silence." The letters must have been faded, the paper brittle, the calligraphy perhaps smudged by time, but the sentiments were still fresh in his memory and thus usable in the text of his "Memorias"—usable as proof that the Nuevomexicano story in the military was not the material of western romance but more like a bad memory.

Of the day his resignation finally went through—September 2, 1864—he writes, "I took off the officer's epaulets, ungirded my sword, with which I had given humble but willing service to my country, and exchanged the blue uniform for the clothing of a civilian. From August 1861 until September 1864, I had passed my time in active campaigns, always earning the confidence of my superiors, and leaving with honor in everything" (303). Yet this moment of self-respecting reflection is unsettled when, in the next paragraph, Chacón remembers that the same Lieutenant Cook who handed him his discharge papers had, less than two months earlier, been one of many Anglo soldiers trying to sabotage his authority, ignoring orders because they were issued in Spanish, "causing discord between the regulars [Anglos] and volunteers [Nuevomexicanos]" and preventing him, as Chacón wrote in the letter of July 21, "from exercising the power that the law and justice extend to me" (282). Moreover, as Chacón implies, he sensed imminent danger. "Until the moment at which I gave up my sword," he remembers, "I made it understood that I was of superior rank and would maintain my authority at all cost" (303).

Even though Chacón narrates a gestured reconciliation with Lieutenant Cook, the micronarrative functions allegorically to suggest how Anglocentric arrogance is disempowered by an unbroken gaze. On the face of it, the scene appears to be a sentimentalized account of intercultural rapprochement between the two men. Yet Chacón is clearly the dominant character in the scene, reminding his readers that the anti-Mexicano military abuses he suffered never disempowered him, never stripped him of his dignity, never threatened his Christian calm, but, on the contrary, brought shame on the perpetrator. "Upon receiving my discharge I gave him my hand, looked directly into his eyes and he, embarrassed and ashamed, lowered his head and squeezed the hand I had extended, and we parted from one another without rancor and without resentment" (303). Chacón's final official encounter with the U.S. Army in the figure of Lieutenant Cook provides him fifty years later with material for a scene in which the New Mexican officer's challenging gaze functions as a mirror of conscience: the Anglo lieutenant is forced to see his own ethnocentrically corrupt visage, and what he sees shames him.

The scene may or may not have been enacted just so in 1864. That is, perhaps Chacón's reading of Cook's averted face may be misremembered, perhaps the "lowered head" and "embarrassed and ashamed" gesturing was an act of disdain, or a show of false sentiment before assuming Chacón's command. We cannot know the event's alternate narrative readings since we have neither a confirming nor a contestatory statement by Cook. Hence, Chacón's version assumes authority by virtue of his politicized composition of an event present only in the old man's memory. Chacón's text of memory becomes a vanquishing ethnic text at the moment two competing cultural characters are written into an autobiographical scene in which the Nuevomexicano author knowingly shames Lieutenant Cook, the Anglo Other, whose own textual space is empty and, since empty, powerless.

V

> Since this trip . . . was in all ways typical of an emigration much like that which might have been made in colonial times by our ancestors, for curiosity's sake I wanted to keep a concise diary of the journey, and from the rough drafts that I made then I take the notes for this part of my memoirs.
> —Rafael Chacón, "Memorias"

Whereas the middle section of the "Memorias" is a record of Chacón's military service and his struggle to return to his home and family, the final section is about his discovery that this home was not a circle of familial and material security to which he could summarily return. Rather, when he did return to Peñasco he found that the "battles to make an honorable living" had exacted a series of economic reversals that made his removal to a new locale and his reconstruction of home necessary. The brief closing pages of the "Memorias" describe his efforts to locate the family in a permanent home and then end with Chacón, the aged patriarch, bequeathing a permanent textual location for the family name, a space in which he could gather the names of family, relatives, and friends in a closing utterance of genealogical identity and cultural tracing.

Although Rafael Chacón lived another thirteen years after completing the "Memorias," the concluding passages of the narrative read like an old man's deathbed words. He pictures himself alone in a room with his wife and compañera, Juanita, hearing the absent voices of those friends who "during the epoch of my prosperity . . . would," he writes, "follow me anywhere, hanging upon my slightest whim or my voice" (332). Alone and no longer prosperous, all he has left is an honorable name and the language with which to purchase permanence within an intimately matrixed familial and cultural text. Keenly conscious of the autobiographical responsibility he assumes in "shaping these last lines," Chacón knows that his narrative constitutes the intersection between his children ("the extension of my hopes and my ambitions") and the "intrepid spirit of their grandparents" (333). Stressing the cultural presence of the colonial "abuelos," or "ancestors," Chacón announces the genealogical tradition he extends to his posterity. "Through their veins runs the blood of gentlemen, of those gentlemen who, with a sword on their belt and with combat spurs, traveled to posts all over the American world" (333). Once again calling attention to the Spanish term for "gentlemen"—"hidalgos"—Chacón reconstructs a line of descent between his children and the Spanish colonial settlers. However much some of us may chafe at such an imperial gesture, for Chacón the articulation of genealogical connection with the colonial ancestors acts as a socially empowering reassertion of cultural continuity in the face of an American hegemony that, as Chacón has repeatedly shown, operated to deracinate Nuevomexicanos.

In the passage I cited as this chapter's epigraph, Chacón's reference to the diary he kept while relocating his family in 1870 resounds with a historically conscious desire to map his family's movement over the same terrain that the Spanish-Mexican colonists—his own "abuelos"—had once traveled, upon which they had settled, and where they had constructed their villages. That Chacón kept a record of the journey, moreover, is remarkable as evidence of his conscientious documenting of what he considered a long tradition of the *crónicas* (chronicles) and *diarios* of colonial settlement in *Nuevo Mexico*. The Chacón family had long been settled in the tight circle of villages surrounding Santa Fe, the city of his birth and early childhood, and now the Chacón relocation to Trinidad affirmed a similar resolve to expand the circle of the homeland. Keeping a journal and then incorporating it into his "Memorias" some thirty-five years later constitutes evidence of a Hispano alive to his place in history, alive to his position within a family and cultural structure of relations, and alive to the power of language as a signatory warrant of culturally matrixed subjectivity.

Chacón's discursive reaffiliation with an older Spanish-Mexican practice, moreover, reveals a tense social relationship with the American territorial regime. The cultural-genealogical impulse contains an implicit critique of an American hegemony that was in the process of erasing such filiations. Keeping a journey diary, a practice that was common during the Spanish colonial period, appears to have declined sharply in the nineteenth century, largely, one may argue, as a result of social displacement. So, Chacón's diary of his own journey to resettle his family represents his desire to situate himself within a discursive tradition of settlement narratives that date to 1598 when Juan de Oñate led a group of colonists to settle *la Nueva Mexico*. Reconstructing a set of relations between his own historical moment (post-1900) and one that preceded him by some three hundred years reestablishes a discourse of cultural continuity that elided the American homesteading period and in so doing imaginatively restored the connection between the emerging twentieth-century Chicano community and its pre-American sources. For Chacón, reaffirming the cultural and familial descent line was requisite to closing the "Memorias."

Just as the military sections of the narrative are motivated by Chacón's topocentric desire, so his narrative of resettlement is permeated with a desire to sustain familial and cultural relations: nearly everyone he greets along the trail is either a blood relative, an in-law, or a *compadre*, a sacramental family friend. Along with his wife and children, two of his brothers-in-law help him make the journey to the "new country," which, although not yet a made home, is already familial. The diary section begins, "On November 9, [1870], a Wednesday, I left Peñasco, Taos County, to settle in Las Animas County, Colorado" (315). A few days later, on November 13, he writes that just when he was "in very reduced circumstances" he happened to meet a "Señor Ortiz . . . who had come to deliver a herd of heifers at El Moreno" and it "turned out that he was a relative of mine, and he supplied me with meat, flour, and other provisions" (318). On November 19, the first houses they come to "were those of our relatives Isidro Medina and Salvador Córdova [who] received us with much friendliness and happiness" (319). And the next day, when they arrive in the "new country," they are welcomed by *familia:* "We were received with tears of joy. Heading the welcome by everyone was my venerable father-in-law, Don Rafael Paez, one of the most noble and generous men that I have ever known" (319).

A particularly poignant voicing of his admiration for his wife, Juanita, and their shared affection and concern for their small children may be seen in another entry. On the morning of November 11, Chacón leaves his family train camped at the mouth of a canyon while he rides into the town of Fernandez for supplies. Away the entire day and late into the night, he returns to camp to find Juanita waiting alone by the light of the fire. The scene gives him pause to consider their bond from a distance.

> When I arrived a moving spectacle presented itself to my eyes, and for a moment I was unable to hold back the tears. Everyone was asleep, except Juanita, my noble spouse. She, who drank with me from the chalice of misfortune, was sad and silent by the fire, awaiting my return, keeping vigil and praying for the tender pieces of our heart that were going with us to test what destiny would hold in a strange country and among strange people.

The "tender pieces of our heart" to whom he lyrically refers are, of course, his "little children, Gumecinda, Antonio, and the baby Eusebio, who was not yet a year old" (316). Juanita had had the misfortune of losing other children at birth, as well as experiencing the severe economic instability that forced the Chacóns to leave northern New Mexico for an uncertain future in southern Colorado. One wonders whether the diary entry for November 11, 1870, actually conveyed such sentiments or whether the old autobiographer transformed the entry into the lyrical meditation on his family we discover in the "Memorias." However interpolated the diary-memoria may be, the passage resonates with Chacón's esteem for Juanita, who has kept vigil during this and other of his absences.

Even though he says that he kept "a concise diary of the journey" it appears that Chacón continued to make diary notations intermittently during the next two years. And although the diary entries are brief and their transformation into the "Memorias" succinct, the daily notations ring with a meaningfully affectionate and celebrative gathering of names. He notes that "on April 20, 1872, Don Felix Cruz and his wife, Doña Feliciana, came to visit us and he helped with the planting until April 26" (321). For April 1873, he remembers planting the fields with only the help of his small children. "Gumecinda, then eleven years old, and Antonio, nine, drove the oxen for me, one on one side and the other on the other side. . . . In that solitude, walking behind the furrow, the work of my children gave a prediction of prosperity on that land, blessed by their angelic presence, their youthful happiness united with the songs of the birds; and those songs and that joy, consecrated like incense with the fragrance of the countryside, had to have been what later brought to my hands a torrent of prosperity" (321). These and each of his eleven children are named at the end of the "Memorias" where he comments on their fates, for most happy but for others tragic. Gumecinda "married Carpio Córdoba, son of Don Juan Córdoba and Doña Quirina Sánchez de Córdoba, residents of Hoehne, Colorado," and Antonio, the other angelic presence of the passage, was "treacherously killed by a cowardly assassin in Tijeras, Colorado, on October 18, 1898" at the age of thirty-eight. Even those who died at or shortly after birth are not only recalled by name but by place of birth. "The eldest, Juliana Basilia, was born in Santa Fe on January 9, 1859 and died the eighteenth of the same month. My fifth child was Máximo, who was born in Peñasco on May 11, 1866, and died three hours after he was born" (332). And his compañera, Juanita, is remembered most prominently in the last paragraph of the "Memorias."

> Upon shaping these last lines, my elderly wife, my noble companion[25] is seated by my side, waiting, in silence, for me to speak to her. Her head and mine are covered with white hair; our home is lonely. . . . Seeing the face of my beloved Juanita, to me she has never become old; to me she is always the youthful slender enchantress of Rio Lucia. She and I have been close together now almost to the end of our mortal life, and with a tranquil conscience we await the eternal departure. (333)

Before departing, however, Chacón, cognizant of the social finality of anonymity, entitles his narrative with the names of relatives and friends, even those of adversaries, which provide the matrix for his own name. Names are marked into a memoir that shall function as a textual marking of people with whom he conducted the business of his life: among those "que fueron amados" (who were beloved) were, for example, "Don Jesús María García, a man of very noble sentiments," "Don Juan Gutierrez, a faithful and good friend of mine," and a host of other men and women whose names are inscribed in an act of filial respect. Their names are inscribed in a narrative history alive to the necessity of protecting the name against the flood of time and political disaster and the distortions of adversaries. Although he is never vituperative, those who discredited the Chacón name are disremembered in an act of narrative retribution. He recalls an incident from 1873 in which a district judge—strategically unnamed but identified as "addicted to liquor and, consequently, with an elastic conscience"—publicly libeled him. Chacón remembers confronting the judge in his hotel room with these words: "I am poor and my only inheritance is my honor. . . . I want to make it known that with this dagger I avenge myself of a tyrannical judge, if necessity obliges me to do so. The thing is public and well known and my pride will also be well known" (324). The "inheritance" Chacón refers to, of course, is his honorable name, a name he has proven many times he is willing to uphold with his life. The judge, who like other "cowards," issues insult only when "wholly supported by a phalanx of power that protects their miserable bodies," recants and pleads that "no mention be made of that episode to a living soul" (324). Chacón keeps the episode secret for over thirty years and then, as he writes, mentions it "now only to leave that very disagreeable moment recorded" (324). Recorded. The power of text to protect the name against the false accusation of those who would damage it. In recording an event long past but not forgotten, an old man writing himself against death ensures that his "inheritance" will be preserved against negative texting of the Chacón name.

This is akin to the Chinese discursive tradition of preserving the descent line, honoring the family name by keeping it "clean and honorable" and then passing the name forward as a container of clean habitation for the next generation. As Stephen Durrant suggests in an essay on Chinese autobiographical writing, the Chinese autobiographer acts as family scribe, or historian, whose narrative presence is important only insofar as it "centers upon the Confucian virtue of filial piety; his future opens up to the expectation that he will 'glorify his name in later generations.'"[26] Such a filial autobiographer discovers meaning not in detaching himself from tradition or culture to assert his uniqueness, as does the Rousseauian autobiographer, but, on the contrary, "could not locate himself, could not even interpret his most intense experience, outside a network of historical relationships and precedents." The genealogical imperative—the bios—subsumes the individuating claim that "auto" demands in Western indentitarian narrative. Inscribing the genealogy of the family is tantamount to inscribing the self, since "the self is a point at which various strands from the past intersect"; hence, the tradition-centered autobiographer "defines his existence not in substance, some inner core of private and personal meaning, but in a series of relationships" (39). Chacón's fixing of his own "existence . . . in a series of relationships" in the last few pages of the "Memorias" draws a genealogical circle of relations around himself. Not only temporally sequential but spatially mapped, the genealogical chronology of the family's presence confers textual certainty within a social terrain undergoing enormous transformation. Indeed, the names and relationships mapped by the old man fix the Chacón name in history at the precise moment that New Mexico passed from territorial status to statehood in 1912, a date that for Nuevomexicanos legislatively closed off the territorial frontier more starkly than Turner did in 1890. By narratively mapping the family's name, Chacón superscribes his own location on that map of the cultural homeland, a homeland that, although undergoing a final geopolitical hardening of boundaries, fixes ontological certainty in the signatory warrant of name(s) situated in distinct cultural space.

The "Memorias" closes with an indefeasible valorization of the Chacón name, not the baptismal name of José Rafael Sotero Chacón, in ego-centered marking, but a familiocentric name, the culturally matrixed name he and Juanita leave to their posterity. Less an autobiographical than a genealogical enunciation, Chacón's last words quite literally constitute a last will and testament. The old man writes, "Upon passing from this scene we do not leave property or great wealth but we do leave for our children a clean and honorable name" (333). Chacón's entire text, one realizes all at once, has been a narrative about the name, a remarkably filial narrative in which the autobiographer functions as family scribe, here an old man prevailing over memory's lapse so as to gather a circle of words around "a clean and honorable name." Chacón: not an egocentric and excluding demarcation but the name as a container of multiple historical experiences, the intersection of many lives, a common tonal ground upon which the family centers itself, an inscription on textual stone that recedes into the Spanish-Mexican colonial past and succeeds beyond the American presence into the future of the Chacón posterity.

6
Lies, Secrets, and Silence
Cultural Autobiography as Resistance in Cleofas Jaramillo's *Romance of a Little Village Girl*

> One professor was writing a book. Would I permit him to use two or three of my stories in his book? I then understood. All they wanted was to read my manuscript and get ideas from it, so I decided to have it published by a small private press here in my city.
>
> —Cleofas Jaramillo, *Romance of a Little Village Girl* (1955)

I

In the 1930s, a diminutive woman residing in Santa Fe, after having, as she writes, "caught the fever from our famous 'cinco pintores' and author Mary Austin," began recording her culture and her life. She first published *Cuentos del Hogar* (1939), a collection of twenty-five tales her mother had related when she was a child, tales that her own daughter encouraged her to preserve. She then compiled a cookbook called *The Genuine New Mexico Tasty Recipes/Potajes Sabrosos* (1939).[1] Some fifteen years later, she remembered this period, the difficulty she had in forcing language onto the page, especially a language in which she did not feel comfortable, and the distinct sense she had that people from outside of the culture were literally trying to steal her writing. As the epigraph above suggests, she understood that cultural outsiders were little interested in granting her authorship, but they were eager to base their own work on the authority of her rich cultural knowledge. "All they wanted was to read my manuscript and get ideas from it," she recalls, "so I decided to have it published by a small private press here in my city" (1955:168). What Jaramillo means, of course, is that rather than give up her knowledge and voice to a cultural stranger, she paid a printer to have the manuscript published with the authority of her own signature. Encouraged by the success of her first two folkloristic chapbooks, she completed another, the nearly pirated *Shadows of the Past/*

Sombras del Pasado (1941), a book in which she labored to "preserve some of the folklore of New Mexico,"² providing an insider's account of religiocultural practices of northern New Mexico. *Shadows of the Past*, however, is a folkloristic narrative that opens toward autobiographical articulation when she situates herself and her family within a set of cultural practices that define personal subjectivity. The autobiographical space opened by *Shadows of the Past* is filled by *Romance of a Little Village Girl*, a sustained personal narrative, published a year before she died, in which she expansively remembers herself as a girl steeped in traditional culture during the last quarter of the nineteenth century and as a woman writing that culture in the first half of the twentieth century.

Cleofas Martínez Jaramillo was this woman who by the late 1940s was being visited by people "from all over our states," who, having read her books, were "doing research" for which they requested her help. Always happy to share her knowledge of "our folk customs," Jaramillo welcomed visitors into her home, consented to interviews with scholars and journalists, contributed short articles on her family's cultural history, and with the expressed "aim of preserving our language, customs and traditions" (1955:176) organized a Spanish-language folklore group in 1935, *La Sociedad Folklórica*, which participated in the swirl of folkloristic and historical preservation activities sweeping New Mexico from the 1920s through the 1940s.

The autochthonous imperative underlying her folkloristic activities and her two cultural autobiographies will here be reconsidered as a discursive activity that was scripted for her by what she more than once refers to as the "newcomers," yet reappropriated by her when it became evident that her cultural knowledge was being plundered. Given her simultaneous sense of ethnographic responsibility to the community from which she sprang and her autobiographical desire to inscribe her own experience, *Shadows of the Past* and *Romance of a Little Village Girl* collapse the lines between ethnography and autobiography. Jaramillo's own explanation of this unavoidable imbrication is voiced in "Memorias," a chapter in *Shadows of the Past:* "The memory of my grandfather and grandmother and many of my aunts is also the memory of old-time customs and ways of living." As we have seen with Rafael Chacón, memory recovers personal experience within a matrix of family and cultural practice. However, unlike Chacón, who by 1906 seems cynical about the efficacy of preserving the fragments of the culture's oral poetics—the *romances*, for example, "have been forgotten or have

been corrupted until they now [circa 1900] remain completely distorted"—Jaramillo assumes responsibility for writing her culture.
For Jaramillo, actively recovering and recording the old-time customs and linguistic practices had a distinct and necessary sociohistorical purpose: she translated and published *Cuentos del Hogar* at
her own expense because they "would soon be lost if someone did
not put them down in writing" (1955: 167); if she "accomplished at
least one thing" in *Shadows of the Past*, she "preserved in writing
our rapidly vanishing New Mexico Spanish folk customs" (168); and
she organized the *Sociedad Folklórica* "in the hope that it will carry
on the work of preserving the Spanish language and customs after I
am gone" (1941: Introduction). Conscious of herself as an interme-
diary between traditional culture and "modern Anglo customs," Jaramillo put herself to work constructing an edifice that would simultaneously mark her own presence in the world as it marked the
presence of a people whose cultural practices were ostensibly vanishing. To reconstruct the cultural legacy was for Jaramillo to reas-
sert those cultural filiations produced over time in a distinct locale
that constituted her own subjectivity. "My pioneer forefathers," she
writes in *Shadows of the Past*, "searching through rugged mountains and hills . . . found the beautiful hidden little valley of the Rio
Hondo, in northern New Mexico. In this isolated nook . . . my ancestors built strong walled houses, and here they left a most interesting folklore, the history of which fills the pages of this book, dating back to my grandmother's time, as far as I can remember"
(Introduction). Like Chacón, again, permanence is fixed within the
lineage of family and culture as it recedes into the past of the colonial ancestors.

But there is a problem: Jaramillo's reconstruction of such filiations takes place at a time and in a place—Santa Fe in the 1930s—
when the reconstruction of the history and culture and lore of the
Southwest was being enacted by nonnative fabulists whose vision
of the land and its people produced a just-so story of the Southwest,
steeped in romance and fantasy that glossed over strained intercultural relations because it occluded the social history of the region.
Writing to preserve her culture during this period, Jaramillo's work
discloses the stresses and contradictions of articulating resistance in
a language, idiom, and sociodiscursive configuration determined by
the cultural Other. Jaramillo's work—as well as that of other Mexican American writers, amateur folklorists, and historians working
during this period—was not only encouraged but, as we shall see,

directed by the very Anglo presence she fears has disrupted the "old-time customs." On the one hand, her work resisted the "rapid adoption of the modern Anglo customs by the new generation" which eroded cultural practice; on the other, since one of these "Anglo customs" was the fetishizing of Mexican American and Native American people, she unwittingly participated with them in constructing a version of culture that dehistoricized social relations, substituting a romanticized culture.

Both *Shadows of the Past* and *Romance of a Little Village Girl*, therefore, raise questions about the politics of cultural and self-representation: both are texts in which the "I" and the cultural community constantly identify and valorize each other in an articulation of resistance to social erasure; yet the ideological configuration of Jaramillo's historical and cultural tropes can be squarely situated within a discourse produced by Anglos which had the purpose of containing resistance by deflecting attention from social and material issues with a theater of southwestern romance. The cultural self-representation Jaramillo produces accommodates itself to social displacement by fashioning an acceptable, or nonthreatening, cultural physiognomy. Such sociodiscursive divisions in cultural representation complicate and undermine autobiographical representation as well. Jaramillo's self-fashioning as a privileged figure within a valorizing cultural text has the effect of decentering and contradicting her own experience. That is, while the ethnographic component of her narrative enterprise tends toward romanticized, often idyllic description of herself within a kind of cultural time machine, the autobiographical component discloses an increasingly anguished personal history. This is especially the case with *Romance of a Little Village Girl* in which memory of day-to-day and year-by-year complications in the personal life contends for space with a sentimental narrative of ethnohistorical events. Although she opens by saying that she intends to expand on the ethnographic function of *Shadows of the Past*—"Some of the material in my first book I have used in this work, . . . a sequel to my first book"—*Romance of a Little Village Girl* turns toward intimate and often painful self-disclosure. It recombines those chapters of *Shadows of the Past* that, for example, explain prescribed cultural practices and festivities: in both books, there are chapters entitled "The Indian Feast of San Geronimo"; "The Penitente Brotherhood" and "Holy Week in Arroyo Hondo," chapters in *Shadows of the Past*, are recirculated as "Penitente Ceremonies of Holy Week" in *Romance of a Little Village Girl.* Yet the latter also opens to a personal terrain that cannot pretend to the kind of harmonious experience—cultural, economic, or familial—one discovers in the former.

There are autobiographically stunning moments in *Romance of a Little Village Girl* where Jaramillo discloses a darkness of spirit that contradicts the willfully naive romance of the title. When her husband, Venceslao, dies of cancer in his thirties, she remembers the very moment "the cord of his life broke" (128), her "crushing grief" (128), and her feeling, disclosed some thirty years later, that with his death "the happiest epoch of my life had ended" (130). Yet she also remembers the "muddle" in which she found his estate, her long and difficult struggle to save their sheep ranch, their farm, and their homes—all while raising her small child, Angelina, alone. Her efforts to stave off bankruptcy, however, were to no avail. "My last thread of hope in saving a home for my daughter broke, after nine years of hard work trying to save something" (137). Following the rupture in what was once a historical and culturally sustained lineage, she is reduced to living in a small apartment in Santa Fe. Yet she provides an atmosphere in which Angelina is encouraged to excel in school, theater, and dance—only to experience a parent's deepest loss when an intruder breaks into their apartment late one Sunday night in 1931 and rapes and murders the seventeen-year-old girl.

Jaramillo's moving account of her daughter's murder, the grief and emptiness she felt thereafter, and her attempt to fill the gap of loneliness by participating in the cultural preservation activities in Santa Fe during the 1930s is an autobiographically astonishing moment buttressed against narrative that has been mostly appropriated by that very swirl of cultural romance about the Spanish Southwest being constructed at the time of Angelina's murder. The result is that a folkloristics of memory, encouraged by people from outside the culture and region, contends for control of the narrative over and against the kind of autobiographical intimacy and urgency one reads in those chapters that describe Jaramillo's grief and confusion over the death of Angelina, her mother, her husband, and two other children who died during infancy. *Romance of a Little Village Girl,* therefore, stands as an example of a narrative divided between Jaramillo's self-assumed responsibility for writing her culture and a desire for writing her life.

At stake in our reading of Jaramillo's autobiography is not only determining the ownership of a text but marking off the ways in which such ownership constructs the "I" in both its cultural and personal configuration. That is to say, *Romance of a Little Village Girl* reads as both a romance about culture and, where the personal life is privileged, a painful account of Jaramillo's devastating loss of her family and her socioeconomic status. Understandably, such narrative tends to be conflicted, contradictory, split between duty to an ethnographics of "rapidly vanishing" cultural practices articulated in a little village girl's voice, and a personal narrative in which Jaramillo's anguish, spiritual doubt, social anger, and reaffirmation of life and purpose in social activity after Angelina's death is articulated in an autobiographically mature voice. Reading *Romance of a Little Village Girl*, therefore, is like reading two books about two different people: one, a story about a woman whose life has been injured by personal tragedy and social displacement; the other, a masquerade produced by the "stranger" in which a woman, costumed in Spanish lace mantilla, is made to play the role of a pure descendant of the Spanish *conquistadores*. It is this latter book about which I will have most to say in this chapter.

II

> The first white speck on the
> Western sea was made by a Spanish
> sail
> And the first lonely grave on the
> plains,
> Was dug by a Spanish trail.

Romance of a Little Village Girl opens with a wistful epigraph to an imperial Spanish presence in the New World from which Jaramillo plots her cultural identity. The cultural "I" is produced by the representation of a glimmering sixteenth-century Spanish colonial enterprise in the "first white speck on the Western sea" and the first mark of colonial habitation in a grave "dug by a Spanish trail." Here is what in New Mexico had by the 1920s become the fabulous story of sixteenth-century Spain brought uncontaminated to the verdant little valley where she was born some three centuries later. Her people's historical configuration and Jaramillo's own evolution through time and space collapse into a string of historical *non sequiturs* celebrating the "romance and adventure [that] have always ridden hand in hand with the Spanish race."

> Intrepid Cortez [1520], Coronado [1540] and Oñate [1598] and brave De Vargas [1692] and many other explorers and colonizers

followed after him ['wise Columbus'], with the same urge. They brought with them colonists and missionary priests. Toiling and suffering under untold hardships, they penetrated through mountain passes, across vast prairies, conquering savage Indian tribes and establishing settlements in the wilderness. Developing farms, they raised scant crops for their maintenance. The missionaries built churches appalling in their construction. They helped carry the faith and culture of old Spain into these remote worlds. Hardships only meant exciting adventure: they did not discourage the Spaniards' desire to discover and conquer. (2)

Within a few paragraphs, Jaramillo has narratively transported herself from the "first white speck on the Western sea" to sometime in the nineteenth century when her family (the Martinezes and the Luceros), having traversed the centuries in an unspoiled genetic and cultural line from De Vargas, situate themselves in northern New Mexico. Such history spares itself the complexities of sociohistorical process, geographic exigency, profound Native American influences, not to mention intermarriage with many "savage Indian tribes," and sociocultural evolution consequent to the long migrations into the far northern provinces of colonial Spain. History is reified out of a desire for a story of Spanish adventure, conquest, settlement, isolation; especially isolation and, its adjunct, genealogical "purity"—uncontaminated sixteenth-century Spain reproducing itself ever purely in an insulated corner of the world. Where Spanish colonial history is concerned, here or anywhere else in the narrative, one discovers little more than just such fantasy, a wish-fulfillment narrative that sets history into relation with a cultural unity Jaramillo believes underlies the "melting ruins" of traditional Nuevomexicano life.

This romance of the Southwest, installed by American intellectuals, writers and artists, and tourists who traveled to New Mexico at the turn of the century, deeply inscribed itself upon the popular and political consciousness, providing a master narrative that strategically concealed deforcement by superordinating a heroic Spanish colonial past that would salve a colonized people's psychological wounds, even while they continued to surrender their land and social status. Along with this master narrative came an entire structure of troubling assumptions about native culture, history, language, and the cultural subject. When Nuevomexicanos were authorized to compose their lives for public view it was not usually as

Mexican Americans but as representatives of a timeless yet always vanishing culture, a species of quaint and colorful primitive, a cultural reliquary of the Spanish colonial period.

Should a Nuevomexicana wish to write during the first half of the twentieth century, she would be coerced (perhaps not verbally or otherwise directly coerced) into composing a text—ethnographic, fictive, or autobiographical—determined by the overwhelmingly nonnative discursive terrain that tightly controlled the grid of articulation. Jaramillo's writing, as we shall see, was subject to the force of a discursive grid that mythified (read: dehistoricized) the Southwest. Nina Otero de Warren was another native whose folkloristic reminiscence, *Old Spain in Our Southwest* (1936), slotted itself comfortably, title and nostalgic contents, into a shelf of New Mexican sentimental *Spanish* exotica. There were others—Cecil Romero, Aurora Lucero White-Lea, Fabiola Cabeza de Baca—whose narratives were arrogated, whose voices blended into this mass romanticizing project, whose texts were, in their ideological structures, prescripted by outsiders. When in the act of remembering they confront the unpleasant reminders of their own conquest and subordination, they often retreat into whispers of discomfort, confused historiography, muted social criticism, or silence.

For example, while describing the deforcement of her family ranch in *We Fed Them Cactus*, Cabeza de Baca offers pointed social commentary on the subject of land grant fraud in New Mexico and then abruptly silences herself.

> When General Kearny talked to the citizens of Las Vegas on August 15, 1846, he promised protection for the New Mexicans and their property. . . . He also promised that the Spanish and Mexican land grants would be respected. But New Mexico, isolated for so many centuries, did not have enough lawyers to plead the cause for its own people. The owners of the grants and other lands were unable to pay for the surveying and gradually most of the land became public domain. Unaccustomed to technicalities, the native New Mexicans later lost even their homesteads because of ignorance of the homestead laws, but all this belongs to a subject too vast to discuss in this history of the Llano. (176)

One the one hand, then, Cabeza de Baca is precise on the date and content of Kearny's statement; on the other, she lapses into the historically facile tale of New Mexico's long centuries of isolation. And given the topic of the chapter, the loss of her father's land to swarms of homesteaders, it should be clear that at the center of the "history of the Llano" is the subject of legal fraud that she dismisses as inappropriate to her narrative.

Much New Mexican discourse of this period reads like Cabeza de Baca's diffident, abruptly self-censoring, sentimental narrative. One cannot but agree with Raymund Paredes who contends that there is "something profoundly disturbing about this body of work [Mexican American literature in English that emerged from New Mexico during the 1930s]. It seems a literature created out of fear and intimidation, a defensive response to racial prejudice, particularly the Anglo distaste for miscegenation."[3] Paredes's concern is legitimate. It is difficult to read a literature that "described a culture seemingly locked in time and barricaded against outside forces . . . confronting the harsh environment with a religiosity and resolve reminiscent of the conquistadors themselves" (Paredes 1982 : 56) without feeling an aversion for the historical amnesia and self-deluding class pretensions displayed by many of these native writers. What feminist critics like Rebolledo have taught us, however, is that given the "overwhelming dominance of Anglo culture and language and . . . patriarchal norms" under which they lived, added to the fact that "most women had no education and even those who did had little leisure to write, . . . it is a wonder they wrote at all."[4] Moreover, Rebolledo has gone on to argue that these women were generally conscious of the oppositional function of their work, even as they were romanticizing the past.[5] Before derogating these writers to the political rubbish heap to which we have often consigned our acquiescent, ideologically imprisoned *antepasados*, what I wish to consider more closely are the socioliterary exertions that account for the construction of a cultural identity stabilized by a unifying metaphor of the "uncontaminated Spanish past" and, where such an imagined past, a present absolved of its social reality. Paredes's unsparing reading of this "defensive" literature opens space for a critically reaccentuated reading if it encourages us to consider the forces at work in shaping such "defensive" strategies. As profoundly disturbing as this literature may be, therefore, we must not dismiss it before engaging in a more thorough analysis of the ideological and discursive exertions at work in its formation.

Consider, once again, the case of Cabeza de Baca. When we situate *We Fed Them Cactus* within the context of the wider Anglo discourse, as well as within Cabeza de Baca's own folklore preservation activities at the time of its composition, we must alter our reading of its "disturbing" contents. Cabeza de Baca was a prominent member of the New Mexico Folklore Society during the 1950s: she was elected second vice-president in 1952, first vice-president in 1954, and state president in 1955, the year after her book appeared. In the 1955 issue of the *New Mexico Folklore Record,* there is notice of a reception in her honor. Cabeza de Baca is referred to not by the name she signed on the book but by the married name to which she refers neither on the cover nor within its pages.

> On January 29, 1955, the Santa Fe Group of the New Mexico Folklore Society, led by Ina Sizer Cassidy, gave a *merienda* and autograph party in honor of our State President, Fabiola Cabeza de Baca Gilbert, whose book, *We Fed Them Cactus* was published by the University of New Mexico Press. The social occasion was held from 3:30 to 5:30, at the home of Mrs. John A. Lowe. At four o'clock, Mrs. Gilbert gave a short resumé of her book and related some of her memories from her childhood on a New Mexico hacienda.[6]

After reading the review of "Mrs. Gilbert's" book, together with the *NMFR* editorial notes, the list of contributors—most of whom were nonnatives (Cassidy, E. W. Baughman, T. M. Pearce, Julia Keleher, Mary Wheelwright)—and the contents of the issue (a compilation of folktales and ballads, Indian myths, ghost town stories, and local outlaw legends), it becomes increasingly apparent that the society was in the business of producing the lore of the Southwest, sans unpleasant political complications. So, the company in and for which Cabeza de Baca's narrative was written may be said to mediate her memoirs, laying a romanticizing folkloristic discourse upon it through which its own voice is split between discomfort and accommodation, chagrin and sentimentality. No need for historical or political tendentiousness when one could be quaint. *We Fed Them Cactus,* however, does here and again disclose fissures of disquietude opening to critique that we must consider more closely. As Rebolledo points out, "Cabeza de Baca describes what is left of a vanishing people as she traces the arrival of the American homesteaders who plow and ruin the land and the loss of land grants. Bitterness over lost land and nostalgia over lost culture are implicit in her description of a barren wasteland in what once had been paradise" (1987:101). Even her abrupt self-silencing may be read as strategic: what she says about land fraud voices an issue that the narrative form does not sanction, nor that its intended audience wishes to hear, but like someone muttering under her breath, gets said just enough to raise an eyebrow.

Even those studies from the same period that otherwise astutely analyze the material consequences of land deforcement and economic retrogression after the American takeover contain puzzling contradictions. George I. Sánchez's classic *Forgotten People: A Study of New Mexicans* (1940) offers a critique of American economic, political, and social policies that effected the dispossession and impoverishment of Nuevomexicanos; yet it surrenders at significant junctures to reductive ethnohistoricism, social ambivalence, and ideological contradiction. The narrative is generally characterized by a judicious voice that, in deflating the "pomp and splendor" that "cloak the Spanish colonial endeavor" (1940:3), exposes the political and economic policies that systematically dispossessed New Mexicans. However, Sánchez's reasoned social critique ends up repeatedly qualifying itself in ways that are conspicuously at cross purposes. It is not unusual to find Sánchez, in one paragraph, commenting on the Nuevomexicanos' rugged struggle and cultural synthesis ("The colony gave birth to a new people, people whose mode of life tempered their Spanish heritage and caused them to create social and economic patterns that fitted their environment" [13]) and, in a following paragraph, bemoaning the damaging effects of cultural isolation ("Their struggle is, in reality, not one against material factors. They battle their own cultural inadequacy. They are unprepared to act in their new environment—unprepared because of centuries of isolation. They have no tradition of competition, of education, or of Western civilization beyond the sixteenth century" [13]). And throughout the study, Sánchez's vigorous opposition to the socioeconomic consequences of the American "march of imperialism" ends up, as on the last page, recontained by assimilationist rhetoric: "The ultimate goal that underlies the thesis of the study is the proper incorporation of the New Mexican into the American fold. That incorporation requires that the New Mexican be fitted to make his contributions to the American civilization" (ibid., 197). Consequently, the ideological configuration of Sánchez's narrative, notwithstanding its progressive intention, reveals numerous contradictions effected by the "power of constraint" at work in discursive practice, as well as the hegemonic exertions of the dominant culture toward consensus. Sánchez criticizes the cultural deracination of his people and yet acts as an agent in the process:

> Almost a hundred years after becoming American citizens, a broad gap still separates them from the culture which surrounds them. In lieu of adequate instruction, they have clung to their language, their customs, their agricultural practices. Though no fault can be found with a society because it seeks to perpetuate worthy elements of its culture, it is to be regretted that, in this instance, the process has not been accompanied by suitable adaptations. (Ibid., 28)

Such marks of contradictory consciousness are all too common in this and other narratives of the period—whether sociological, ethnographic, or autobiographical. Nuevomexicanos celebrate their customs and yet blame themselves for failing to adapt to the dictates of the dominant culture. Historical memory evokes articulations of resistance and within the same breath gestures of retraction. Those writers to whom I refer—Cleofas Jaramillo, Nina Otero de Warren, Fabiola Cabeza de Baca, and George I. Sánchez—voice their resentment, at moments their anger, and then, as though surprised by the harsh sound of their own words, placate their audience, reconceal resentment to keep speaking.

What I wish to propose, therefore, is a contextually reaccentuated reading of Jaramillo's culturally romanticizing autobiographical narrative, a reading that restores the discursive grid in which a subordinate text appears and in so doing discovers the sociodiscursive forces that conspire for control of the text, encouraging its cultural romanticizing and historical concealment, muting it where it raises troublesome questions, and eliding unpleasant socioideological issues. The proliferation of nonnative, Anglo-American cultural discourse in New Mexico between 1900 and 1940 led to what Michel Foucault identifies as "systems of exclusion for the control and delimitation of discourse" that, in effect, exercise a "power of constraint upon other forms of discourse."[7] This "system of exclusion," I contend, was so powerful that the literary activity of an entire generation of Nuevomexicanos was at once selected, organized, and controlled by a powerful nonnative discursive network that divided their ability to see straight to the heart of their own historical and material condition, or, to the extent that they did, muted their capacity to speak without fear of nullification or erasure.

III

> Life is the least vital feature of New Mexico. The present is a husk—the past
> was a romance and a glory.
> > —Charles F. Lummis, *The Land of Poco Tiempo*

There are other texts with which one might begin tracing this discursive formation—Josiah Gregg's *Commerce of the Prairies* (1844),
Lewis H. Garrard's *Wah-to-Yah and the Taos Trail* (1850), and
W. W. H. Davis's *El Gringo, or New Mexico and Her People*
(1854)—but Charles F. Lummis's famous *The Land of Poco Tiempo*[8]
is the generative text in which New Mexico was reconstructed as a
"picturesque" social utopia. Lummis, who had written rather extensively on his southwestern travels[9] for *Harper's Weekly, Century,*
and *Survey Graphic* and had published a book of short stories along
with a travel book based on his experience in New Mexico[10] put
himself at the center of what he determined would be a widely influential enterprise for promoting and preserving the "romance" underlying the history, culture, and lore of the entire West. As Lawrence Clark Powell writes, Lummis threw himself into the task of
re-presenting a region that remained a dark spot in the American
mind: "Although there have been more polished writers on the
Southwest than Lummis, none has equalled his genius for seeing,
understanding, and popularizing the region. It was he who first
called it 'The Southwest.'"[11] Because it was so immediately and
widely popular, *The Land of Poco Tiempo* turned out to be just the
authorizing statement he needed to press ahead with his "common
weal" project of reconstituting a Southwest romance.

Focusing at length on the landscape as well as on the physiognomy and cultural practices of the native people, Lummis's book
was a combination of topographic description, sentimental and sen-
sationalistic ethnography, impressionistic and rather reductive history of the region, and a folkloristic receptacle for "the folk-songs of
the Spanish and Indian Southwest" (Lummis [1893] 1973:165). Opening with what Powell says "is often quoted as the motto of the Land
of Enchantment" (49)—a motto the native people of the state have
never gotten over—Lummis authorized and instituted a language
that has reverberated in other travel narratives, magazine articles,
scholarly studies, poetry, novels, and theater of the region down to
the present.

> Sun, silence, and adobe—that is New Mexico in three words.
> Here is the land of *poco tiempo*—the home of "Pretty Soon."

Why hurry with the hurrying world? The "Pretty Soon" of New Spain is better than the "Now! Now!" of the haggard States. The opiate sun soothes to rest, the adobe is made to lean against, the hush of day-long noon would not be broken. Let us not hasten—*mañana* will do. Better still, *pasado mañana*. . . .

"Picturesque" is a tame word for it. It is a picture, a romance, a dream, all in one. It is our one corner that is the sun's very own. Here he has had his way, and no discrepancy mars his work. It is a land of quaint, swart faces, of Oriental dress and unspelled speech; a land where distance is lost, and the eye is a liar; a land of ineffable lights and sudden shadows; of polytheism and superstition, where the rattlesnake is a demigod, and the cigarette a means of grace, and where Christians mangle and crucify themselves—the heart of Africa beating against the ribs of the Rockies. ([1893] 1973:1)

The influence of Lummis's theatrical anacoenosis in describing cultural practice was extraordinarily wide, the breathless hyperbole and the generally ethnocentric ideological content of the text circulated and recirculated in scores of books, articles, and studies of the Southwest. As Paul Walter comments in the foreword to the fourth edition of the text, "'The Land of Poco Tiempo,' when it first appeared . . . aroused the interest not only of the traveling public, but also writers, painters, scientists, to whom the volume disclosed an inexhaustible vein of subjects of pen, brush, and research" (1952:xi). During the 1890s, Lummis edited the *Land of Sunshine*, a travel magazine of the West, into which he "poured riches on the Southwest—articles and photographs by himself and others, documents and translations—at the same time that he encouraged new writers and artists such as Mary Austin, Sharlot Hall, Eugene Manlove Rhodes, Ed Borein, and Maynard Dixon. Nearly all [of whom] remained devoted to the patron."[12] Lummis, "a wiry bundle of energy, intellect, learning and zest, and above all, a compulsion to communicate and educate" (Powell 1974:44), placed himself at the center of this circle and was enormously influential in directing these and numerous other novelists, poets, ethnographers, historians, and artists to move to New Mexico where, once settled, they participated in the "preservation" of Indian and Mexican cultural practices.[13] The textual production of this intellectual emigration dating from 1900 to 1940, to choose an important discursive enclosure, consisted of scores of novels, volumes of poetry, plays, literary magazines, not to mention professional and amateur ethnographic narratives that, as the WPA Writer's Project publication, *New Mex-*

ico: A Guide to the Colorful State, pointed out, "began to appear, first slowly and then with an accelerated pace, until their number now [1940] is almost bewildering" (1940:134). A short list of some of the books published during the 1920s and 1930s, by their very titles, suggests the formation of a certain discursive concentration on landscape and the exoticism of native New Mexican cultures: Spud Johnson's *Red Earth* (1920) and *Yellow* (1935); Harvey Fergusson's *Blood of the Conquerors* (1921) and *Wolf Song* (1927); Willa Cather's *Death Comes for the Archbishop* (1927); Mary Austin's *An American Rhythm* (1923), *The Land of Journey's Ending* (1924), *Starry Adventure* (1931), and *One Smoke Stories* (1934); Paul Horgan's *The Royal City of the Holy Faith* (1936); Raymond Otis's *Miguel of the Bright Mountain* (1936) and *The Little Valley* (1937); Oliver La Farge's *Laughing Boy: A Navajo Romance* (1929); Leo Crane's *Desert Drums* (1928); Erna Fergusson's *Dancing Gods* (1931); Frank G. Applegate's *Native Tales of New Mexico* (1930); J. Frank Dobie's *Coronado's Children* (1930); and Peggy Pond Church's *The Burro of Angelitos* (1937).

However much they may have considered themselves intellectually and socially progressive, these artists and intellectuals who retreated to the Southwest to escape the dehumanizing effects of an alienating industrial and urban society on the East Coast often participated in the dehumanization of their subjects, or better put, their objects—Mexicans and Native Americans. Although they believed that their work constituted a gesture of intercultural rapprochement which would reverse a welter of negative representations that had accrued in the literary discourse of the nineteenth century,[14] their own representations essentialized native people, at every turn sedimenting their cultural practices in a kind of deanthropomorphization—D. H. Lawrence's "pine tree" Apaches and Cather's Acoma "crustaceans in their armour."[15] Instead of relating to people as social subjects, the "newcomers" mystified and occulted native cultural practices, as in Lummis's sensational account of the Penitentes,[16] and reified their social history, as one sees in scores of newspapers, magazines, and books that celebrated the legendary Spanish conquistadores.

And, of course, there was D. H. Lawrence who Mabel Dodge-Luhan had lured to her desert mountain home in 1922 to interpret "the true, primordial, undiscovered America that was preserved, living, in the Indian bloodstream."[17] Lawrence never wrote the "magnificent creation" Dodge-Luhan had hoped for; rather, he left a scattering of predictably insistent Lawrentian essays, a parcel of very bad poems, even a fragment of a drama—a kitchen piece set in Taos. In his first essay on New Mexico, "Indians and an Englishman" (1922), Indians are imagined as the veil between the preanimal life impulse and life itself. They are figured as a mysterious indecipherable, a "strange" linguistic space between preconsciousness and rational cognition, witnessed in awe by Western man in the person of Lawrence. Here is a description of an Apache tribal ceremonial: "Strange dark faces with wide, shouting mouths and rows of small, close-set teeth, and strange lines on the faces, part ecstasy, part mockery, part humorous, part devilish, and the strange calling, summoning sound in a wild song-shout. . . . The strange yell, song, shout rising so lonely in the dusk, as if pine trees could suddenly, shaggily sing. Almost a pre-animal sound."[18] Such audacious nullification of Native American consciousness was actually intended to valorize the Indian, who in Lawrence's estimation possessed the primal life force from which Western consciousness had been severed. In another essay on Taos, Lawrence's search for nodes of primal power is elaborated thus: "Places can lose their living nodality. Rome, to me, has lost hers. In Venice one feels the magic of the glamorous old node that once united East and West, but it is the beauty of an afterlife. Taos pueblo still retains its old nodality, . . . the old nodality of the pueblo still holding, like a dark ganglion spinning invisible threads of consciousness."[19] Perhaps because they were examples of Western devolution rather than his privileged figures of the "pre-animal" life force, Lawrence had little to say about Mexicans, except, of course, that "Mexicans insist on being Mexicans, squeezing the last black drop of macabre joy out of life."[20]

Lummis, however, had a good deal to say about Mexican social and cultural practices in The Land of Poco Tiempo. Once again, his remarks were intended to valorize a people who had been the objects of derision and willful ignorance. In The Spanish Pioneers, a romanticized history of the Spanish conquest, he argued against ethnocentric slurs to which the Mexican had long been subjected but did so simply by skipping backward over the social history of the moment: "In this country of free and brave men, race-prejudice, the most ignorant of all human ignorances, must die out. We must respect manhood more than nationality, and admire it for its own sake wherever found. We love manhood; and the Spanish pioneering of the Americas was the largest and longest and most marvelous feat of manhood in all history."[21] Lummis's phallic paean to the fifteenth-century Spanish conquistador was strangely refigured in The Land of Poco Tiempo. "The Mexican is popularly listed—thanks to the safely remote pens of those who know him from a car window, and who would run from his gray wrath—as cowardly and treacherous. He is neither. The sixth generation is too soon to turn coward the blood which made the noblest record of lonely heroism that time ever read" (14). That heroism had, unfortunately, turned inward on itself, so much so that Lummis—and nearly every other observer—described Nuevomexicanos as a people who, over a period of three hundred years, had been isolated from social and cultural events, had drifted inward, wrapped themselves in a kind of geocultural cocoon in which they were still sleeping when Lummis and other Americans discovered them at the end of the nineteenth century: "The most unsleeping vigilance wrested this bare, brown land to the world; and having wrested it, went to sleep. . . . It never has wakened—one does not know that it ever can" (2). New Mexico's comatose "Mexicans" were further characterized by Lummis as the "inbred and isolation-shrunken descendants of the Castilian world-finders" (3). *The Land of Poco Tiempo*, contrary to its announced reestimation of the Southwest, simply reinforced a representation of cultural isolation, loneliness, inwardness that figured the Mexican's culturally distinct organization of everyday life as an experience outside of time, as revery, daydream, a kind of utopian elsewhere that Americans simultaneously desired and abhorred. The American work ethic was nowhere to be found among those "inbred and isolation-shrunken" *paisanos* who fed on dreams and religious visions: "The native, stirred to unwonted perspiration by the one-time advent of the prodigal *peso*, has dropped back to ease with dignity—dignity with rags, mayhap, but always dignity. To the old ways he has not wholly returned—just to the old joy of living, the broad content of sitting and remembering that one has lungs for this ozone and eyes for this day-dream. I would not be understood that it is idleness. This is work, but such unfatal work!" (7) In such a daydream culture, sucking ozone the entire day in a "simple, restful, patriarchal, long lonely world" (18) presumably produced a hallucinatory state that conjured witches and developed an "infinitely complicated superstitio-religion" from which the *Penitentes*, *brujos*, and *curanderas* would emerge to dominate New Mexican life.

To this sociogeographically fabulous world, mañana would truly never come—nor need it—when Lummis's generative text exercised its ethnographic authority over the formation of metaphors for describing the social practices of Mexicans, often by Mexicans themselves. Cecil Romero, for example, uncritically mimicked Lummis's rhetoric in an essay on the archaic Spanish of northern New

Mexico: "Left thus for centuries to a self-sufficient existence in that lonely, gaunt land, the inbred descendants of the Conquistadores lost the color and fire of those bold spirits and settled down to the prosaic life of tending their flocks and coaxing a simple living from the mountain soil. It was a life peacefully primitive, almost patriarchal in its simplicity."[22] And some thirty years after it was first published, Lummis's racial romance would authorize the sociological analysis of the Mexican family in a scholarly article entitled "The Land of 'Poco Tiempo': A Study of Mexican Family Relationships in a Changing Social Environment."

> The title chosen for this study may be translated 'pretty soon,' or 'after a while.' It is not only the usual response to what an American deems an urgent social situation, but it is a fixed Mexican attitude toward trouble: 'Your troubles will vanish if you wait.' . . .
>
> The Mexican shares this attitude with many primitive peoples: Why hurry with the hurrying world? The sun is hot, the adobe is made to lean against, the quiet of the long afternoon should not be broken, let us not hurry. *Mañana* (tomorrow) will do; better still *pasada mañana* (the day after). The only hurry in Mexico is the foliage and the roses, which grow with a rush to cover mouldering walls.[23]

IV

> Under the apparent deadness of our New Mexico villages there runs a romantic current invisible to the stranger and understood only by their inhabitants.
> —Cleofas Jaramillo, *Romance of a Little Village Girl*

Only a detailed recontextualization allows us to read and understand Jaramillo's autobiography as a narrative mediated by a powerful nonnative discourse that authorized her textual presence in history just as it determined the shape such presence would assume. Embodied within this discursive configuration, however, is a structure of cultural representations reverberating with cultural difference about native cultural practice which blind "the stranger" to the currents of sociocultural significance and, therefore, open space for voicing resistance to imprisonment in Lummis's Southwest museum. Just as the early chapters remember her early life steeped in those cultural practices that psychologically and socially center her, the later chapters recall her work during her middle and late years of reappropriating and restoring a wide range of customs and traditions distorted by fascinated "American newcomers." Jaramillo's own attempts to restore cultural purity, as I have already argued, are troubled by an obsession with the Spanish past, but, as we shall see, the autobiographical reconstituting of a contrived "Spanish" subjectivity arms itself against historical erasure by inscription within a text that will not be erased, even though the content of the text tends toward a romanticized cultural history.

Jaramillo's desire for an original simplicity and purity embedded in New Mexico "Spanish" culture is marked out in the preface to *Romance of a Little Village Girl.* The prefatory remarks disclose Jaramillo's wish to return to a harmonious and ahistoric plane of edenic cultural experience. Jaramillo figures herself as a young rural Eve who once lived in an isolated valley, a veritable edenic locale. "In this little valley of the Arroyo Hondo, situated in the northern part of the state of New Mexico, hemmed in by high mountains and hills, sheltered from the contamination of the outside world, the inhabitants lived peacefully, preserving the customs and traditions of their ancestors" (1955 : vii). The autobiographical act that restores her own experience as one of these inhabitants is a kind of postlapsarian enterprise, an attempt to imagine herself not only in another era but in another life, an alternate experience uncontaminated by the tragedies Jaramillo experienced once she left her edenic Arroyo Hondo. She wishes to "live again in memory the girlhood years that were enriched with comfort and love, innocent of any wickedness, sheltered from all care and grief" (ibid.), but to carry out this plan means repressing the care and grief that have repeatedly punctured her personal and social life. This she cannot ultimately do.

As aged narrator, as the woman who moved away from innocence into the contaminated world of social experience, Jaramillo wishes to retrieve a coherence that may be traced, she insists, to a cultural locale still in force "under the apparent deadness" of village life. That this "romantic current" remains "invisible to the stranger and understood only by [the] inhabitants" suggests the degree to which she posits a subjectivity grounded in culturally coded experience. Sprung from native soil, she is vitally connected with this "romantic current" and, therefore, alone authorized to interpret the indentitarian cultural codes embodied by her people. Here and elsewhere she insists that despite all of the ethnography recorded by nonnative observers, the true current of cultural meanings remains invisible, except to the native inhabitants themselves. What is set at odds with this deep romantic current, however, is the surface of sociohistorical events that have leveled village life. The "apparent deadness" of village life may be attributed to social and economic transformations that altered the complex ecology of villages like Arroyo Hondo, but the specifics of material transformation lie outside of the legitimate folkloristic discourse prevailing during the moment she composed her life; consequently, reaching for what she believes to be a deep spiritual well of cultural meanings replaces a narrative that might well exercise its right to describe those hard surfaces of material reality—land usurpation, social and linguistic hegemony, corporate banking practices, taxation, and probate laws— that are responsible for the "deadness" of village life. Jaramillo's repression of material specifics, however, cannot be entirely flattened by a romance of the past, because although it is the very function of her romance to provide a substitute narrative that will occlude material history, resentment, anger, grumblings of various kinds surface in the narrative as irregularities, irruptions of oppositional articulation.

Northrop Frye's comments on the social motive underlying the romance are directive here. Jaramillo's "quiet romance" constitutes a nostalgic mythos that represses historical specificity simply because the truth of social displacement is too painful to think about; hence, the text of social history is replaced by an alternate narrative, a retrospective of an imagined earlier moment—in Jaramillo's book, a "traditional" cultural world that is always "rapidly vanishing" and yet always being restored in memories of earlier cultural life as well as in the costume of fiestas and pageants. As Frye notes,

> The romance is nearest of all literary forms to the wish-fulfillment dream, and for that reason it has socially a curiously paradoxical role. In every age the ruling social or intellectual class tends to project its ideals in some form of romance. . . . Yet there is a genuinely "proletarian" element in romance too which is never satisfied with its various incarnations, and in fact the incarnations themselves indicate that no matter how great a change may take place in society, romance will turn up again, as hungry as ever, looking for new hopes and desires to feed on. The perennially childlike quality of romance is marked by its extraordinarily persistent nostalgia, its search for some kind of imaginative golden age in time or space.[24]

Nostalgia for an imaginative golden age functions to occlude harsh social transformation throughout much of Jaramillo's narrative, but, while it accommodates itself to domination at one rhetorical level, it also opens toward a rhetoric of nonappeasement. Although she and other native "inhabitants" may gravitate toward a romanticizing and nostalgic discourse, they are never entirely absorbed by it; otherwise, articulations of resistance, hinging as resistance does on sustaining a social ego, would be impossible. As it turns out, therefore, because it articulates a collective desire for self-management, a fabulous historical romance articulated in native voice, however costumed in nostalgia and however much it relies on nonnative representations, is preferable to silence. Given the alternatives—cultural maceration in the material domain and ideological reification in the social—the ambivalent colonized subject is coerced into participating in a masquerading of history grounded in the dominant cultural production of the "newcomer." The erasing of history, or its radical revision, by the dominant group and the aporia that opens when native people do not imagine themselves as historical subjects may well lead to self-negation unless, in combination with sustained cultural practices, the forms made available to members of the subordinate group—cultural romance, folklore, a theater and masquerade of the Spanish golden age brought whole to New Mexico—are appropriated and turned to oppositional use.

Articulating an uncontaminated "Spanish" past came rather easily given the exogenous discourse operating in New Mexico, perhaps especially in Santa Fe during the 1930s and 1940s when Jaramillo was preserving her "Spanish" culture in *Sombras del Pasado*, helping Anglo-Americans organize the annual "Spanish" fiesta, and organizing a "Spanish" folklore group. As early as 1914, *Harper's Weekly* carried an article entitled "Our Spanish-American Fellow Citizens" in which "Spanish" blood lines in New Mexico were declared pure hundreds of years after the Spanish colonial enterprise. "The Spanish people in New Mexico . . . are not of the mixed breed one finds south of the Rio Grande, or even in Arizona, where there is a small remnant of Spanish blood. Indeed, it is probable that there is no purer Spanish stock in Old Spain itself."[25] And Mary Austin, mentioned as a vital inspiration to Jaramillo's writing, was another newcomer who during the 1920s was largely responsible for shoring up the residue of the "Spanish" past, embellishing "Spanish" cultural fragments where necessary, and inventing "Spanish" cultural practices where there were visible gaps. In a 1931 special issue of *Survey* magazine, "Mexicans in Our Midst," intended to quiet anxiety about rising Mexican immigration to the United States, Austin distinguished between pure and contaminated genealogy in New Mexico.

> There is reason to think that the first settlement was direct from Spain, but later the country filled slowly with disappointed gold seekers from the cities of Mexico, deracinated

descendants of the Spanish-Mexican politicians. There was, however, enough uncontaminated Spanish blood to give the dominant Spanish tradition to the social life of the colonies; at the same time there went on, at the lower social levels of population, the fusions of Spanish peasants, Moorish slaves, Mexican and New Mexican Indian, which produced the peon class of old Mexico itself.[26]

In her autobiography, *Earth Horizon*, of the following year, however, Austin occluded such genealogical "fusions."

> The colonists who came here originally came direct from Spain; they had not much tarrying in Mexico. They brought with them what they remembered, and as soon as they began to create, they made things in the likeness of old Spain. . . . They made *santos* and *bultos* [church altar statues carved in wood] in the pattern of the holy images of sixteenth-century Spain.[27]

While it is certainly true that New Mexicans had sustained a sense of themselves as a group with a distinct regional history that receded to the Spanish colonizers—the marking of such lines is clear in Vallejo's "Recuerdos históricos y personales" and Chacón's "Memorias"—the commemoration of such an affiliation was seldom marked by the kind of theatrical kitsch introduced by Anglo-Americans. What had been a local, primarily religious commemoration of the Spanish reconquest in 1692,[28] for example, was refashioned by Austin and her Anglo compatriots into a cultural event that insistently reconstructed the "dominant Spanish tradition" that had apparently not been sustained by the natives. As Austin writes in *Earth Horizon*,

> There was an annual fiesta at Santa Fe which was attended by the natives, but not very successfully. There was a tendency to divert it to tourist uses. This grew to be an offense to the artists, so that Witter Bynner, John Sloan, Gus Bauman, Will Shuster, and a dozen other artists set out to create a fiesta that should be Spanish; they persuaded the natives and finally the rest of the community. It has grown to be notable, and thoroughly, alively native. (358)

Never mind that significant elements of this "thoroughly, alively native" fiesta were invented by Anglo-American artists and scholars before consulting with those natives. Perhaps it was enough that the natives were persuaded somewhere along the way that they should follow their Anglo-American benefactors in recovering purer Spanish traditions than they alone had managed to maintain. As the editor of *El Palacio,* the "Weekly Review of the Arts and Sciences in the Southwest," suggested in 1925, the fiesta required the kind of professional molding that would ensure preservation of the Spanish cultural legacy through pageantry.

> Pronounced success attended the further effort of Director Edgar L. Hewett of the School of American Research and the Museum of New Mexico to mould the annual Santa Fe Fiesta into a folk festival that would reflect and preserve the distinctive characteristics of Southwestern culture as it has been developing during the march of the centuries since the beginnings of man on this Continent. . . . The Santa Fe Fiesta emphasizes chiefly the state's heritage from the Spanish civilization—that remarkable, almost indelible culture. . . . Men in glittering casques and corselets, . . . the picture springs faithfully out of the far past, to the smallest detail; our thrill comes from the fact that the environment and the setting have changed but little in three centuries.[29]

Precisely such extracultural intercessions in recovering and purifying the region's ostensibly *true* cultural past are discursively superimposed on Jaramillo's autobiography to such an extent that it is no surprise to see her agreeing with Austin and *El Palacio* in a chapter of her own on "The Santa Fe Fiesta."

> It's now the year 1935 in the present city of Santa Fe, but the calendar has been turned back to the year 1672 [*sic*] to commemorate the re-conquest of the capital of the Royal Kingdom of New Spain. There is a great contrast between the weary remnants of the army of Gen. Diego de Vargas which entered the city in that year and the resplendent De Vargas pageant now entering the city, as also is the gay, colorful crowd which fills the capital today to celebrate its annual fiesta, commemorating its victory. Many additions have lately been brought about to make it a genuine Spanish fiesta. It now starts with the burning of the *Zozobra,* the Spanish effigy of gloom. Into the huge image are placed all the afflictions and troubles of mankind, amid loud grunts and groans and the hissing and spitting of fire, Zozobra burns, writhing in agony. (1955 : 170)

Yet what neither Austin nor Jaramillo say is that *Zozobra* was the creation in 1926 of the artist Will Shuster, who took the idea not from Spain but from someone else who had seen something of the sort in Mexico.

Jaramillo's own additions may be regarded as disruptions of the fiesta. Her desire to believe in a genuine Spanish legacy often confuses the fact that making "additions" to the fiesta—or to any cultural event—disrupts what is taking place at the level of everyday practice over a period of time. Nevertheless, I would argue that hers are disruptions strategically intended to counter those additions that did not emerge out of Nuevomexicano society. As Jaramillo writes, "If we were to ransack our mother's old trunks, I believe we would find some find old-fashioned silk gowns and jewels. So far we have been seeing mostly what Americans have arranged." Much of what had been arranged by Americans must have seemed ludicrous to people like Jaramillo. Among the events installed during the 1930s were decidedly nonreligious carnivalesque affairs, one the Historical/Hysterical Parade, the other the Pet Parade in which family pets were costumed and then marched through the streets. The Historical/Hysterical Parade of 1934 must have been an extraordinary event, for as the *Santa Fe New Mexican* reported,

> It was a vast conglomeration, taking an hour or more to pass, of dinosaurs, sultans, monstrosities, pioneers, sacred cows, federal codes, Chinese, Scotch, Spanish, Mexican, Hindustani, Indian and Annamese characters, scientists, explorers, Dionne quintuplets, burros, Matachines, bagpipers, gaily caparisoned horses, hundreds of peoples in gorgeous costumes, ancient flivvers and steamers, ox-carts, wagons of every size and shape, rancheros, musicos, payazos, world without end.[30]

So much for "genuine" native New Mexico religious and cultural festivities.

In a string of four chapters in *Romance of a Little Village Girl*, Jaramillo organizes her recollections of the years from about 1934 to 1955 as a memoir of her own folkloristic activities in Santa Fe and her struggle to intervene in the planning and production of events in which her people's history and culture were being stupidly carnivalized by Anglos. In "Spanish Folklore Society Organized," Jaramillo recalls her "plan . . . to arouse more interest amongst our Spanish-speaking population in taking part in the fiesta," by calling on a group of Hispanas who would enter the annual Parade of the Cross, dressed in "old-fashioned gowns" and riding on horseback as *"Las Galleras de Santa Ana"* (the Ladies of Saint Anne); afterward they would offer a "chocolate *merienda"* where fiesta-goers would be serenaded by "Spanish songs" (174–175). The genteel *merienda* may have fostered class pretensions on the part of the "elite" families, but the "addition" of the horsewomen's procession emerged from long-standing church holy societies (societies to which many of our mothers and grandmothers still belong) whose members devote themselves to patron saints or the Blessed Virgin. Emerging as it did from religiocultural practice, *Las Galleras de Santa Ana* must be considered a culturally countermanding "addition" to the grotesque conglomeration of the Historical/Hysterical Parade. As she explains in her chapter "The Coronado Centennial," whereas the Coronado Cuarto Commission put on a "gorgeous pageant" commemorating the 400-year anniversary of Francisco Vásquez de Coronado's exploration of the Southwest in 1540,[31] Jaramillo's group sponsored a more modest but culturally imperative staging of the Spanish-language play, *Los Moros y los Cristianos*, "the first drama," Jaramillo writes, "given by the Oñate expedition in New Spain" (178) in 1598 when he and a group of Spanish colonists settled Santa Fe.[32] The chapters describing such activities end with "Again La Villa Celebrates," in which she encourages her people to take active interest in the "preservation of the old Spanish customs and the study of our traditions." Recognizing the potential for losing control of a centuries-old legacy, she pleads with her people to assume proprietary responsibility for cultural maintenance.

> The glamour and beauty which appeals to the senses of the artists and the writers who have come into our country, should appeal more forcefully to us, the heirs of the artistic culture and of the poetry and the religious traditions our Spanish ancestors left to crystallize on the crests of our New Mexico mountains. (183)

V

> This quiet romance I will try to describe in the following pages of my autobiography, although I feel an appalling shortage of words, not being a writer, and writing in a language almost foreign to me.
> —Cleofas Jaramillo, *Romance of Little Village Girl*

Jaramillo's desire to reconstruct the "quiet romance" of a Spanish heritage, however illusory given our understanding of the mestizo heritage of almost all New Mexicans, must be read as a sociopsychological compensation for her actual social and economic status through the 1930s and 1940s as a financially troubled widow living in a small apartment off the main plaza in Santa Fe. Forced by

Cleofas Jaramillo in traditional dress for Santa Fe Fiesta. Photograph courtesy of the Museum of New Mexico, negative #9919.

circumstances as well as encouraged by Anglos who yearned to see living representations of the romantic Spanish past, it is little wonder that like other women from once elite families, she would costume herself in "old-fashioned" finery, silk shawls, and heirlooms in an annual fashion show that glimmered of an imagined colonial golden age.[33] Even though she had lost her home and land to American bankers who were not interested in the imaginative currency of her genealogical ascendency, like other Hispanos of her generation she was simply trying to hold onto her dignity as it might be imagined in class and genealogical status. For Jaramillo, then, constituting herself as a pedigreed Spanish lady, a direct descendant of the Spanish *conquistadores*, absolved everyone of history—those Anglo-Americans who wished to gloss a troubling history of the area and those New Mexicans like Jaramillo who wished to draw imaginary distinction between themselves and those other "isolation-shrunken-descendants of the Castilian world finders" who were having a tough time in the everyday world.

The image of the Spanish figure imposed by the cultural Other exerts a heavy toll on Jaramillo's autobiography just as it does on the cultural narratives of other New Mexican writers of the period: the appropriation of the figure of the Spanish conquistador legitimizes their discursive, if not social, existence. Although marked by ideological figurations of containment constructed in the imagination of the dominant group, the Spanish "I" provided a symbolic identity, which however much a contradiction in terms ensured survival in the social domain. Hence, the double bind of contradictory posturing may also be read as strategic double consciousness and multiple address of the kind seen in Vigil y Alaríd, Seguín, and Vallejo a century earlier.

So our *antepasados*—Cleofas Jaramillo among them—were not fools. There are moments of recognition throughout their work, when with profound clarity, they voice their understanding of the social predicament in which they found themselves: they knew they were engaged in a battle for social, cultural, and linguistic survival, they understood the condescending rhetoric that daily glossed the material displacement to which they were subject, and they understood the sociodiscursive power that shaped and perpetuated a racial romance about them. Consequently, when they did speak in the public realm, they spoke their resistance through the master romance of the colorful Spanish past. To figure into the public discourse on New Mexico's Spanish colonial history may, on one hand, be regarded as a gesture of blind acquiescence to the dominant hegemony; on the other, we may read romanticizing memorials about the past as attempts to exercise some control over the discourse in which native people were represented. In intercultural discourse between a dominant and subject group, survival is predicated on strategically voicing one's presence. Often, simply being able to open one's mouth signals a moment of affirmation, notwithstanding the uncertainty, hesitance, nostalgic sentiment that belie unclarified resentment and opposition. So, yes, hegemonic discourse had the effect of lulling the Nuevomexicano into a realm of fantasy that *was* just fantasy, self-conceit, illusion but was *also* a way of saying "No!" to cultural effacement. The discourse of the Spanish colonial period provided a means for authorizing "native" status, even though the authorizing apparatus was a parcel of historical distortions; moreover, it tended toward a double-, sometimes a multiple-voiced discourse that served the simultaneous purpose of being hospitable toward the *extranjeros* while providing a socially symbolic form of control for Nuevomexicanos, whose world, it may have seemed, was dissolving like the adobe structures to which Jaramillo more than once refers.

Jaramillo may be considered a Hispanophile, but it would be a mistake to think her therefore passive. She understood the exploitative motive underlying the behavior of those newcomers who were infatuated with Nuevomexicano culture. Her almost single-handed organization of *La Sociedad Folklórica* in the 1930s must be regarded as a gesture of resistance to Anglo domination of cultural preservation activities in Santa Fe. Although the idea for *La Sociedad* was influenced by similar Anglo folklore preservation projects, specifically J. Frank Dobie's Texas Folklore Society (176), she seized on a decidedly political strategy when forming the group: the romanticized genealogy and melodious language celebrated in *extranjero* discourse about New Mexico would be used to exclude non-natives. Jaramillo writes, "The first rules which I drafted still govern the organization. These rules were that the society should be composed of only thirty members, all of whom must be of Spanish descent, and that the meetings must be conducted in the Spanish language, with the aim of preserving our language, customs and traditions" (1955 : 176). Such rules, clearly a form of ethnocodifying, effectively excluded the likes of Austin, Shuster, Bynner, and other "writers and artists who have come into our country." In the same chapter where she describes her efforts to organize *La Sociedad Folklórica*, she makes a number of comments that mark conscious resistance to cultural hegemony: her efforts to "arouse more interest amongst our Spanish-speaking population in taking part of the fiesta" is described as a direct response to cultural activities controlled by Anglo-Americans, she says, because, "so far we have been seeing mostly what Americans have arranged" (174); she remembers that the "Fiesta Council, having heard about my activities, elected me to be a member and sent me an invitation to attend the weekly meetings" (174), asked her group to elect the fiesta queen, and then, for "political reasons" told the group "we would have to choose another" (175), which, she writes, they refused to do. And in the same chapter where she voices gratitude to one American woman ("Miss Hazel Hyde was kind enough to lend me her lovely patio for a Spanish card party" [177]), Jaramillo also shows that she is capable of outright sarcasm when referring to an article published in *Holland Magazine* about New Mexican cooking by a "Mrs. D." The article, she remembers, was "nicely written and illustrated, but very deficient as to the knowledge of our Spanish cooking. In giving the recipe for making tortillas it read, 'Mix bread flour with water, add salt.' How nice and light these must be without yeast or shortening! And still these smart Americans make money with their writing, and we who know the correct way sit back and listen" (173).

Quibbling over the fiesta queen and the ingredients in tortillas seem small enough gestures of resistance, but, taken together with other articulations of resistance in Jaramillo, just such voicings add up to *coraje*. Such *coraje*, or anger, has to alter our reading of a text as seemingly innocuous as *The Genuine New Mexico Tasty Recipes*. We no longer have a recipe book of "quaint Spanish" dishes but a complex cultural narrative in which the repossession of food preparation is described as one activity within a cultural matrix. As Rebolledo has pointed out, precisely because a "sense of place and belonging can be connoted by such mundane activities as regional food traditions, . . . the Cookbook . . . preserves these traditions."[34] Interspersed between the recipes, Jaramillo remembers familial and community occasions that contextualize the very preparation and consumption of food. On the one hand, *The Genuine New Mexico Tasty Recipes* represents the popularization of ethnic cuisine and, in that respect, caters to members of the dominant culture; on the other, Jaramillo contextualizes consumption in an explicitly cultural manner and, therefore, suggests how intimately food is related to lived cultural experience. Hence, we discover a form of culinary resistance: Anglo-Americans can follow the recipe and still not eat Nuevomexicano cooking.[35]

I am being somewhat facetious, of course, but Jaramillo was not when referring to Americans making "money with their writing," while the natives who live the culture "sit back and listen." She did not. *The Genuine New Mexico Tasty Recipes* opens an interstice for counterhegemonic expression at a level that is all but overlooked, unless one is listening for articulations of opposition. In this case, what seems the ideologically neutral compilation of a cookbook becomes an "embryonic" site of contention of the kind that Gramsci identifies in his comments on folkloristic expressions of counter-hegemony.[36] What at first may seem acquiescence on closer reading reveals verbal gestures of discontent and anger. Jaramillo may open her mouth initially to share a recipe with the newcomers, but that she has opened her mouth to correct the recipe is the beginning of assertion. As Anne Goldman has recently argued, *The Genuine New Mexico Tasty Recipes* "is not simply a catalogue of recipes correcting the absence of yeast and shortening. Instead, it represents food and its preparation, within the context of personal narrative, as metonyms for the reaffirmation and maintenance of traditional Hispano cultural practices as a whole."[37]

Likewise, her *Romance of a Little Village Girl* may begin in apology and verbal hesitation, but it opens to a life disclosed within a troubling context of social transformation that refutes its own sentimentality. In fact, the prefatory hesitance Jaramillo discloses about writing the "quiet romance" turns out to be a crucial site of negotiation for control of the text, given its projected readership. "This quiet romance I will try to describe in the following pages of my autobiography, although I feel an appalling shortage of words, not being a writer, and writing in a language almost foreign to me. May I offer an apology for my want of continued expression to some parts of my story" (Preface). To whom is she explaining if not to an Anglo-American readership? She is apologizing for writing haltingly, perhaps inaccurately, crudely, in a foreign literary idiom. She wishes to inscribe her experience, to utter herself into textual permanence; yet she concedes her relative inability to do so in the idiom determined by those Anglo writers occupying Santa Fe whose work had shaped an entire set of readerly expectations. As she explains later in the narrative, she began writing about her culture and herself because "writing and painting are contagious in this old town"—Santa Fe in the 1930s. One might speculate that being a writer of the kind typified by Mary Austin, Alice Corbin, and Peggy Pond Church would not, under native circumstances, have appealed to Jaramillo. Not that Nuevomexicanos did not write, but the forms Nuevomexicano writing took were not ethnographic and even more certainly not self-ethnographic. And I have not even mentioned her apology for writing in English—"a language almost foreign" to her. Jaramillo's admission is appalling if one considers that she is saying (without saying) that she is thinking herself in Spanish, remembering herself in her native tongue, but writing herself in English, a nearly foreign language. One can speculate that writing in Spanish might have produced a different narrative voice, one more given to addressing her people without restraint about a shared predicament.

That she wrote in English is a troubling but necessary contradiction. She authors her own cultural preservation activities, in English, for an Anglo-American readership, to forestall another Anglo from describing her people's cultural history. On this issue, Jaramillo is strategically ethnocentric if one recalls her claim that the cultural life "of New Mexico villages" appears dead only because it is "invisible to the stranger," and where apparent in any guise is nevertheless misread because the cultural codes can be "understood only by their inhabitants."[38] Jaramillo's renunciation of nonnative ethnographic discourse is here doubled, complete. Whereas she altogether refuses to authorize nonnative discourse, however eloquent, she authorizes herself to speak in a "foreign language," however awkwardly. Jaramillo may apologize for her "want of continued expression," yet she expropriates the discourse of the newcomer as a resistive gesture against another Anglo-American legitimizing the wrong ingredients for making tortillas, so to speak, and, in the process of being appropriated by, actually appropriates the discourse of the *extranjero.*

In the closing chapter, "Rhythm in Adobe," Jaramillo remarks that writing had increasingly taken on life-sustaining significance for her. Along with reading, the "work of writing" kept her from "becoming too lonely and discouraged" while living alone in her seventy-fifth year. Authorship had become a life-extending activity. Or, rather, it had become her life. Like the hot mineral spring of Ojo Caliente to which she refers in the chapter, writing renewed the "spirit and the mind." The book must close, but the final chapter echoes with reasons not to: "Each time I come to the end of my story, something happens to incite me to continue writing a little longer" (198).

In this final chapter, Cleofas Jaramillo discloses an uncanny sense of the textuality and intertexuality of her life. "I must try to put this little work on the market and, also, the two plays I 'snitched' from my first book. For now at this book's close, I am also coming to the close of my seventy-fifth year of my life" (199). She and her autobiography have become coterminous. She must finish the book because she senses the end, but to stop writing is to come to the end. And while she awaits a natural death for herself, *Ro-*

mance of a Little Village Girl projects a critique of the numerous technological threats her people must endure, from the urban sprawl, noise, and "speedy striving of competition" (189) to the ultimate threat to us all, "the proximity of the atomic hatchery [in Los Alamos] holding us for better or for destruction" (190). Despite an "appalling shortage of words" or a "want of continued expression," even despite her discomfort with English, Cleofas Jaramillo has, by the end of *Romance of a Little Village Girl,* seized the discourse of the newcomer as a palliative against death—her own and that of the culture from which she springs.

Conclusion
Other Voices and Other Subjects, Continuities of Autobiographical Desire

I

As I have argued at length in this book, the Mexican Americans with whom I deal articulate a desire, a longing, a nostalgia for a homeland here, a cultural habitat ruptured in 1848 and for the next century and a half surviving by sheer force of communitarian will. Although, as many social historians have suggested, Mexicans crossed the imaginary (but also real) border to settle in the Rio Grande Valley of Texas, in the Mesilla Valley of New Mexico, in Tucson, Arizona, in Los Angeles, in the Imperial Valley in California, most Mexican American communities in the United States at the turn of the century considered themselves the permanent inhabitants of the soil they occupied but no longer owned.

Although as early as the 1840s Mexicanos throughout the Southwest had become Seguín's "strangers in their native land," as a group they sustained a cultural epistemology situated in an idea of the homeland. This trope of the homeland structures much of our cultural narrative. Whether we read Juan Seguín or Cleofas Jaramillo, Rafael Chacón or Apolinaria Lorenzana, Mariano Vallejo or Fabiola Cabeza de Baca, we hear sighing, muttering, or outright anger for a homeland seized by Americans in 1848 and after, for a culture threatened or actually stripped of its land and social economy, its language, daily cultural practices, aesthetic production. In each of the autobiographical texts I read there is an echo, and a reverberation of that echo, as of a way of life lost irretrievably, yet never lost to the imagination since remembering the homeland is always a form of retrieval, a strategy for sustaining a complex of daily cultural practices even as culture is changing, a way of never letting go of the idea of a past reconstituted in the present in however transformed and contingent a manner. The figuration of loss, grievance, and resistance survives into the present in Chicano historical and literary study in which loss of the homeland and the ensuing resistance to American domination is privileged in such histories as Rudolfo Acuña's *Occupied America* (1981) and John R. Chávez's *The Lost Land: The Chicano Image of the Southwest* (1984) and in such literary studies as Ramón Saldívar's *Chicano Narrative: The Dialectics of Difference* (1990) and José Limón's *Mexican Ballads, Chicano Poems* (1992).

However, some thirty years before these scholars radicalized the trope of the homeland, Jaramillo and also Cabeza de Baca, who died in 1990 at the age of ninety-one, gave expression to a fierce desire to sustain the cultural cogitos over and against the social, political, and epistemological hegemony of gringo ways of experiencing the world. When Cabeza de Baca catalogs the Spanish-language geography and familial genealogy of the *llano,* she is doing more than grieving over lost land and dead *parientes* and *familiares:* she is giving textual permanence to a cultural configuration located within an identifiable geographic and social space that, while no longer titled by her people, is nevertheless anchored to a region claimed by the native language that names its topography.

> The Hispano has almost vanished from the land . . . but the names of hills, rivers, arroyos, canyons, and defunct plazas linger as monuments to a people who pioneered into the land of the buffalo and the Comanche. These names have undergone many changes, but are still known and repeated. Very likely many of those who pronounce them daily are unaware that they are of Spanish origin. (66)

Such sociotopographic mapping projects an epistemological matrix of identity transmitted textually to a posterity displaced from the land itself but positioned to reconstruct filiations with a community resettled in the imagination of the reading present. That Cabeza de Baca refuses to jettison the genealogy of the homeland argues for the force of identitarian will sustained by ethnic and cultural communities that paradoxically refuse to forget the past while tending toward the occlusion of the present.

Indeed, this tendency to occlude the social conditions of the present seems apparent in recent autobiographical narrative that emerges from the narrative formation I have examined. What at first appears to be a textual residue of Jaramillo's and Cabeza de Baca's narrative nostalgia for an earlier moment is also a nostalgia deeply politicized by the alienations of modern life. In California, Arnold Rojas's narrative paean to a rural, ranching California is something of a throwback of desire to Vallejo's beloved Sonoma valley of the 1830s. His tribute to the past is announced in the titles of his many books, among them, *California Vaquero* (1953), *Lord of the California Vaquero* (1958), and *Last of the Vaqueros* (1960). Alfonso Griego's *Good-bye, My Land of Enchantment* (1981) and Eva Wilbur-Cruce's *A Beautiful, Cruel Country* (1987) are personal narratives that loop back to turn-of-the-century communities. Thirty years after the appearance of *Romance of a Little Village Girl* and *We Fed Them Cactus*, Wilbur-Cruce inclines once again to an image of the socially utopian past that narratively closes around 1910. "I constantly thank God for the privilege I have had of having seen and ridden the open range, back in the days when the national forest was open country and not crisscrossed with barbed-wire fences and riders everywhere. . . . One reason I have finally written this book was to evoke that beautiful, cruel land of solitude for others in a form more accessible and permanent than it can take in my own memory."[1] Wilbur-Cruce completely smooths over the difficulties and disruptions of the social present, but it is apparent that such difficulties and disruptions generate a narrative of longing for an imagined community of the past, a community less divided by competition, by greed, by the Anglo machine of progress. Griego's narrative is generally a wistful autobiographical reconstruction of a cultural economy ostensibly uncontaminated by "the machine" and by "progress." However politically inefficacious his idealisms may seem, he remembers a set of communitarian filiations he believes is retrievable not only in the imagination but in the practice of everyday life.

> Just as the farmer, the cattlemen, the sheep-raisers came to each other's aid for the hunt, the harvest, the lambing season, and, just as neighbors helped each other in times of sickness and death, so we too must come together and fill some of each other's needs without the exchange of money, just like our ancestors did in their days. . . . For our labor in the common market is never justly repaid. We come away after eight hours of hard work with not enough to live on. . . . We must begin to help each other again. We have so much to give, little things that don't cost us. We are builders, doctors, lawyers, mechanics, plumbers, and most of all, we are still neighbors. . . . High school students could adopt a granny. Someone in one of those rest homes. They could learn from them. . . . They could go and read to them, or

write letters for them, or play cards with them. Then maybe we could insist that our children receive an education that would be meaningful in their everyday life, that it be full of experience, rather than just 'book learning.'"[2]

Griego may pine for "the ancestors" and their way of life, however idealized, but his politicized understanding that people are not fairly compensated for their labor cannot be argued. Most Mexican Americans (indeed most Americans) live in a labor economy in which the loss of familial intimacy and friendship is purchased with the illusion of more money and greater leisure, but Griego, in a classic articulation of a worker's knowledge of the world, recognizes that "the more money we receive for our labor today . . . more is extracted from us for those things which have become the necessities of today" (77). His worry is that in "our haste to race into a better future," we have lost a vital connection with the communitarian affiliations practiced in an earlier period; indeed, his narrative recovery is an attempt to restore his own severed affiliations since he had lived much of his adult life not in a utopian village but as a machinist in a shipyard and a carpet cleaner in the urban mess of California.

In large measure, as I have argued, a retrospective narrative habit has developed in Mexican American autobiography which goes beyond reconstructing an individual life. Rather, an individual life is measured within a communitarian configuration and against the disruption of identity as identity is situated within an imagined cultural community of the past. Autobiography functions not only to reconstruct "a life" but to save some idea of "lives" as they might be lived in another time and place. The overarching ideal of a homeland, whether framed as the homeland of the pre-American Southwest, the mythic Aztlán, or barrio of the "homey," remains a deeply embedded—if metaphorically fluid—unifying symbol for a community that in its various manifestations and regional developments remains recalcitrant in the face of social domination since 1848. This impulse requires an imaginative move largely dominated by nostalgia for social control in a prior condition.

For members of the social elite like Vallejo and Jaramillo, such a move was especially necessary since their displacement had been so galling. But even people in the lower social strata—Apolinaria Lorenzana, for example—also felt deeply displaced from their social and cultural habitat. Although class divisions and patriarchal constraints remained unresolved, there was an idea of a homeland sustained by a complex system of cultural practices and productions.

Autobiographical narrative—along with such forms as the *décima* (folk poetry), the *corrido* and the *cuento*—have given voice to grievance, to personal narrative tied to the community's material displacement and yet privatized by personal loss and a longing for an idea of a homeland in which the "I" may settle into the comfort and security provided by a filiative culture of the kind many of our writers have imagined for well over a century.

II

In 1959, three years after Cleofas Jaramillo passed away in her beloved Santa Fe, José Antonio Villarreal published *Pocho*, an autobiographical novel that describes a family's forced exodus from Mexico during the Revolution of 1910 and their uneasy adaptation to life in the United States. As Villarreal wrote of that separation from another homeland, Mexicans crossed the border into a social space of economic exploitation, ethnocentric exclusion, and social uncertainty.

> By the hundreds they crossed the Rio Grande, and then by the thousands. They came first to Juárez, where the price of the three minute train ride would take them into El Paso del Norte—or a short walk through the open door would deposit them in Utopia. The ever-increasing army of people swarmed across while the border remained open, fleeing from squalor and oppression. But they could not flee reality, and the Texans, who welcomed them as a blessing because there were miles of cotton to be harvested, had never really forgotten the Alamo. The certain degree of dignity the Mexicans yet retained made some of them turn around and walk back into the hell they had left. Others huddled close to the international bridge and established a colony on the American side of the river, in the city of El Paso, because they could gaze at their homeland a few yards away whenever the impulse struck them. The bewildered people came on—insensitive to the fact that even though they were not stopped, they were not really wanted. It was the ancient quest for El Dorado, and so they moved onward, west to New Mexico and Arizona and California, and as they moved, they planted their new seed.[3]

The exodus and diasporic proliferation throughout the United States with which Villarreal's novel opens represents a major shift in Mexican American social presence in the United States, just as it signals a shift in the narrative figurations of immigrant experience and sociocultural adjustment to life in the United States. The internal social trauma caused by the Mexican Revolution and the severe economic destabilization of the country, coupled with the rise in industrial and agricultural business in the western United States from 1900 to 1930, created what Paul Taylor referred to as the "push" and "pull" of a massive labor pool to the border states.[4] In the years between 1880 and 1900, only some 3,000 Mexicans crossed the border; between 1900 and 1930, more than 750,000 people crossed over.[5] However, because these are official figures that cannot measure undocumented immigration, they are undercounts. Over the ten-year period from 1910 to 1920, as Lawrence Cardoso argues, "The number of border crossings was nearer a total of 2,000,000 than the 330,000 counted by the United States Immigration officials."[6]

Whereas at the turn of the century there was a Mexican American population of 120,000, by 1955, with the revolutionary exodus, the agricultural, railroad, and industrial development in California and Texas that led to the recruitment of tens of thousands of Mexicans, and the Bracero Program initiated during World War II, there was a stable Mexican immigrant population of well over two million. It is this immigration and the sociocultural difficulties of language loyalty and loss, assimilation and acculturation, intergenerational cleavage between the Mexican-born parents' nostalgia for a homeland *allá en Mexico* and the second generation's adaptation to and acceptance of the new home of the United States that opens a distinct narrative activity among Mexican American writers. For members of the first generation, immigration usually was (and still is) figured as necessity rather than desire, with the projection of return to native soil an ideal; for second and subsequent generations, and even for Mexicans who have been in the United States for many years, the idea of return has been transformed into a socially symbolic metaphor for resistance to acculturation and assimilation by American society.

For first-generation immigrant Mexicans crossing the border after 1910, the memory of the homeland produced a fierce loyalty for Mexico that reproduces many of the idealities of and about the past that I have identified throughout this study. Ernesto Galarza's *Barrio Bay* (1971), for example, is as sentimental a remembrance of his beloved Mexican village of Jalcocotán as Cleofas Jaramillo's recollection of Arroyo Hondo in *Romance of a Little Village Girl*. Much like

Jaramillo and Griego, Galarza locates his childhood in a utopian space of village cooperation and edenic isolation from the contaminations of the outside world. Even when the Revolution of 1910 brings an end to village life and his family is forced to flee north to the United States, Galarza writes the past as an adventure rather than as the tragedy of death, starvation, and displacement it was for millions of Mexican people.

Well before Galarza wrote his autobiography, however, Manuel Gamio, a Mexican anthropologist, conducted an expansive study of Mexican immigrants that among other data collected autobiographical statements from a large field of informants—the majority of whom, like Galarza and the Rubio family in *Pocho*, had been forced to leave Mexico for an uncertain future in the United States. In *The Mexican Immigrant: His Life Story* (1931),[7] Gamio published a cross section of these statements under categories that showed just how loyal people remained to the mother country, even though in many cases they had already lived in this country for many years. One immigrant, Gonzalo Galván, a resident of the United States for sixteen years, is unreconciled to life here and bitter about the exploitation he had experienced: "This is only a jail in disguise. One's life is a real struggle [to] endure these *bolillos* [Americans] who do whatever they want to do with one especially when one doesn't know English. One lives here to leave one's strength and then go back to Mexico when one is old like I am. That is why I am taking my son while he is young so that he won't forget his country" (25). Another man, Carlos Ibañez, claimed, on one hand, that he liked the United States and lived "in peace with everyone," but, on the other hand, although he had lived twenty-five consecutive years in the United States, he had no intention of becoming a citizen. "I would rather cut my throat before changing my Mexican nationality. . . . I haven't lost hope of spending my last days in my own country" (46). One woman, Soledad Sandoval told Gamio, "I can't adapt . . . to certain customs in this country," and went on to say that she was "opposed to its tendencies of dominion and of power" (64). And Juan Berzunzolo, in the United States for seventeen years, figured himself as a body summarily exploited for its labor capital and then discarded. "I have left the best of my life and strength here, sprinkling with the sweat of my brow the field and the factories of these gringos, who only know how to make one sweat and don't even pay any attention when they see that one is old" (147). Berzunzolo's own children have grown to adulthood in the United States, but he dreams nevertheless of taking his grandchildren back to Mexico, be-

cause he does not want them to become *"pochos"* (147). Berzunzolo's plan for returning to Mexico sounds much like the father's in
Pocho, who proclaims "next year we will have enough money and
we will return to our country" (31). But, of course, the family never
returns, and the father's nostalgia gives way to the children's acculturation in the new country.

Even very recent journalistic and ethnographic collections of autobiographical statement by Mexican immigrants disclose the tena-
city with which people sustain and act upon an idea of the homeland
as the center of communitarian identity (see Ted Conover, *Coyotes, a Journey Through the Secret World of American's Illegal A-
liens* [1987]; Marilyn Davis, ed., *Mexican Voices/American Dreams*
[1990]). In *Diary of an Undocumented Immigrant* (1991), Ramón
"Tianguis" Pérez recalls his odyssey of labor and daily insecurity in
the United States and then closes with his decision to return to
Mexico rather than apply for resident status primarily on the basis
of cultural loyalty. "It *does* seem easier to qualify for residency under the new law, but I don't plan to try. Ever since the day in which
I made my plans to come to the United States, it has been with the
idea of earning dollars to change into pesos when I go back" (232).⁸
Pérez's desire to return to Mexico is expressive of a pervasive distrust and disregard for life in the United States that is a haunting
echo of attitudes articulated by Gamio's immigrant speakers seventy years earlier. "Even most of those townsmen who've been able
to establish legal residency don't plan to stay in the United States
for the rest of their lives. For example, my Uncle Vicente. . . . While
he is working here, his children are in Mexican universities. Had he
brought them here, it is unlikely they would have pursued higher
education. What's more likely they would have fallen prey to drugs,
and my uncle would have spent his last days like the old man in
black gabardine that I knew in Houston" (232).

What we hear from Gamio in the 1920s to Pérez in the 1980s is
a profound and painful recognition in people voicing the dilemma of
destabilized subjectivity in the cross-cultural terrain they inhabit.
Pérez may return to Mexico thinking it will be for good, but, like
the majority of immigrants, necessity and habit will very likely bring
him back across the border. Indeed, like many immigrant workers,
Pérez may stand for us here as the figure of the Mexican immigrant
who crosses and recrosses the border so many times that he becomes
a person neither Mexican nor American but a kind of transcultural
subject, neither a victim nor a liminal figure but someone adept at
traversing the border with confidence and integrity. Yet this projec-

tion of a stable subjectivity lived between borders may be an intellectualizing conceit not easily borne out in the experience of immigrants themselves. That is, such transcultural subjectivity is not easily attained because it emerges from exclusions on both sides of the border that are psychologically divisive and emotionally painful. The divided subjectivity of Mexicans confounded by their intercultural identity was eloquently articulated long ago by numerous of Gamio's informants, one of whom describes the displacement the Mexican(American) feels in both countries.

> Such a person, when he goes to Mexico, wearing American clothes and speaking Spanish with a foreign accent, calls himself Mexican because he is accustomed to being called a Mexican in the United States. Nevertheless, Mexicans in Mexico, knowing nothing of this, become indignant of the idea of such a person being a Mexican, while on the other hand, Americans find it strange that he calls himself an American, since in the U.S. he is always a Mexican." (263)

The inevitable destabilization of unitary identification with either country or culture that marks post-1848 narratives like Seguín's *Personal Memoirs* and Chacón's "Memorias" can be seen as a condition of intercultural ambiguity that remains continuous, albeit variously nuanced by class, regional, and immigrant status in contemporary Chicano autobiographical narratives like Oscar Zeta Acosta's *The Autobiography of a Brown Buffalo* (1972) and *The Revolt of the Cockroach People* (1973), Anthony Quinn's *The Original Sin* (1972), Cherríe Moraga's *Loving in the War Years*, Richard Rodriguez's *Hunger of Memory* (1982) and *Days of Obligation: An Argument with My Father* (1992), and Gloria Anzaldúa's *Borderlands/ La Frontera: The New Mestiza* (1987).

In 1972, Acosta gave voice to the formation of a historical subjectivity located in the space between binary categories. "I am neither a Mexican nor an American. . . . I am a Chicano by ancestry and a Brown Buffalo by choice."[9] Like the figure in Gamio's study, Acosta visits Mexico, seeking his roots, only to be rightfully incarcerated for his "gringo arrogance and americano impatience" and then told by the judge to "go home and learn to speak [his] father's language." Yet before Acosta can "go home," a border guard challenges him to produce an I.D., telling him, "You don't look like an American, you know." To be a "Chicano by ancestry" means recognizing the historical formation of identity shaped from and by the exclusions on both sides of the border. In a poem in Anzaldúa's *Bor-*

derlands, the speaker identifies the multiplicity of negative exclusions from a single identity of blood or monolithic cultural identity.

> To live in the Borderlands means you
> are neither *hispana india negra española*
> *ni gabacha, eres mestiza, mulata*, half-breed
> caught in the crossfire between camps

Living in the borderlands, moreover, requires recognizing the ideological contradictions of various self-deceits, that is, "means knowing / that the india in you, betrayed for 500 years, / is no longer speaking to you, / that *mexicanos* call you *rejetas* / that denying the Anglo inside you / is as bad as having denied the Indian or Black."[10] Anzaldúa imagines as necessary, because inevitable, the social and racial mestizaje that emerges from multiple intercultural encounters in the social spaces of modern life.

Yet Anzaldúa and other recent Chicano autobiographers, although recognizing themselves as occupying a social space of multiple identities, speak another (contradictory?) desire for a unitary and collective cultural economy imagined in the past, or on the other side of the border. Behind such a reaffirmation of multiple presence is the uneasy memory of an imaginary unity elsewhere, whether of the barrios in Los Angeles or Albuquerque or San Antonio or Chicago, the agricultural valleys of the West, or the pueblos and villages of a remembered Mexico. Chicano autobiographers cannot quite forget what they perceive to be the historical rupture, the violence of displacement, exploitation, and denigration voiced again and again by their *antepasados*— Seguín, de la Guerra, Vallejo, Chacón, Jaramillo—and deeply embedded in the collective psyche through our cultural narratives, which bring us to the juncture of loose ends from which we (re)build new subjectivities, new communities, and new idealities. It is precisely this troubled relationship with the past, the past as narrated to us by our *antepasados*, through which contemporary Chicano writers affirm a relationship with an imagined community, a metaphorical homeland distinct from the material surface of society, the land from which—like Juan Seguín in the 1840s—we have been made strangers.

Rather than inhabit a borderless mestizaje, Anzaldúa, Acosta, Moraga, and even Rodriguez premise a condition of empowered multiple identity that is the result of living in the marginal space to which history (and the dominant society) has consigned them. Acosta calls into question the legality of being conferred citizenship by the conqueror: "No one ever asked me or my brother if we wanted to be American citizens. We are all citizens by default. They stole our land and made us half-slaves" (198). Anzaldúa, in a poem that closes *Borderlands*, imagines an earlier moment, an "age before the Gringo when Texas was Mexico," a time when "roots like those of the mesquite / [were] firmly planted" in the "Valley near the Rio Grande." However "firmly planted," Anzaldúa recalls those violations suffered by her people at the hands of the gringos who "have taken our lands" and have broken a people's connection with the community of its dead ancestors: "Not even the cemetery is ours now / where they buried Don Urbano / your great-great-grandfather." She imagines a future horizon of mestiza reclaiming of the land "when the Gringos are gone," but this contestatory assertion is a form of nostalgia for the future, imagining a landscape of the past as yet uninhabited by "the Gringo" then projecting a vision of a future purged of the gringo and "very much alive" in a utopian landscape "carrying the best of all cultures" (202).

Nostalgia, whether for the past or for the future, has played a central part in our survival in this country, even though one can argue that nostalgia perpetuates an identitarian illusion shot through with contradiction. As Moraga writes, "Every oppressed group needs to imagine with the help of history and mythology a world where our oppression did not seem the pre-ordained order. Aztlán for Chicanos is another example. The mistake lies in believing in this ideal past or imagined future so thoroughly and single-mindedly that finding solutions to present-day inequities loses priority, or we attempt to create too-easy solutions for the pain we feel today."[11] Much recent Chicano autobiographical narrative attempts to reconcile the dilemma between utopian desire for an "ideal past or imagined future" and the startling realities of a present in which too many of our children are the victims of drugs and barrio warfare; a present in which most of us remain day laborers, maids, service workers subsiding on minimum wages and no health insurance; a present in which immigrants are commonly exploited by agricultural and industrial corporations as well as by small businesses and individuals looking for cheap labor and child care; a present in which less than half of our young people ever finish high school and less than 30 percent of those high school graduates ever enroll in college, with fewer than 40 percent ever completing degrees.

That handful of us who teach in American universities learn from our research and the daily information we gather that our condition in this country has not greatly changed in the last century and a half. Those of us who do literary history and what is loosely defined as cultural studies know from our reading of the historical and social text that our cultural production has been largely ignored, dismissed, and suppressed by a mean-spirited and ethnocentrically arrogant intellectual elite. Our job is to restore the full genealogy of our cultural text—autobiographical narrative included—by recovering our literary production from obscurity and suppression, recalculating the reciprocal consciousness that may be seen to give unity in plurality to our historical experience, that specifically traces the cultural and ideological connections between the idea of a homeland *aquí* and a homeland *allá en Mexico.*

For those of us doing work on Mexican immigrant autobiography, we must reclaim cultural ownership of immigrant narrative by calling into question the ethnographic function such narrative has been made to serve from Manuel Gamio's work of the 1920s to that of the present in which, even when softened by journalistic popular representations like Davis's *Mexican Voices/American Dreams,* Mexican immigrants are figured as objects of curiosity for an American reading audience sentimentally interested in *the plight of illegal aliens.* I believe that we must also question the current practice fashionable among critical anthropologists of calling their own imperial practices into question, many of whom are shaping powerful academic careers for themselves by speaking in a confessional mode, a self-reflexive narcissism that further displaces Third World people by making them the objects of theoretical speculation. Although this kinder, gentler anthropology calls for collaborative, dialogic ethnographic exchange, it is in my estimation just another strategy for focusing attention on the anthropologist rather than on the people whose lives are confiscated in one way or another by strangers. Like the professor in Cleofas Jaramillo's *Romance of a Little Village Girl* who wants more and more information about Jaramillo's Nuevomexicano culture because he was "writing a book," the new anthropology continues to plunder different cultural groups for its own professional interests.

My own reading of Mexican immigrant autobiography, while in part implicated in the current debate, is intended to restore the autobiographical authority of personal stories and human voices *de una manera digna de ellos.* It is the small stubbornness of individual vocality and the narrative desire of people for speaking the fullness of their experiences in a sustained and self-sufficient manner that I wish to consider in a larger study. Mexican immigrant narratives largely have operated as part of a generalizing sociological and anthropological project to construct a representation of the immigrant writ large. For Mexicans crossing the border, this ethnographic scrutiny and narrative construction begins with Gamio, is elaborated and popularized in Oscar Lewis's "multiple autobiographies" (*Five Families*, 1959, and *The Children of Sanchez*, 1961), and continues in such ethnographic autobiographies as *Between Two Cultures: The Life of an American Mexican* (1973), John Poggie's editorial construction of a man pseudonymously referred to as Ramón Gonzales. Even Davis's *Mexican Voices/American Dreams* seems a throwback to Gamio in its construction of a master narrative about immigrant experience, reconstituted from scores of brief autobiographical statements that are the textual equivalent of "sound bites," those twenty- to thirty-second media clips that squeeze *essential* information into the smallest possible narrative space.

My next project, therefore, will begin with Gamio's construction of the Mexican cultural subject, simultaneously privileged as autobiographical agent and undermined by social science for its part in a larger scheme of social understanding. I will be less interested in establishing intertextual origins than in thinking about the sociodiscursive formation of the immigrant subject as the specimen-object of social science research, a bodied voice whose story serves a sociological function, a man or a woman with a life history whose narrative operates as a representation for a set of generalizations about immigration and THE immigrant. For my interests as an autobiography scholar, I wish to discover how and when *the immigrant Mexican* ceases performing the role of the body-cum-object of social science and becomes the autonomous subject of his or her own narrative fascination, an autobiographical agent rather than the dehumanized and usually denamed object of speculation.

Notes
Works Cited
Index

Notes

Chapter 1. The Formation of Autobiography in Mexican American Culture

1. Throughout this study, I interchangeably use the terms "Mexican American," "Mexicana/o(s)," and "Hispano/a" as well as regional self-designations: "Tejanos," "Nuevomexicanos," and "Californios." Both the general and the regional terms identify that group of people of Mexican ancestry who, as I indicate in the study, became American citizens after 1848 but usually referred to themselves by such terms. Although I think of this project as a study in the formation of autobiography in Chicano culture, I use the term "Chicano" only for the contemporary period because it was not commonly used during the period I am studying.

2. David J. Weber, *Foreigners in Their Native Land: Historical Roots of the Mexican Americans* (Albuquerque: University of New Mexico Press, 1973): 140. See Weber's excellent discussions of events leading up to and the effects of the U.S. war against Mexico, 88–100, 140–160.

3. See chapter 3, "The Lost Land," in *The Lost Land: The Chicano Image of the Southwest*, John R. Chávez (Albuquerque: University of New Mexico Press, 1984).

4. Leonard Pitt records one such example of correspondence between brothers Antonio María and Pablo de la Guerra, members of an affluent and politically influential California family: "As he set out for the 'new world' of the north [northern California], Antonio vowed to his brother to 'write something of my compañeros that will entertain you.' He did so in a series of lively letters which illuminate the Californio's sense of alienation outside his home precincts." *The Decline of the Californios: A Social History of the Spanish-Speaking Californians, 1846–1890* (Berkeley: University of California Press, 1971): 141, 141–147.

5. See Luis A. Torres's poetry anthology, *The World of Early Chicano Poetry, 1846–1910*, Vol. I: *California Poetry, 1855–1881* (Los Angeles: Floricanto Press, 1993).

6. Pitt, for example, devotes an entire chapter to the work of Francisco P. Ramírez, who edited and published *El Clamor Público*, a Los Angeles newspaper that in addition to carrying general news about Latin America, argued

forcefully on behalf of Mexican Americans; Pitt writes, "Crusading editor Ramirez licensed himself to serve his people in many ways. As their chronicler he revived little-known historical facts, such as how Sonorans had discovered gold in Mexican California long before the advent of Señor James Marshall. As their public defender he chronicled all their expulsions from the mines, lynching, and courtroom difficulties." (*The Decline of the Californios*, 184, 181–189).

7. As early as 1973, Leal called for "an effort . . . to trace the historical development of Mexican American literature." He also recognized the need for, and then set out to train, a generation of "Chicano specialists conversant not only with American literature but with Mexican letters and Chicano culture" whose own work would "accelerate the formation of a tradition of Chicano literary criticism." See "Mexican American Literature: A Historical Perspective," *Revista Chicano-Riqueña*, I, 1 (1973): 32:44; reprinted in *Modern Chicano Writers: A Collection of Critical Essays*, ed. Joseph Sommers and Tomás Ybarra-Frausto (New York: Prentice-Hall, 1979): 18–30.

8. See Genaro M. Padilla, "Self as Cultural Metaphor in Acosta's *The Autobiography of a Brown Buffalo*," *Journal of General Education* 35 (1984): 242–58; Antonio C. Marquez, "Richard Rodriguez' *Hunger of Memory* and the Poetics of Experience," *Arizona Quarterly* (Winter 1984): 130–41; and Ramón Saldívar, "Ideologies of the Self: Chicano Autobiography," *Diacritics* (Fall 1985): 25–34. These are the first essays dealing exclusively with autobiography as a genre.

9. *The Americas Review: A Review of Hispanic Literature and Art of the USA* 16, nos. 3–4 (Fall-Winter 1988). Among this collection of nine essays, only my essay on nineteenth-century California women's personal narrative deals with earlier autobiographical formations.

10. See John Blassingame, *Slave Testimony: Two Centuries of Letters, Speeches, Gilbert Interviews, and Autobiographies* (Baton Rouge: Louisiana State University Press, 1977); Osofsky, ed., *Puttin' on Ole Massa: The Slave Narratives of Henry Bibb, William Wells Brown, and Soloman Northrup* (New York: Harper & Row, 1969); Arna Bontempts, ed., *Great Slave Narratives* (Boston: Beacon Press, 1948); Robert Stepto, *From Behind the Veil: A Study of Afro-American Narrative* (Urbana: University of Illinois Press, 1979); Joanne Braxton, *Black Women Writing Autobiography: A Tradition within a Tradition* (Philadelphia: Temple University Press, 1989).

11. *For Those Who Come After: A Study of Native American Autobiography* (Berkeley: University of California Press, 1985): 33.

12. *Sending My Heart Back Across the Years: Tradition and Innovation in Native American Autobiography* (New York: Oxford University Press, 1992): 57.

13. Henry Louis Gates, Introduction, *The Classic Slave Narratives* (New York: New American Library, 1987): x.

14. Madie Brown Emparan, *The Vallejos of California* (San Francisco: University of San Francisco Press, 1968): 36.

15. *To Tell a Free Story: The First Century of Afro-American Autobiography, 1760–1865* (Urbana: University of Illinois Press, 1988): 5.

16. *Altered Egos: Authority in American Autobiography* (New York: Oxford University Press, 1989): 120.

17. *The Journey Back: Issues in Black Literature and Criticism* (Chicago: University of Chicago Press, 1980): xv–xvii.

18. *To Tell a Free Story*, 4.

19. There have been scores of essays by Chicano scholars which seek to recover the connections to pre-Columbian literature and culture. For the most complete collection of essays on the appropriation of pre-Columbian myth, metaphor, and culture, see Rudolfo A. Anaya and Francisco Lomelí, eds., *Aztlán: Essays on the Chicano Homeland* (Albuquerque: Academia/El Norte Publications, 1989).

20. Miguel León-Portilla, *Pre-Columbian Literatures of Mexico* (Norman: University of Oklahoma Press, 1969): 78; see also León-Portilla's *The Broken Spears: Aztec Account of the Conquest of Mexico* (Boston: Beacon, 1961), and *Los Antiguos Mexicanos a través de sus Crónicas y Cantares* (Mexico City: Fondo de Cultura Económica, 1961), and José María Vigil, *Nezahualcoyotl, el rey poeta* (Mexico: Ediciones de Andrea, 1957).

21. León-Portilla, *Pre-Columbian Literatures*, 82.

22. *Journal of the First Voyage to America* (New York: Albert & Charles Boni, 1924): 26.

23. As Leal says, "We shall consider works especially dating before 1821, written by the inhabitants of this region with a Spanish background, to belong to an early stage of Chicano literature." "Mexican American Literature: A Historical Perspective," in *Modern Chicano Writers*, 22.

24. Here I accept Bruce-Novoa's recent "compromise" of his original proposition that the space signified "the intercultural *nothingness*" in "The Space of Chicano Literature Update: 1978," *RetroSpace: Collected Essays on Chicano Literature* (Houston: Arte Público Press, 1990): 98.

25. For useful accounts of the Mexican War, as well as the social, political, and cultural transformations that resulted, see Carey McWilliams's *North from Mexico: The Spanish-Speaking People of the United States* (New York: Greenwood Press, 1968); Rodolfo Acuña's *Occupied America: A History of Chicanos* (New York: Harper & Row, 1981); and Leonard Pitt's *The Decline of the Californios*.

26. Raymund Paredes, "The Evolution of Chicano Literature," in *Three American Literatures*, ed. Houston A. Baker, Jr. (New York: Modern Language Association, 1982): 36.

27. Emory Elliott, ed., *Columbia Literary History of the United States* (New York: Columbia University Press, 1988): 800–810.

28. Weber, *Foreigners in their Native Land*, vi.

29. This is an echo of Joseph Sommers's dismissive commentary of Rudolfo Anaya's *Bless Me, Ultima* as a novel "harking back in sadness and nostalgia to a forgotten, idealized and unobtainable past." See "Critical Approaches to Chicano Literature," in *Modern Chicano Writers*, 38.

30. Menchaca's "Reminiscences" (MS), Seguín's *Personal Memoirs* (see chap. 2 for full citation), and Pérez's "Memoirs" (MS), Barker Texas History Center, University of Texas, Austin; Tafolla's "Nearing the End of the Trail" (MS), and Garza's "La lógica de mis hechos" (MS), Benson Latin American Collection, Mexican American Archives, Univerisity of Texas, Austin: Rodríguez, *"The Old Guide": His Life in His Own Words* (Dallas: Methodist Episcopal Church, 1897).

31. Padre Martínez's "Relación de méritos," first published by Martínez himself in 1838, may be found in the Benjamin Read Papers, State Records Center, Santa Fe, New Mex., and also in translation in the *New Mexico Historical Review* (Oct. 1928), trans. Cecil Romero.

32. See Fray Angelico Chávez's *But for Time and Chance, the Story of Padre Martínez of Taos, 1793–1867* (Santa Fe: Sunstone Press, 1981); Ray John de Aragon, *Padre Martínez and Bishop Lamy* (Las Vegas, New Mex.: Pan-Am Publications, 1978); and E. A. Mares's edition, *Padre Martínez: New Perspectives from Taos* (Taso: Millicent Rogers Museum, 1988).

33. *My Life on the Frontier, 1864–1882* (New York: Press of the Pioneers, 1935); *My Life on the Frontier, 1882–1897* (Albuquerque: University of New Mexico Press, 1939); and *My Nine Years as Governor of the Territory of New Mexico, 1897–1905* (Albuquerque: University of New Mexico Press, 1940). Otero also wrote *The Real Billy the Kid: With New Light on the Lincoln County War* (New York: R. F. Wilson, 1936).

34. Tey Diana Rebolledo, "Tradition and Mythology: Signatures of Landscape in Chicana Literature," in *The Desert Is No Lady: Southwest Landscapes in Women's Writing and Art,* ed. Vera Norwood and Janice Monk (New Haven: Yale University Press, 1987): 102.

35. Anne Goldman, "'I yam what I yam': Cooking, Culture and Colonialism," in *De/Colonizing the Subject: Politics and Gender in Women's Autobiographical Practice,* ed. Sidonie Smith and Julia Watson (Minneapolis: University of Minnesota Press, 1992): 172.

36. Tey Diana Rebolledo, "Narrative Strategies of Resistance in Hispana Writing," *Journal of Narrative Technique* 20, 2 (Spring 1990): 135. Rebolledo's essay provides a provocative and thoughtful exchange with views I had expressed in a 1987 conference paper that became "Imprisoned Narrative? Or Lies, Secrets and Silence in New Mexico Women's Autobiography," in *Criticism in the Borderlands: Studies in Chicano Literature, Culture and Ideology,* ed. Hector Calderón and José David Saldívar (Durham: Duke University Press, 1991): 43–61.

37. Michel Foucault, *The Archaeology of Knowledge, and the Discourse on Language* (New York: Pantheon, 1972): 149–156, 162–165, 218–220.

38. *History of California,* 7 vols., and *Pastoral California,* like all of Bancroft's historical work, were published by his own San Francisco publishing house, the History Company.

39. H. H. Bancroft, *Literary Industries* (San Francisco: The History Company, 1890): 282.

40. Both Cerruti and Savage left manuscript reports of their ethnographic

expeditions which contain valuable insight into their collection methods. See Savage's "Report on Labors on Archives and Procuring Material for the History of California, 1876–1879," and Cerruti's more autobiographical "Ramblings in California" (1874), both in the Manuscript Collections, Bancroft Library, University of California at Berkeley.

41. All of these manuscripts are held in the Bancroft Library.

42. Georges Gusdorf, "Conditions and Limits of Autobiography" (1956), in *Autobiography: Essays Theoretical and Critical*, ed. James Olney (Princeton: Princeton University Press, 1980): 36.

43. Pitt, *The Decline of the Californios*, 281.

44. "History of the 'Osos,'" 1876, MS, Bancroft Library.

45. *The Poetics of Women's Autobiography: Marginality and the Fictions of Self-Representation* (Bloomington and Indianapolis: Indiana University Press, 1987): 50.

46. Editorial, *La Voz del Nuevo Mundo*, March 7, 1876, California newspaper collection, Bancroft Library.

47. Krupat (1985: 34–35) notes that although Indian autobiography is "produced as an acknowledgment of Indian defeat, in the ideological service of progressive expansionism, . . . by admitting an Indian to the ranks of the self-represented, [it also] questioned progressivist expansionism. For the production of an Indian's own statement of his inevitable disappearance required that the Indian be represented as speaking in his own voice. Unlike Indian biographies, Indian autobiographies require contact with living Indians, for it is the central convention of autobiography that the subject speaks for himself. And it is in its presentation of an Indian voice not as vanished and silent, but as still living and able to be heard that the oppositional potential of Indian autobiography resides."

48. Philippe Lejeune, "The Autobiographical Contract," in *On Autobiography* (Minneapolis: University of Minnesota Press, 1989): 3–30. Lejeune also insists that such forms as the memoir, diary, and autobiographical poem do not properly satisfy the "conditions" of autobiography. There is, of course, a rather large body of critical literature that has moved well beyond a rigid definition of autobiography as a singularly self-disclosing text that reads something like St. Augustine's or Rousseaus' *Confessions.*

49. In addition to the work of Krupat, Gates, Wong, Smith, and Lionnet, I have been influenced widely by numerous scholars whose thinking has substantially reshaped the critical contours of autobiographical study. I cite here a group of studies and anthologies that have influenced my own thinking: Susan Groag Bell and Marilyn Yalom, eds., *Revealing Lives: Autobiography, Biography, and Gender* (Albany: State University of New York Press, 1990); Shari Benstock, ed., *The Private Self: Theory and Practice of Women's Autobiographical Writings* (Chapel Hill: University of North Carolina Press, 1988); Bella Brodzki and Celeste Schenck, eds., *Life/Lines: Theorizing Women's Autobiography* (Ithaca: Cornell University Press, 1988); H. David Brumble, *American Indian Autobiography* (Berkeley: University of California Press, 1988); Joy Webster Barbre/The Personal Narratives

Group, eds., *Interpreting Women's Lives: A Feminist Theory and Personal Narratives* (Bloomington: Indiana University Press, 1989); Paul John Eakin, ed., *American Autobiography: Retrospect and Prospect* (Madison: University of Wisconsin Press, 1991); Shirley Neuman, ed., *Autobiography and Questions of Gender* (Portland, Ore.: F. Cass, 1991); James Olney, ed., *Studies in Autobiography* (New York: Oxford University Press, 1988); James Robert Payne, ed., *Multicultural Autobiography: American Lives* (Knoxville: University of Tennessee Press, 1992); Sidonie Smith and Julia Watson, eds., *De/Colonizing the Subject: The Politics of Gender in Women's Autobiography* (Minneapolis: University of Minnesota, 1992); Valerie Smith, *Self-Discovery and Authority in Afro-American Narrative* (Cambridge: Harvard University Press, 1987); Domna C. Stanton, ed., *The Female Autobiography: Theory and Practice of Autobiography From the Tenth to the Twentieth Century* (Chicago: University of Chicago Press, 1984).

50. *Autobiography: Toward a Poetics of Experience* (Philadelphia: University of Pennsylvania Press, 1982): 142.

51. Richard Rodriguez, *Hunger of Memory: The Education of Richard Rodriguez* (Boston: David R. Godine, 1981).

52. *Hunger of Memory* has received hostile reviews from most Chicano critics, while it has, in general, been favorably reviewed by Anglos. See, for example, Cordelia Candelaria's "Hangup of Memory: Another View of Growing Up Chicano," *American Book Review* 5 (May-June 1983): 4. Also Paul Zweig, "The Child of Two Cultures," *New York Times Book Review,* April 5, 1982, 1.

53. *"The Old Guide,"* 94.

54. An example of Pérez's "Memoirs": "In March 15/1889 . . . I was enlisted in Co. B of the Texas Ranger Under Capt Lee Hall we was send to Alice San diego and Concepsion Catarino Garza is [i.e., Garza's] Revulusion was going on wee arrested Encarnacion Garza[,] Catarino is [i.e., Catarino's] Father-in Law also arrested Encarnacion Garza Catarino is brother took them to San Antonio on the 18 of May mi and Paulino Coy went to arrest Rafael Peña and Maruicio Vela for Horse steeling we met Manuel Ochoa and a girl that had run away with him the Girl had men is cloths and hat they was riding the same horse when wee saw them they was wattering the horse in a lake . . . we was on one side of the lake and he was in the other when he saw us he put the bridle on the horse right quick and gat on the horse and was trying to get away . . . when we was close to him he shot at Coy and the bullet went in about 3 inches and went out again right close to the left hip at that time me and Coy shot at Ochoa and he was hit Just below the left ear he was Killed instantly . . . when wee saw the girl we asked her what she was doing with men is cloth she told us that Ochoa had been at a dance and he told her that if she wond go with him that night he will Killed her" (12).

55. A short list of gringo Texas Ranger memoirs published around the time Pérez composed his 144-page memoir is as follows: James B. Gillet's *Six Years with the Texas Rangers, 1875–81* (New Haven: Yale University

Press, 1925); Claude L. Douglass's *The Gentlemen in the White Hats: Dramatic Episodes in the History of the Texas Rangers* (Dallas: Turner Co., 1934); and Jennings Napoleon Augustus's *A Texas Ranger* (Dallas: Turner Co., 1930).

56. *Autobiographical Voices: Race, Gender, Self-Portraiture* (Ithaca: Cornell University Press, 1989): 18.

57. See *"With his pistol in his hand": A Border Ballad and Its Hero* (Austin: University of Texas Press, 1958): esp. 7–32, 119–125, 147–150.

Chapter 2. Autobiographical Prefigurations

1. *The History of the Military Occupation of the Territory of New Mexico from 1846 to 1851* (Denver: Smith Brooks Co., 1909): 52.

2. See Benjamín R. Read, *Guerra Mexico-Americana* (Santa Fe: 1910), for other Bent letters disclosing *anti-Mexicano* attitudes during the period immediately preceding the occupation of New Mexico by Kearny.

3. *Occupied America*, 50.

4. For details of the Americanization of New Mexico and the events of the period in 1846–47, see Twitchell 1909:38–149; Lamar 1966:56–82; Read 1910:171–219; and Acuña 1981:48–52.

5. Wayne A. Harper, "Juan Bautista Vigil y Alaríd, a New Mexico Bureaucrat, 1792–1866" (M.A. thesis, Brigham Young University, 1985): 159.

6. Jacqueline Dorgan Meketa, *Legacy of Honor: The Life of Rafael Chacón, a Nineteenth-Century New Mexican* (Albuquerque: University of New Mexico Press, 1986): 67.

7. Rosalía Vallejo de Leese, "History of the 'Osos,'" MS, Bancroft Library.

8. Dana's complimentary remarks about Vallejo were culled from a diary entry of December 27, 1835. See *Two Years Before The Mast* (New York: New American Library, 1964): 217.

9. Dana, *Two Years Before the Mast*, 217–218.

10. J. Hector St. John Crevecoeur, "What Is an American," in *Letters from an American Farmer* (New York: Fox, Duffield, Co., 1904): 69–72.

The following description in a more recent history of the period echoes Crevecoeur, if not exactly my Hell's Angels metaphor: "They were reckless and unprincipled fellows with nothing to lose but their lives who would as soon fight Californians as Indians to gratify a taste for violence, revenge, and personal advantage. Others, restless and careless of Mexican rights, were carriers of Manifest Destiny who sought by espousing independence and annexation to the United States to secure land and freedom, even power and wealth. Some were there only in self-defense; though ready to believe the worst about Mexicans they had probably seldom met." Neal Harlow, *California Conquered* (Berkeley: University of California Press, 1982): 101.

11. *California, from the Conquest in 1846 to the Second Vigilance Committee in San Francisco: A Study in American Character* (Boston: Houghton Mifflin, 1886; reprint ed. New York: Alfred Knopf, 1948): 48–49.

12. Bancroft, *History of California*, 5:111.

13. See Reuben L. Underhill, *From Cowhides to Golden Fleece: A Narrative of California, 1832–1858, Based Upon Unpublished Correspondence of Thomas Oliver Larkin* (Stanford: Stanford University Press, 1939): 115.

14. Bancroft, *History of California*, 5:79n.

15. Ibid., 78n.

16. *The Year of Decision: 1846* (Boston: Little, Brown & Co., 1943): 224.

17. William B. Ide, "A Biographical Sketch of the Life of William B. Ide" (1880), in *The Conquest of California by the Bear Flag Party* (Glorieta, New Mex.: Rio Grande Press, 1967): 125.

18. "Ten thousand pounds of flour were purchased on the credit of the Government, and deposited within the garrison; an account was opened for the supply of beef, on terms agreed upon. . . . Whiskey was altogether a contraband article" (Ide 1967:131).

19. Bancroft, *History of California*, 5:113n.

20. Bancroft, *History of California*, 5:125.

21. Emparan, *The Vallejos of California*, 36.

22. For more detailed descriptions of Californio social manners in Dana, *Two Years Before the Mast*, see chapter 13, "Monterey," and chapter 21, "California and Its Inhabitants."

23. John N. Seguín, *Personal Memoirs: From the Year 1834 to the Retreat of General Woll from the City of San Antonio, 1842* (San Antonio: Ledger Book and Job Office, 1858).

24. As David Montejano has argued in *Anglos and Mexicans in the Making of Texas* (Austin: University of Texas Press, 1988), such seemingly contradictory claims were common, among the elite especially. "The Tejanos, or Texas Mexicans, were, as historian James Crisp aptly put it, a 'people of paradox.' José Antonio Navarro and others like Juan Seguín had believed it possible to be both a proud Mexicano and a loyal Tejano. During the rebellion against the Santa Anna dictatorship, such beliefs were not contradictory" (26).

25. Letters of John A. Veach to General Mirabeau B. Lamar, February 23, 1848. *The Papers of Mirabeau Buonaparte Lamar*, ed. Charles A. Gulick (Austin: Von Boeckmann-Jones, 1924).

26. See entry for Juan Nepumuceno Seguín in *The Handbook of Texas, A Supplement*, Vol. III, ed. Eldon Stephen Branda (Austin: Texas State Historical Association, 1976): 868.

27. Ibid., p. 868.

Chapter 3. "It is my history, not yours I propose to tell"

1. See Emparan, *The Vallejos of California*, 76: "On the 19th of February [1851], Vallejo gave bond for $500,000. . . . He swore he was worth in property, real and personal, one million dollars."

2. Emparan, *The Vallejos of California*, 113.

3. See Pitt, *The Decline of the Californios*, 148–166, 195–213, 229–248);

also see Weber, *Foreigners in Their Native Land,* for commentary, "Yankee Infiltration and the Hardening of Stereotypes" (52–61), before 1846 and the cultural conflict ("Cultures Collide," 88–100) after 1846.

4. Vols. 1–5, Manuscript Collection, Bancroft Library; see also Earl R. Hewitt, typescript translation, "Historical and Personal Memoirs Relating to Alta California," Manuscript Collection, Bancroft Library. In my comments on Vallejo's "Recuerdos" I quote interchangeably from Vallejo's own Spanish text and Hewitt's English translation. It should be noted that although Vallejo had a rudimentary use of English, he wrote almost exclusively in Spanish; the Emparan and Brown essays referred to below make use of English translations of letters and other personal statements. My use of English translations is intended as a convenience to the general English reader.

5. Bancroft, *Literary Industries,* 285.

6. Bancroft, *History of California,* vol. 5, Pioneer Register and Index, 757.

7. Emparan, *The Vallejos of California,* 122.

8. See Madie D. Brown, "Gen. M. G. Vallejo and H. H. Bancroft," *California Historical Society Quarterly* 29, 2 (1950): 153.

9. Emparan, *The Vallejos of California,* 226.

10. Emparan, *The Vallejos of California,* 140.

11. Vallejo, MS, 4:199.

12. Whether there actually was a Joaquin Murieta is debatable, but he became the composite name of Mexican social bandits who resisted Americans throughout California in the 1850s. In fact, Joaquin Murieta became what Pitt aptly terms "California's foremost folk legend," a ubiquitous Robin Hood-like hero who filled newspaper columns and who John Rollin Ridge made famous in a popular novel called *The Life and Adventures of Joaquin Murieta* (1854). See Pitt, *The Decline of the Californios,* 77–82.

13. Vallejo, MS, 5:238.

14. "In the schools of San Francisco French and German are taught. Why does there not also exist at least one class in Spanish? Is the Californian population perchance less worthy than the French or German? Is it perchance less intelligent? Perhaps it is and in that case the only remedy that will save it is education. Why is it denied to it? The reason is clear, the German population controls thirty thousand votes, while the number of voters belonging to the Spanish-American races [razas hispano americanas] scarcely amounts to four thousand. The former are fawned upon and the latter despised" (5:189).

15. Emparan, *The Vallejos of California,* 125.

16. Emparan, *The Vallejos of California,* 126.

17. John Frisbie, Vallejo's son-in-law, was president of the Vallejo Savings and Commercial Bank at the time. Vallejo was livid, as a letter to Platon shows: "I am so beset with so many evils that have befallen me since the failure of Frisbie. . . . Frisbie ought not to have jeopardized or risked what was not his, neither in his speculations nor in the stocks." See Emparan, *The Vallejos of California,* 138–40.

18. *History of California,* 5:62.

19. Brown, "Gen. M. G. Vallejo and H. H. Bancroft," 156–157.

20. Letter to Bancroft of Nov. 16, 1875; see Emparan, *The Vallejos of California,* 130.

21. *Literary Industries,* 306.

22. Emparan, *The Vallejos of California,* 174.

Chapter 4. "Yo sola aprendí"

1. This and each of the women's personal narratives to which I refer is housed in the Bancroft Library, University of California at Berkeley. Unless otherwise indicated, references to the manuscripts will be cited by manuscript page (e.g., MS, 5) within the chapter; see Works Cited.

2. MS, Bancroft Library, 87.

3. MS, Bancroft Library, 99.

4. 5:337 (my translation).

5. "Times Gone By in Alta California" (Recollections of Señora Doña Juana Machado Alipaz de Ridington), translation and annotation by Raymond S. Brandes, *Historical Society of Southern California Quarterly* (September 1959): 195–240.

6. In Vivian C. Fisher, ed., *Three Memoirs of Mexican California* (Berkeley: Friends of the Bancroft Library, 1988).

7. Dana, *Two Years Before the Mast,* 162. In "California and Its Inhabitants," chap. 21, Dana goes on to report: "A few inches of cold steel has been the punishment of many an unwary man, who has been guilty, perhaps, of nothing more than indiscretion. The difficulties of the attempt are numerous, and the consequences of discovery fatal, in the better classes." Of Native Americans, Dana is ruthless: "Indeed, to show the entire want of any sense of morality or domestic duty among them, I have frequently known an Indian to bring his wife, to whom he was lawfully married in the church, down to the beach, and carry her back again, dividing with her the money which she had got from the sailors."

8. Alfred Robinson, *Life in California* (New York: Wiley & Putnam, 1846; reprinted ed., New York: Da Capo Press, 1969): 73.

9. Castañeda, "The Political Economy of Nineteenth-Century Stereotypes of Californianas," in *Between Borders: Essays on Mexicana/Chicana History,* ed. Adelaida R. Del Castillo (Encino: Floricanto Press, 1990): 215.

10. Castañeda, "Political Economy," 225.

11. The sense I had of Bancroft's private joke with American readers, especially male readers, emerges throughout *California Pastoral* where Bancroft presents himself as a champion of Mexican women but always with them and their male counterparts as the butt of historiographic humor. Bancroft's opening comments suffice to make my point here: "Before penetrating into the mysteries of our modern lotus-land, or entering upon a description of the golden age of California, if indeed any age characterized by ignorance and laziness can be called golden" (1). Chapter 10, "Woman and

Her Sphere," opens thus: "Women were not treated with the greatest respect: in Latin and in savage countries they seldom are" (305). He also delights in comparing Mexican women with their more *beautiful* American sisters, to the merit of neither: "The beauty of women is of shorter duration in Spanish countries than in the United States; but the monster Time behaves differently in the two places. In the states, the sere and yellow leaf of beauty shrivels into scragginess in the extremes of the type; but in Spanish-speaking countries it is not the withering of the gourd of beauty that those have to deplore who sit beneath its shadow with so great delight, but it is the broadening of that shadow. Without altogether indorsing sylph-like forms, it is yet safe to affirm that degrees of beauty in women are not in direct ratio to the degrees of the latitude of their circumference" (324). Otherwise, Bancroft asserts that "among the married women of the common class, there was looseness—not remarkably so, but they were less strict than American women in this respect" (321).

The text, some 800 pages of ethnographic information on Mexican society before and shortly after 1848, is simply saturated by this form of ethnocentric, sexist consciousness.

12. I argued in "Yo Sola Aprendí: Mexican Women's Personal Narratives from Nineteenth-Century California" (*Revealing Lives: Autobiography, Biography, and Gender* ed. Susan Groag Bell and Marilyn Yalom (State University Press of New York, 1990), that "aside from the accounts of political intrigues, revolts against various Mexican officials, the war with the United States that Bancroft wished to elicit from all of his informants, from the women he also wanted 'information on manners and customs of the Californians.' He wanted the women to remember social events, their favorite dances and songs, their marriages, children's births—in short, their domestic lives as diminutive reflections of the lives of Hispano men. This directive, ironically, meant that memory was pointed back towards women's activities" (119). But as I rethink the women's narratives, what Bancroft wanted from the women and what he got were two different things: women remembered themselves in the public social life of California.

13. See Dana's general description of Ana María de la Guerra's wedding to Alfred Robinson in chap. 27.

14. See Bancroft's Pioneer Register and Index entry, *History of California,* 4:759.

15. Her brother Pablo, for example, was *alcalde* of Santa Barbara in 1847 and after the Americanization served as one of the few Mexican American state senators for several terms, was acting lieutenant governor, U.S. marshal, and district judge from 1864 to 1874. See Bancroft, *History of California,* Pioneer Register and Index, 769.

16. Bancroft, *History of California,* 3:436.

17. See Bancroft, *History of California,* 4:309 (n. 19), and entire chap. XII for an account of Commodore Jones at Monterey, 298–329.

18. She also refutes the widely circulated story that, in apology for his gaffe, Commodore Jones gave a ball to the people of Monterey. As she says,

"It would have been impossible for me not to have known it in so small a place. . . . The truth is there never was such a ball" (53–54).

19. 5:372.

20. *Historical Society of Southern California Quarterly* 8 (1926): 343–344.

21. Pérez is figured into Bancroft's extensive commentary on the development of the mission in the late eighteenth century, the lives of various missionaries, the ecclesiastical and socioeconomic mission of Christianizing the surrounding tribes, and the daily operation and manufacturing process of the missions.

22. Although Pérez does not mention the specifics, she and Mariné apparently split up after a few years. Marie Northrup points out that their separation led to Pérez eventually losing grantee rights to Mariné for the 3-1/2-square-league Rancho el Rincón de San Pascual in what is now Pasadena: "They did not seem to get along together very well so separated, with Doña Eulalia taking the house and Mariné taking land. Eulalia Pérez was granted the Rancho but had never bothered to have her deed recorded in the civil records. No doubt she did not realize the importance of this act. But Mariné did, so he applied to Governor Figueroa for the land. It was granted to him on 18 February 1835. . . . In the Archives of Los Angeles are recorded the unsuccessful attempts she made to regain possession of her land." "Searching for the Birth Date of Eulalia Pérez de Guillén de Mariné," *Historical Society of Southern California Quarterly* 40 (1958): 183.

23. See "Times Gone By in Alta California," 195–240.

24. In a note on the San Diego ranchos occupied by private citizens, Bancroft mentions that Jamacha was granted "in 1840 to Apolinaria Lorenzana, who had asked for it and obtained the necessary certificates from the padres in 1833–34." *History of California*, 3:611.

25. "Times Gone By in Alta California," 201.

26. Weber, *Foreigners in Their Native Land*, 128.

Chapter 5. Leaving a "clean and honorable name"

1. In addition to editing a number of Spanish-language newspapers, Felipe Chacón published a volume of poetry and short prose in 1924 entitled *Obras de Felipe Maximiliano Chacón, "El Cantador Neomexicano" Poesía y Prosa* (Works of Felipe Maximiliano Chacón, "New Mexican Singer": Poetry and Prose). See Erlinda Gonzales-Berry's discussion of Chacón's poetry, "Vincente Bernal and Felipe M. Chacón: Bridging Two Cultures," in *Pasó por Aquí: Critical Essays on the New Mexico Literary Tradition, 1542–1988*, ed., Erlinda Gonzales-Berry (Albuquerque: University of New Mexico Press, 1989): 185–198.

2. Eusebio Chacón published *El hijo de la tempestad* (Son of the Storm) and *Tras la tormenta la calma* (The Calm after the Storm) in 1892. For an excellent discussion on his ground-breaking work as a novelist, essayist, and cultural spokesman, see Francisco Lomelí's "Eusebio Chacón: An Early Pioneer of the New Mexican Novel," in *Pasó por Aquí*, 149–166.

3. I received this manuscript information in a letter (July 13, 1988) from David M. Hays, librarian at the Western Historical Collections, University of Colorado Library, Boulder.

4. All references to the Meketa text, unless otherwise noted, will appear by page number.

5. Like the terms "Californio" and "Tejano," "Nuevomexicano" is a self-designation commonly used by people in the Spanish colonial province and, after 1821, the Mexican department of Nuevo Mexico.

6. Paul Radin, *Crashing Thunder: The Autobiography of an American Indian* (Lincoln: University of Nebraska Press, 1983): ix–xviii.

7. See Krupat, *For Those Who Come After.*

8. As Francisco Lomelí defines them, *inditas* are "songs or poems that use the capture of women by Indians as their central motif," and *cuandos* are poems or ballads "using 'when' as their point of departure." "A Literary Portrait of Hispanic New Mexico: Dialectics of Perception," in *Pasó por Aquí,* 138.

9. By the early 1840s, New Mexicans were well aware that the United States had designs on Mexico's northern territory, and Armijo did attempt to prepare his compatriots for the impending invasion many expected.

10. For useful accounts of resistance to the invading American forces see Rodolfo Acuña's *Occupied America,* and Robert J. Rosenbaum's *Mexicano Resistance in the Southwest: "The Sacred Rights of Self-Preservation"* (Austin: University of Texas Press, 1981).

11. Meketa notes that about this time "an interest in the history of Trinidad and the colorful characters who had participated in the settlement of the Southwest arose in the area. The Early Settler's Association was then formed, as the forerunner of the present-day Trinidad Historical Society, and regional historians began questioning Chacón and other pioneers about their memories of earlier times, both in person and by letter" (308).

12. Although Chacón does not say as much, he must be referring here to the same Juan Bautista Vigil y Alaríd, who he refers to as "Doctor Alaríd," a title that would be appropriate for an apothecary.

13. See "New Mexican Spanish Folk-Lore," *Journal of American Folklore* 26, 100: (April–June 1913): 97.

14. Rowena Rivera, "New Mexico Colonial Poetry: Tradition and Innovation," in *Pasó por Aquí,* 83–84.

15. Rivera, "New Mexico Colonial Poetry," 97. Rivera, while suggesting that certain forms have "miraculously survived . . . up to the 1960s," notes the erosion of traditional practice: "In northern New Mexico and southern Colorado, one can still find a few surviving fragmented texts representing the fullest traditional form of the secular *décima* or the religious *décima-a-lo-divino.* And occasionally, one also finds, especially in southern Colorado, an older poet who can chant the *planta* [introductory quatrain for the *décima*] and a few stanzas." Ibid., 90.

16. See Genaro M. Padilla, ed., *The Short Stories of Fray Angelico Chávez* (Albuquerque: University of New Mexico Press, 1987), and Rudolfo Anaya's *Bless Me, Ultima* (Berkeley: Quinto Sol, 1972), *Heart of Aztlán* (Berkeley:

Editorial Justa, 1976), and *The Silence of the Llano* (Berkeley: Tonatiuh-Quinto Sol, 1982).

17. See Herbert Eugene Bolton, *Spanish Exploration in the Southwest, 1542–1706* (New York: Charles Scribner's Sons, 1916): 223–232.

18. My thinking here on the deeply ingrained desire to protect the homeland has been much influenced by Tobias Duran, a historian at the University of New Mexico.

19. Darlis A. Miller, "Hispanos and the Civil War in New Mexico: A Reconsideration," *New Mexico Historical Review* 54, no. 2 (1979): 107.

20. As Chacón writes toward the end of the narrative, generations of Chacóns had fought against the Navajos with substantial losses. "The terrible Navajos . . . had deprived me of those who were dear to me, my grandfather Don Francisco Lopez, my god father, Captain Blas de Hinojosa, and so many other officers from my family who perished in the wars against that tribe" (303). Although he offers no apologies for waging war against the Navajos, Chacón opposed the inhumane conditions to which they were subjected in forced removals by the United States during the 1860s. In a letter to the *Santa Fe Gazette* (April 1863), Chacón balked at the plan to remove the Navajos to a location he thought impossibly severe: "The place is unfit, it will not even grow grass. . . . The winters are very cold and the summers are unpleasant. No people have ever lived in this area; it is a desert" (Meketa 1986: 248).

21. Ralph Emerson Twitchell, *The Leading Facts of New Mexican History*, vol. 2 (Cedar Rapids: Torch Press, 1912): 33n.

22. The original history was the Spanish *Historia Ilustrada de Nuevo Mexico* (Santa Fe: Compañia Impresora de Nuevo Mexico, 1911).

23. Meketa's text is the product of such appropriation of autobiographical narrative to generalizing historical ends.

24. Read had called on "Captain Chacón," who was living in Trinidad at the time, to supply him with information on the American invasion of 1846 and other significant events of the territorial period. The *Illustrated History of New Mexico*, for example, includes a long letter, dated May 4, 1910, in which Chacón recounted events from 1846; in the letter, Chacón says, "I wrote in 1906 part of my memoirs and thence I copy what follows" (Read 1912, 432). As Meketa says, "About the time that Rafael Chacón began writing his memoirs an interest in the history of Trinidad and the colorful characters who had participated in the settlement of the Southwest arose in the area . . . and regional historians began questioning Chacón and other pioneers about their memories of earlier times, both in person and by letter" (Meketa, 1986: 308). Chacón, however, seems to have had little interest in being a colorful character whose memories would supplement the legend of the West.

25. Rather than the stiff rhetorical endearment it sounds like in English, in Spanish, the term "compañera" has particular cultural significance: a couple who refer to each other as "compañeros" means that they trust and rely on each other, that they enjoy each others' company; it is also term equivalent to "sweetheart," etc.

26. Durrant, "Self as the Intersection of Traditions: The Autobiographical writings of Ssuma Chien," *Journal of the American Oriental Society* 106, no. 1 (1986): 33–40.

Chapter 6. Lies, Secrets, and Silence

1. Jaramillo's privately printed edition 1939 was republished in 1942 by Seton Village Press in Santa Fe.

2. Introduction, *Sombras del Pasado/Shadows of the Past* (Santa Fe: Ancient City Press, 1941).

3. Paredes, "The Evolution of Chicano Literature," in *Three American Literatures*, 56.

4. Rebolledo, "Tradition and Mythology: Signatures of Landscape in Chicano Literature," in *The Desert Is No Lady*, 98.

5. Rebolledo, "Narrative Strategies of Resistance in Hispana Writing," 135.

6. *New Mexico Folklore Record* IX (1954–55): 3.

7. Foucault, *The Archaeology of Knowledge, and the Discourse on Language*, 149–156, 162–165, 218–220.

8. The University of New Mexico Press bought publication rights in 1952 and has continued to print *The Land of Poco Tiempo* as one of its staples.

9. *A Tramp Across the Continent* (New York: Charles Scribner's Sons, 1892).

10. See *A New Mexico David and Other Stories and Sketches of the Southwest* (New York: Charles Scribner, 1891) and *Some Strange Corners of Our Country: The Wonderland of the Southwest* (New York: Century, 1892).

11. *Southwest Classics: The Creative Literature of the Arid Lands* (Tucson: University of Arizona Press, 1974): 44.

12. Powell, *Southwest Classics*, 51.

13. Lummis helped to establish the Landmarks Club (1895), an organization committed to preserving the California missions, historic homes, and locales; and he also established the Southwest Museum in Los Angeles in 1907.

14. For a detailed examination of the figure of the Mexican in American literature and culture, see Cecil Robinson's *With the Ears of Strangers* (Tucson: University of Arizona Press, 1963).

15. Cather, *Death Comes for the Archbishop* (New York: Alfred A. Knopf, 1927): 103.

16. See "The Penitent Brothers" in *Land of Poco Tiempo*. The account of the complex socioreligious ritual Lenten practices of the Penitente Brotherhood, a long misrepresented lay religious group in New Mexico, opens with Lummis's typical sensationalizing: "So late as 1891, a procession of flagellants took place within the limits of the United States. A procession in which voters of this Republic shredded their naked backs with savage whips, staggered beneath huge crosses, and hugged the maddening needles of the cactus; a procession which culminated in the flesh-and-blood cruci-

fixion of an unworthy representative of the Redeemer. Nor was this an iso-lated horror. Every Good Friday, for many generations, it has been a staple custom to hold these barbarous rites in part of New Mexico" (56).

For further reading on the Penitentes, see Marta Weigle's intelligent an-thropology in *Brothers of Blood, Brothers of Light: The Penitentes of the Southwest* (Albuquerque: University of New Mexico Press, 1976).

17. Keith Sagar, ed., *D. H. Lawrence and New Mexico* (Salt Lake City: Peregrine Smith, 1982): 3.

18. Ibid., 3.

19. Ibid., 11.

20. Ibid., 2.

21. Lummis, *The Spanish Pioneers* (Chicago: A. C. McClurg, 1893): Preface.

22. Cecil Romero, "A Unique American Chronicle," *El Palacio* 24, no. 9 (March 3, 1928): 159.

23. Orfa Jean Shontz, *The Family* 8 (May 1927): 74.

24. Northrop Frye, *Anatomy of Criticism* (Princeton: Princeton Univer-sity Press, 1957): 186.

25. McGregor, "Our Spanish-American Fellow Citizens," *Harper's Weekly* (June 13, 1914): 7.

26. Mary Austin, "Mexicans and New Mexico," *The Survey* 66, no. 3 (May 1931): 141.

27. Mary Austin, *Earth Horizon: Autobiography* (New York: Houghton Mifflin, 1932): 352.

28. In 1680, a confederation of Pueblo tribes successfully rebelled against the Spanish, driving them from the entire province to El Paso del Norte, where the colonists remained until Diego de Vargas led an expedition back to Santa Fe in 1692 where he reconsolidated colonial authority.

29. "The 1925 Fiesta," *El Palacio* IX (September 1, 1925): 88, 109. The article ends on a note encouraging the "amalgamating force" of the fiesta: "One of the fine things about the Fiesta is its influence toward welding together more in spirit and sympathy the people of these two main branches of our population; Anglos reenacting the role of heroic Spaniards, native people commemorating the upbuilding of an American state, and venerat-ing the flag for which they have made their fullest sacrifice. The fiesta, we believe, is a strong amalgamating force, striking down what barriers the ignorant and those without vision seek to raise. Celebrating the exploits of the Castilians and perpetuating the beauty they have bequeathed us; hand in hand with an honest and vigorous effort to bring to their descendants every advantage that American progress and enlightenment affords—this is the way to fullest amalgamation" (110–111).

30. *Santa Fe New Mexican* (September 4, 1934).

31. In 1940, New Mexico celebrated the 400-year anniversary of Corona-do's exploratory journey of 1540–1542 through the Southwest in a drama-tization that followed the Coronado trail between seventeen New Mexico, West Texas, and Arizona cities. The historical drama, "Entrada: A Pageant

of the Centuries," was scripted by Thomas Woods Stevens. That year *New Mexico* magazine carried an article (Edmund Sherman, "New Mexico Celebrates," vol. 18, June 1940) that opens with an echo of Lummis's project for restoring the romance of the Spanish conquest. "From the land of *mañana* to that of yesteryear, New Mexico is reaching back into history four centuries to commemorate this summer an event that was the beginning of the American Southwest. . . . Thomas Wood Stevens, internationally known pageant writer, produced the pageant book, a precise and dramatic play which depicts the Coronado *Entrada* on a grand scale. Costuming presented one of the major tasks in the presentation . . . for nearly 1000 pieces of clothing were necessary to clothe the cast of the hundreds. . . . For this job, Miss Lucy Barton, nationally known costume designer, was employed. . . . Then came the problem of a stage upon which to produce a show of the magnitude of that planned for the Coronado celebration. The Jerome H. Cargill production organization of New York, experts in the construction of stage and lighting equipment, has taken charge of this phase of the production. The stage to be used in the featured *entradas* will measure 300 feet in length with backgrounds extending more than 50 feet high, depicting the various locations visited by the *Conquistadores*" (12–13).

32. *Los Moros y los Cristianos* has been identified as one of the first dramas performed in the Americas, versions of which have remained in performance for many generations. For a useful discussion of this and other Spanish colonial drama in New Mexico, see Reed Anderson, "Early Secular Theater in New Mexico," in *Pasó por Aquí*, 101–127.

33. The *Santa Fe New Mexican* of September 16, 1936, expressed the desire for the kind of colonial costuming Jaramillo's *Sociedad* could provide the residents of the state. "The heavy silks, satins and brocades of women's fashionable attire from 1850 to the turn of the century, that years in trunks have not destroyed and scarcely weakened, were once again in their glory during the fiesta when the Sociedad Folklorica entertained with a Spanish-Colonial style show and chocolate merienda at the Sena Plaza. . . . Gowns imported to the frontier country by the Spanish aristocrats, gowns that traveled the Santa Fe trail in pioneer days, were seen in the stunning, historical style show. Those attending believed this to be one of the most interesting new features of the Fiesta and hope it will be repeated in coming years." Jaramillo's Spanish colonial fashion show was repeated during the "coming years"—so much so that it has become an integral part of the Fiesta up to the present.

34. Rebolledo, "Tradition and Mythology," in *The Desert Is No Lady*, 102.

35. Since this chapter was originally drafted, Anne Goldman has written extensively and brilliantly on the subtle contestatory function of both Jaramillo's *The Genuine New Mexico Tasty Recipes* and Fabiola Cabeza de Baca's *The Good Life: New Mexico Traditions and Food*. As she writes of the sociocultural significance of transmitting recipes, "Encouraging readers to reproduce, revise and make a recipe their own enables Cabeza de Baca to call attention to cultural commodification in *The Good Life*. If the text

appears to encourage its audience to make "New Mexico Traditions and Food" their own, however, its author ultimately provides obstacles to such appropriation. 'In order to have the dishes taste as one has eaten them in the New Mexican homes or genuine new Mexican restaurants, one must use New Mexican products,' she counsels (45). As with Jaramillo's text [*The Genuine New Mexico Tasty Recipes*], "genuine" works here not merely as authorization of authenticity (with respect to the writer) but as barrier (vis-à-vis the reader) as well. Ostensibly allowing for the possibility of extracultural access, this admonishment to use 'New Mexican products' works on another level to divide nonnative readers from the Hispano community the book itself so wholeheartedly celebrates, thus resisting cultural abstraction and insisting on rootedness and a sense of place. Appending the book with a glossary of Spanish terms allows Cabeza de Baca to remind her readership that reproducing the recipes of *The Good Life* does not necessarily lead to cultural ownership. "The words in this glossary may have other meanings," she asserts, "but the one given here explains the meaning as used in this composition" (81). By calling attention to what is left over, the remainder which escapes translation, the author problematizes cultural access, depicting a web of associations and meanings ultimately ungraspable by the nonnative speaker." "'I yam what I yam,'" in *De/Colonizing the Subject*, 184.

36. See Antonio Gramsci, "The Study of Philosophy," in *Selections from the Prison Notebooks*, ed. and trans. Quintin Hoare and Geoffrey Nowell Smith (New York: International Publishers, 1971).

37. Goldman, "'I yam what I yam,'" in *De/Colonizing the Subject*, 179.

38. This moment of resistance to the cultural Other is prefigured in earlier Mexican American journalism and scholarship in which there is a critique of the smug pronouncements on native cultural production by Anglos. In 1932, Arthur Campa, in "Religious Spanish Folk-Drama in New Mexico," comments on the "unusual amount of interest . . . in things Spanish" that produced a body of scholarship Campa regards as plagued by cultural misunderstanding, lack of socioaesthetic context, and facile notions about the origins and social use of theater and other literary practices. Campa argued that newcomers authorize themselves to speak on native cultural practices that, as Jaramillo would later write, ran as a "current invisible to the stranger and understood only by their inhabitants." As Campa writes, "Within the last few years, an unusual amount of interest has been aroused in things Spanish, and as a result, charlatan and quack scholars have been induced to break out into print with everything that has a Spanish semblance. Much harm can be done and is done by this sort of work under the name of scholarship." As a corrective to such shoddy scholarship, the middle of Campa's essay—much like the whole of Campa's career as a noted folklorist—provides a contextualized commentary on the performative aspects of literary practices, in this case religious drama. The essay closes by revoicing his criticism of commentary removed from or ignorant of the complex cultural and performative context of the drama. "New Mexico abounds in poetry, drama, and song. All this folk-lore is not the product of

one generation and cannot be studied wholly from the schoolroom or the office. The perspective necessary to interpret the customs and tradition of the Spanish inhabitants in the Southwest is gained only by close observation. It is easy to become charmed and enthused, but quite another thing to understand the object of interest." "Religious Spanish Folk-Drama in New Mexico," *New Mexico Quarterly* 2, no. 1 (February 1932): 3–13.

Conclusion

1. Eva Wilbur-Cruce, *A Beautiful, Cruel Country* (Tucson: University of Arizona Press, 1987): viii.

2. Alfonso Griego, *Good-bye, My Land of Enchantment* (Albuquerque, 1981).

3. José Antonio Villarreal *Pocho* (New York: Doubleday, 1959): 15–16.

4. See Paul Taylor, *Mexican Labor in the United Sates.* 7 vols. Berkeley: University of California Press, 1928–1932).

5. Alejandro Portes and Robert L. Bach, *Latin Journey: Cuban and Mexican Immigrants in the United States* (Berkeley: University of California Press, 1985): 79.

6. Lawrence Cardoso, *Mexican Emigration to the United States, 1897–1931* (Tucson: University of Arizona Press, 1980): 53.

7. Also see Gamio's *Mexican Immigration to the United States: A Study in Human Migration and Adjustment* (Chicago: University of Chicago Press, 1930).

8. Ramón Perez, *Diary of an Undocumented Immigrant* (Houston: Arte Público Press, 1991): 232. The Immigration Reform and Control Act of 1986 made it possible for undocumented workers who had been in the country unlawfully before January 1, 1982, to apply legal resident status. Over three million people applied for residency under the new law; although, as it turns out, there were numerous provisions and exclusions that created obstacles to permanent residence.

9. Oscar Zeta Acosta, *The Autobiography of a Brown Buffalo* (San Francisco: Straight Arrow Books, 1972; reprint ed. New York: Penguin, 1989): 199.

10. Gloria Anzaldúa, *Borderands/La Frontera: The New Mestiza* (San Francisco: Spinsters/Aunt Lute, 1987): 194.

11. Cherríe Moraga, *Loving in the War Years* (Boston: South End Press, 1983): 129.

Works Cited

Books and Theses

Acosta, Oscar Zeta. *The Autobiography of a Brown Buffalo.* San Francisco: Straight Arrow, 1972; reprint ed. New York: Penguin, 1989.

Acuña, Rodolfo. *Occupied America: A History of Chicanos.* 2d ed. New York: Harper & Row, 1981.

Anaya, Rudolfo. *Bless Me, Ultima.* Berkeley: Quinto Sol, 1972.

Andrews, William. *To Tell a Free Story: The First Century of Afro-American Autobiography, 1760–1865.* Urbana: University of Illinois Press, 1988.

Anzaldúa, Gloria. *Borderlands/La Frontera: The New Mestiza.* San Francisco: Spinsters/Aunt Lute, 1987.

Augustus, Jennings Napoleon. *A Texas Ranger.* Dallas: Turner Co., 1930.

Austin, Mary. *Earth Horizon: Autobiography.* New York: Houghton Mifflin, 1932.

Baker, Jr., Houston A. *The Journey Back: Issues in Black Literature and Criticism.* Chicago: University of Chicago Press, 1980.

Bancroft, Hubert Howe. *History of California.* 7 vols. San Francisco: The History Company, 1884–1889.

Bancroft, Hubert Howe. *Pastoral California.* San Francisco: The History Company, 1888.

Bancroft, Hubert Howe. *Literary Industries.* San Francisco: The History Company, 1890.

Blassingame, John. *Slave Testimony: Two Centuries of Letters, Speeches, Interviews, and Autobiographies.* Baton Rouge: Louisiana State University Press, 1977.

Bolton, Herbert Eugene. *Spanish Exploration in the Southwest, 1542–1706.* New York: Charles Scribner's Sons, 1916.

Bontempts, Arna, ed. *Great Slave Narratives.* Boston: Beacon Press, 1948.

Branda, Elson Stephen, ed. *The Handbook of Texas, A Supplement.* Austin: Texas State Historical Association, 1976.

Bruce-Novoa, Juan. *RetroSpace: Collected Essays on Chicano Literature.* Houston: Arte Público Press, 1990.

Cabeza de Baca, Fabiola. *The Good Life: New Mexico Traditions and Food.* 1949. Santa Fe: Museum of New Mexico Press, 1982.

Cabeza de Baca, Fabiola. *We Fed Them Cactus.* Albuquerque: University of New Mexico Press, 1954.

Cather, Willa. *Death Comes for the Archbishop.* New York: Alfred A. Knopf, 1927.

Chávez, Fray Angelico. *But for Time and Chance, the Story of Padre Martínez de Taos, 1793–1867.* Santa Fe: Sunstone Press, 1981.

Chávez, John R. *The Lost Land: The Chicano Image of the Southwest.* Albuquerque: University of New Mexico Press, 1984.

Columbus, Christopher. *The Journal of the First Voyage to the Americas.* Trans. Cecil Jane. New York: Knopf, 1927.

Couser, Thomas G. *Altered Egos: Authority in American Autobiography.* Oxford: Oxford University Press, 1989.

Crevecoeur, J. Hector St. John de. *Letters from an American Farmer.* 1782. New York: Fox, Duffield, Co., 1904.

Dana, Richard Henry. *Two Years Before the Mast.* 1840. New York: New American Library, 1964.

Del Castillo, Adelaida R., ed. *Between Borders: Essays on Mexicana/Chicana History.* Encino, Calif.: Floricanto Press, 1990.

DeVoto, Bernard. *The Year of Decision: 1846.* Boston: Little, Brown & Co., 1943.

Douglass, Claude L. *The Gentlemen in the White Hats: Dramatic Episodes in the History of the Texas Rangers.* Dallas: Turner Co., 1934.

Emparan, Madie Brown. *The Vallejos of California.* San Francisco: University of San Francisco Press, 1968.

Fisher, Vivian C., ed. *Three Memoirs of Mexican California.* Berkeley: Friends of the Bancroft Library, 1988.

Frye, Northrop. *Anatomy of Criticism.* Princeton: Princeton University Press, 1957.

Foucault, Michel. *The Archaeology of Knowledge, and the Discourse on Language.* New York: Pantheon, 1972.

Galarza, Ernesto. *Barrio Boy: The Story of a Boy's Acculturation.* Notre Dame: University of Notre Dame Press, 1971.

Gamio, Manuel. *The Mexican Immigrant: His Life Story.* Chicago: University of Chicago Press, 1931.

Gates, Henry Louis. Introduction. *The Classic Slave Narratives.* New York: New American Library, 1987.

Gillet, James B. *Six Years with the Texas Rangers, 1875–81.* New Haven: Yale University Press, 1925.

Gramsci, Antonio. *Selections from the Prison Notebooks.* Trans. and ed. Quintin Hoare and Geoffrey Nowell Smith. New York: International Publishers, 1971.

Griego, Alfonso. *Good-bye, My Land of Enchantment.* Albuquerque, 1981.

Gulick, Charles A., ed. *The Papers of Mirabeau Buonaparte Lamar.* Austin: Von Boeckmann-Jones, 1924.

Gunn, Janet Varner. *Autobiography: Toward a Poetics of Experience*. Philadelphia: University of Pennsylvania Press, 1982.

Harlow, Neal. *California Conquered*. Berkeley: University of California Press, 1982.

Harper, Wayne A. "Juan Bautista Vigil y Alaríd, a New Mexico Bureaucrat, 1792–1866." M.A. thesis. Brigham Young University, 1985.

Ide, William B. *The Conquest of California by the Bear Flag Party*. Glorieta, New Mex.: Rio Grande Press, 1967.

Jaramillo, Cleofas. *Romance of a Little Village Girl*. San Antonio: Naylor, 1955.

Jaramillo, Cleofas. *The Genuine New Mexico Tasty Recipes: Old and Quaint Formulas for the Preparation of Seventy-five Delicious Spanish Dishes*. 1939. Santa Fe: Seton Village Press, 1942.

Jaramillo, Cleofas. *Sombras del Pasado/Shadows of the Past*. Santa Fe: Ancient City Press, 1941.

Jaramillo, Cleofas. *Cuentos del Hogar*. El Campo, Texas: Citizen Press, 1939.

Krupat, Arnold. *For Those Who Come After: A Study of Native American Autobiography*. Berkeley: University of California Press, 1985.

Lamar, Howard Roberts. *The Far Southwest, 1846–1912: A Territorial History*. New Haven: Yale University Press, 1966.

Lejeune, Philippe. *On Autobiography*. Minneapolis: University of Minnesota Press, 1989.

León-Portilla, Miguel. *Pre-Columbian Literatures of Mexico*. Norman: University of Oklahoma Press, 1969.

León-Portilla, Miguel. *The Broken Spears: Aztec Accounts of the Conquest of Mexico*. Boston: Beacon, 1961.

León-Portilla, Miguel. *Los Antiguos Mexicanos a través de sus Crónicas y Cantares*. Mexico City: Fondo de Cultura Económica, 1961.

Lionnet, Françoise. *Autobiographical Voices: Race, Gender and Self Portraiture*. Ithaca: Cornell University Press, 1989.

Lummis, Charles F. *The Land of Poco Tiempo*. New York: Charles Scribner's Sons, 1893: reprint ed. Albuquerque: University of New Mexico Press, 1973.

Lummis, Charles F. *The Spanish Pioneers*. Chicago: A. C. McClurg, 1893.

McWilliams, Carey. *North from Mexico: The Spanish-Speaking People of the United States*. Philadelphia: J. B. Lippincott, 1948; reprint ed. New York: Greenwood Press, 1968.

Meketa, Jacqueline Dorgan. *Legacy of Honor: The Life of Rafael Chacón, a Nineteenth-Century New Mexican*. Albuquerque: University of New Mexico Press, 1986.

Montejano, David. *Anglos and Mexicans in the Making of Texas*. Austin: University of Texas Press, 1988.

Moraga, Cherríe. *Loving in the War Years*. Boston: South End Press, 1983.

Osofsky, Gilbert, ed. *Puttin' On Ole Massa: The Slave Narratives of Henry Bibb, William Wells Brown, and Soloman Northrup*. New York: Harper & Row, 1969.

Otero, Miguel Antonio. *My Life on the Frontier, 1864–1882*. New York: Press of the Pioneers, 1935.

Otero, Miguel Antonio. *My Life on the Frontier, 1882–1897*. Albuquerque: University of New Mexico Press, 1939.

Otero, Miguel Antonio. *My Nine Years as Governor of the Territory of New Mexico, 1897–1905*. Albuquerque: University of New Mexico Press, 1940.

Padilla, Genaro M., ed. *The Short Stories of Fray Angelico Chávez*. Albuquerque: University of New Mexico Press, 1987.

Paredes, Américo. *"With his pistol in his hand": A Border Ballad and Its Hero*. Austin: University of Texas Press, 1958.

Pérez, Ramón. *Diary of an Undocumented Worker*. Houston: Arte Público, 1991.

Pitt, Leonard. *The Decline of the Californios: A Social History of the Spanish-Speaking Californios, 1846–1890*. Berkeley: University of California Press, 1971.

Powell, Lawrence Clark. *Southwest Classics: The Creative Literature of the Arid Lands*. Tucson: University of Arizona Press, 1974.

Radin, Paul. *Crashing Thunder: The Autobiography of an American Indian*. Lincoln: University of Nebraska Press, 1983.

Read, Benjamín R. *Guerra Mexico-Americana*. Santa Fe: Santa Fe New Mexican Printing Co., 1910.

Read, Benjamín R. *Illustrated History of New Mexico*. Santa Fe: Santa Fe New Mexican Printing Co., 1912.

Rodríguez, José Policarpio. *"The Old Guide": His Life in His Own Words*. Dallas: Methodist Episcopal Church, ca. 1897.

Rodriguez, Richard. *Hunger of Memory: The Education of Richard Rodriguez*. Boston: David R. Godine, 1981.

Robinson, Alfred S. *Life in California*. 1846. New York: Da Capo Press, 1969.

Rosenbaum, Robert J. *Mexicano Resistance in the Southwest: "The Sacred Rights of Self-Preservation."* Austin: University of Texas Press, 1981.

Royce, Josiah. *California, from the Conquest in 1846 to the Second Vigilance Committee in San Francisco: A Study in American Character*. Boston: Houghton Mifflin, 1886; reprint ed. New York: Alfred Knopf, 1948.

Sagar, Keith, ed. *D. H. Lawrence and New Mexico*. Salt Lake City: Peregrine Smith, 1982.

Saldívar, Ramón. *Chicano Narrative: The Dialectics of Difference*. Madison: University of Wisconsin Press, 1990.

Sánchez, George I. *Forgotten People: A Study of New Mexicans*. Albuquerque: University of New Mexico Press, 1940.

Seguín, John N. *Personal Memoirs: From the Year 1834 to the Retreat of General Woll from the City of San Antonio, 1842*. San Antonio: Ledger Book and Job Office, 1858.

Smith, Sidonie. *The Poetics of Women's Autobiography: Marginality and the Fictions of Self-Representation*. Bloomington: Indiana University Press, 1987.

Stepto, Robert. *From Behind the Veil: A Study of Afro-American Narrative.* Urbana: University of Illinois Press, 1979.

Twitchell, Ralph Emerson. *The History of the Military Occupation of the Territory of New Mexico from 1846 to 1851.* Denver: Smith Brooks Co., 1909.

Twitchell, Ralph Emerson. *The Leading Facts of New Mexican History.* Cedar Rapids: Torch Press, 1912.

Underhill, Reuben L. *From Cowhides to Golden Fleece: A Narrative of California, 1832–1858, Based Upon Unpublished Correspondence of Thomas Oliver Larkin.* Stanford: Stanford University Press, 1939.

Vigil, José María. *Nezahualcoyotl, el rey poeta.* Mexico: 1957.

Villarreal, José Antonio. *Pocho.* New York: Doubleday, 1959.

Warren, Nina Otero. *Old Spain in Our Southwest.* New York: Harcourt, Brace & Co., 1936.

Weber, David J. *Foreigners in Their Native Land: Historical Roots of the Mexican Americans.* Albuquerque: University of New Mexico Press, 1973.

White-Lea, Aurora Lucero. *Literary Folklore of the Hispanic Southwest.* San Antonio: Naylor, 1953.

Wilbur-Cruce, Eva. *A Beautiful, Cruel Country.* Tucson: University of Arizona Press, 1987.

Wong, Hertha. *Sending My Heart Back Across the Years: Tradition and Innovation in Native American Autobiography* New York: Oxford University Press, 1992.

Articles

Anderson, Reed. "Early Secular Theater in New Mexico." *Pasó por Aquí: Critical Essays on the New Mexico Literary Tradition, 1542–1988.* Ed. Erlinda Gonzales-Berry. Albuquerque: University of New Mexico Press, 1989.

Austin, Mary. "Mexicans and New Mexico." *The Survey* 66, no. 3 (May 1931): 141.

Brown, Madie E. "Gen. M. G. Vallejo and H. H. Bancroft." *California Historical Society Quarterly* 29 (1950): 150–161.

Burnham, Frederick R. "The Remarks of Major Frederick R. Burnham." *Historical Society of Southern California Quarterly* 8 (1926): 343–344.

Campa, Arthur. "Religious Spanish Folk-Drama in New Mexico." *New Mexico Quarterly* 2, no. 1 (February 1932): 3–13.

Candelaria, Cordelia. "Hangup of Memory: Another View of Growing Up Chicano." *American Book Review* 5 (May–June 1983): 4.

Durrant, Stephen. "Self as the Intersection of Traditions: The Autobiographical writings of Ssuma Chien." *Journal of the American Oriental Society* 106, no. 1 (1986): 33–40.

Espinosa, Aurelio M. "New Mexican Spanish Folk-Lore." *Journal of American Folklore* 26, no. 100 (April–June 1913): 97.

Fierro, Felipe. Editorial. *La Voz del Nuevo Mundo* [San Francisco] March 7, 1876.

Goldman, Anne. "'I yam what I yam': Cooking, Culture and Colonialism." *De/Colonizing the Subject: Politics and Gender in Women's Autobiographical Practice.* Ed. Sidonie Smith and Julia Watson. Minneapolis: University of Minnesota Press, 1992.

Gonzales-Berry, Erlinda. "Vincente Bernal and Felipe M. Chacón: Bridging Two Cultures." *Pasó por Aquí: Critical Essays on the New Mexico Literary Tradition, 1542–1988.* Ed. Erlinda Gonzales-Berry. Albuquerque: University of New Mexico, 1989.

Gusdorf, Georges. "Conditions and Limits of Autobiography." Reprinted in *Autobiography: Essays Theoretical and Critical.* Ed. James Olney. Princeton: Princeton University Press, 1980.

Hays, David M. Letter to the author. 13 July 1988.

Leal, Luís. "Mexican American Literature: A Historical Perspective." *Revista Chicano-Riquena* 1 (1973): 32–44. Reprinted in *Modern Chicano Writers: A Collection of Critical Essays.* Ed. Joseph Sommer and Tomas Ybarra-Frausto. New York: Prentice-Hall, 1979.

Lomelí, Francisco. "A Literary Portrait of Hispanic New Mexico: Dialectics of Perception." *Pasó por Aquí: Critical Essays on the New Mexican Literary Tradition.* Ed. Erlinda Gonzales-Berry. Albuquerque: University of New Mexico Press, 1989.

McGregor. "Our Spanish-American Fellow Citizens." *Harper's Weekly* (June 13, 1914): 7.

Machado, Señora Doña Juana. "Times Gone By in Alta California." Trans. Raymond S. Brandes. *Historical Society of Southern California Quarterly* (September 1959): 195–240.

Marquez, Antonio C. "Richard Rodriquez' *Hunger of Memory* and the Poetics of Experience." *Arizona Quarterly* (Winter 1984): 130–141.

Miller, Darlis A. "Hispanos and the Civil War in New Mexico: A Reconsideration." *New Mexico Historical Review* 54, no. 2 (1979): 107.

New Mexico Folklore Record 9 (1954–55): 3.

Northrup, Marie. "Searching for the Birth Date of Eulalia Pérez de Guillén de Mariné." *Historical Society of Southern California Quarterly* 40 (1958): 183.

Padilla, Genaro M. "Self as Cultural Metaphor in Acosta's The Autobiography of a Brown Buffalo." *Journal of General Education* 35 (1984): 242–258.

Padilla, Genaro M. "Imprisoned Narrative? Or Lies, Secrets and Silence in New Mexico Women's Autobiography." *Criticism in the Borderlands: Studies in Chicano Literature, Culture, and Ideology.* Ed. Hector Calderón and José David Saldívar. Durham: Duke University Press, 1991.

Padilla, Genaro M. "Yo Sola Aprendí: Mexican Women's Personal Narratives from Nineteenth-Century California." *Revealing Lives: Autobiography, Biography, and Gender.* Ed. Susan Groag Bell and Marilyn Yalom. New York: State University Press of New York, 1990.

Paredes, Raymund. "The Evolution of Chicano Literature." *Three American Literatures*. Ed. Houston A. Baker, Jr. New York: Modern Language Association, 1982.

Rebolledo, Tey Diana. "Tradition and Mythology: Signatures of Landscape in Chicano Literature." *The Desert Is No Lady: Southwest Landscapes in Women's Writing and Art*. Ed. Vera Norwood and Janice Monk. New Haven: Yale University Press, 1987.

Rebolledo, Tey Diana. "Narrative Strategies of Resistance in Hispana Writing." *Journal of Narrative Technique* 20, 2 (Spring 1990): 134–146.

Rivera, Rowena. "New Mexico Colonial Poetry: Tradition and Innovation." *Pasó por Aquí: Critical Essays on the New Mexican Literary Tradition, 1542–1988*. Ed. Erlinda Gonzales-Berry. Albuquerque: University of New Mexico Press, 1989.

Romero, Cecil. "A Unique American Chronicle." *El Palacio* 24, no. 9 (March 3, 1928): 159.

Saldívar, Ramón. "Ideologies of the Self: Chicano Autobiography." *Diacritics* (Fall 1985): 25–34.

Sherman, Edmund. "New Mexico Celebrates." *New Mexico* (June 1940): 14–17.

Shontz, Orfa Jean. "The Land of 'Poco Tiempo': A Study of Mexican Family Relationships in a Changing Social Environment." *The Family* 8 (May 1927): 74.

Sommers, Joseph. "Critical Approaches to Chicano Literature." *Modern Chicano Writers: A Collection of Essays*. Ed. Joseph Sommers and Tomas Ybarra-Frausto. New York: Prentice-Hall, 1979.

Wong, Hertha. "Pictography as Autobiography: Plains Indian Sketchbooks of the Late Nineteenth and Early Twentieth Centuries." *American Literary History* 1 (Summer 1989): 295–316.

Zweig, Paul. "The Child of Two Cultures." *New York Times Book Review*. April 5, 1982.

Archival Materials/Manuscripts in Typescripts

Amador, José María. "Memorias sobre la historia de California." MS. Bancroft Library, University of California, Berkeley.

Avila, María Inocente Pico de. "Cosas de California." MS. Bancroft Library, University of California, Berkeley.

Bernal, Juan. "Memoria de un Californio." MS. Bancroft Library, University of California, Berkeley.

Carillo de Fitch, Josefa. "Narración de una Californiana." MS. Bancroft Library, University of California, Berkeley.

Cerruti, Enrique. "Ramblings in California." MS. Bancroft Library, University of California, Berkeley.

Chacón, Rafael. "Memorias." 1912. (Chaps. 1–3) University of Colorado Library, Boulder.

De la Guerra, María de las Angustias. "Ocurrencias en California." 1878. MS. Bancroft Library, University of California, Berkeley.

Garza, Catarino E. "La lógica de mis hechos." 1877–1889. MS. Benson Latin

American Collection, Mexican American Archives, University of Texas, Austin.

González, Rafael. "Experiencias de un soldado." MS. Bancroft Library, University of California, Berkeley.

Lorenzana, Apolinaria. "Memorias de la Beata." 1878. MS. Bancroft Library, University of California, Berkeley.

Martínez, Padre Antonio José. "Relación de méritos." 1838.

Menchaca, José Antonio. "Reminiscences." ca. 1850. MS., TS. Barker Texas History Center, University of Texas, Austin.

Osuña de Marrón, Felipa. "Recuerdos del pasado." MS. Bancroft Library, University of California, Berkeley.

Pérez, Eulalia. "Una vieja y sus recuerdos." 1877. MS. Bancroft Library, University of California, Berkeley.

Pérez, Jesse. "Memoirs." TS. Barker Texas History Center, University of Texas, Austin.

Pico, Pío. "Narración histórico." MS. Bancroft Library, University of California, Berkeley.

Ríos, Catarina Avila de. "Recuerdos." MS. Bancroft Library, University of California, Berkeley.

Sánchez, Vincente. "Cartas de un Angelino." MS. Bancroft Library, University of California, Berkeley.

Savage, Thomas. "Report on Labors on Archives and Procuring Material for the History of California." 1874. MS. Bancroft Library, University of California, Berkeley.

Seguín, John Nepumuceno. *Personal Memoirs.* 1858. TS. Barker Texas History Center, University of Texas, Austin.

Tafolla, Santiago. "Nearing the End of the Trail." ca. 1890. MS. Benson Latin American Collection, Mexican American Archives, University of Texas, Austin.

Vallejo, Mariano Guadalupe. "Recuerdos históricos y personales tocante a la alta California." 5 vols. 1875. MS. Bancroft Library, University of California, Berkeley.

Vallejo, Mariano Guadalupe. "Historical and Personal Memoirs Relating to Alta California." Trans. Earl R. Hewitt. TS. Bancroft Library, University of California, Berkeley.

Vallejo, Salvador. "Notas históricas sobre California." MS. Bancroft Library, University of California, Berkeley.

Vallejo de Leese, Rosalía. "History of the 'Osos.'" 1876. MS. Bancroft Library, University of California, Berkeley.

Vejar, Pablo. "Recuerdos de un viejo." MS. Bancroft Library, University of California, Berkeley.

Index

Marian Anderson
My Lord, What a Morning
Introduction by Nellie Y. McKay

American Women's Autobiography: Fea(s)ts of Memory
Edited, with an introduction, by Margo Culley

Frank Marshall Davis
Livin' the Blues: Memoirs of a Black Journalist and Poet
Edited, with an introduction, by John Edgar Tidwell

Joanne Jacobson
Authority and Alliance in the Letters of Henry Adams

Kamau Brathwaite
The Zea Mexican Diary
Foreword by Sandra Pouchet Paquet

Genaro M. Padilla
*My History, Not Yours: The Formation of
Mexican American Autobiography*

Frances Smith Foster
*Witnessing Slavery: The Development of Ante-bellum
Slave Narratives*

Native American Autobiography: An Anthology
Edited, with an introduction, by Arnold Krupat

American Lives: An Anthology of Autobiographical Writing
Edited, with an introduction, by Robert F. Sayre

Carol Holly
*Intensely Family: The Inheritance of Family Shame and the
Autobiographies of Henry James*